Greek Political Theory

Greek Political Theory

THE IMAGE OF MAN
IN THUCYDIDES AND PLATO

David Grene

Phoenix Books

THE UNIVERSITY OF CHICAGO PRESS

CHICAGO & LONDON

Originally published under the title

MAN IN HIS PRIDE

A STUDY IN THE POLITICAL PHILOSOPHY

OF THUCYDIDES AND PLATO

THE UNIVERSITY OF CHICAGO PRESS, CHICAGO & LONDON

The University of Toronto Press, Toronto 5, Canada

© *1950 by The University of Chicago. All rights reserved. Published 1950. First Phoenix Edition 1965. Third Impression 1967. Printed in the United States of America*

Preface

IN THIS essay I did not intend to treat Thucydides and Plato in the orthodox sense as historian and philosopher, respectively. My aim was rather to establish their intellectual configuration, that is, to establish for each a kind of intellectual personality, complete, alive, and individual. A man's doctrines have a life of their own; they belong in the order of history and the order of logic, for there are alternatives to them which are explored in the course of time or in the range of logical possibility. But the sum total of his doctrines is another thing. The nexus of a human personality has tied these together so that a complete intellectual picture can only be one which implies the impossibility of alternatives for particular aspects of his thought.

The portraits of the two writers are one element in this little book. I wanted, too, to make alive the world of the fifth century from which Thucydides and Plato came, not as they have done—for how should anyone make that world more alive, directly, than the *History* of Thucydides and the dialogues of Plato—but to make it alive in a sense in which the artist and his work have each a place. I wanted not to say what I thought the fifth century was like, nor yet to retell the story in which Thucydides and Plato said what it was like, but to show another kind of picture in which the historian and his historical material and the philosopher and his world of complexity and bareness are all parts of a total canvas. It seemed to me that so the meaning of human society in fifth-century Athens would be more complete for us than in any other way.

That this meaning is more important for us than that of any historical period between us and them I am sure. It is not only the obvious and often stated fact that that period, like ours, was "a time of moral crisis," in which in the minds of many men a traditional ethic had become the subject of doubt and denial.

It is not only the fact that ours has become in large part a government by public pressures, similar in many ways, though on a mass scale, to the direct democracy of Athens. It is not only the occurrence of total war in that time as in ours, and the increasingly technical conception of the manipulation of power, both in peace and war. It is, rather, the total humanity of political life that brings fifth-century Athens so close to us; not, certainly, humanity in the sense of humaneness—for both they and we have had to face, in our different circumstances, the extremes of human cruelty—but humanity in the sense that it is man and man alone, without cosmic or supernatural sanction, who is both the source and the resolution of conflict.

If, however, our affinity with the political life of fifth-century Athens is so striking, why select only two of the figures who have reported it to us, instead of discussing the general concepts which run through Greek political theory? There are, I think, two good reasons for the rather unorthodox procedure I have chosen. In the first place, it is these two authors who have brought the fifth century down to us in living and relevant form, politically. Apart from the minor auxiliary writers, like Xenophon and the Old Oligarch, and the dramatists, whose political information is incidental, the two other authors one might think important in this connection are Herodotus and Aristotle. But Herodotus wrote in the afterglow of the national fervor of the Persian Wars, when Greece stood for freedom against the Eastern despotism of the Great King. The moral climate of that time was one of triumph for what seemed, for a few brief years, a self-vindicated and stable ethic—a world away from the Athens of the Peloponnesian War. And the *Ethics* and *Politics* of Aristotle are as far removed from Periclean Athens on the other side; it is the dead bones of a culture which has lived through its triumph *and* its crisis which Aristotle catalogues.

It is not, however, this rather mechanical reason which is the primary one for choosing these two writers and treating them as I have done. Political ideas do not grow disembodied, and it is only in their growth, in their living presence, however indirectly we must recapture it, that we can understand them. What seems to me vital in our study of the political likenesses and differences between ourselves and the fifth-century Athenians is not so much the consideration of principles as a knowledge of men and situations and men *in* situations. We can learn from knowing them, much as we can learn from knowing our contemporaries. Although the knowledge may grow richer by its very distance, it must, however indirectly acquired, be face-to-face knowledge—in essence like one's understanding of a friend.

Not only our respect for the living totality of each man, moreover, forces us to look at each in his own right—and prevents a glib and easy unification or comparison of the two—but the material we have to deal with is in the two cases of an irreducible disparity. Not only was one a historian, the other a philosopher. But one has left us a work, which, though in part unrevised, presents a single total view of a historical canvas. The other has given us a long series of writings in which, as I shall hope to show, we find not the articulation of a formal system but the development into maturity and old age of a man, and with him of his peculiar vision. Therefore, in terms of problems of evidence, organization, etc., our two portraits are bound to be very different.

Yet out of the totality of each, once we have seen it, we may gain some illumination of the limits within which, in its view of political man, our Western tradition has developed. The eyes of both the historian and philosopher were bent on an identical historical society. In what they saw, the difference of their two temperaments was of supreme importance. And the polarity of their intellectual configuration defined the range within which, in my judgment, all political speculation in the West can be seen to move. Many theories of man in political society not envisaged by Thucydides and Plato have arisen, but the completeness of the view of man, historically and politically, attained in these two different ways, is a kind of alpha and omega.

In treating Thucydides and Plato thus, the establishment of this intellectual personality does not mean an identification with fifth-century Greece which would estrange them from us, for each of these men is especially fitted and perhaps even uniquely fitted to be a medium between that Greece and ourselves. Neither of them is wholly a citizen of his country nor yet a citizen of ours. They stand consciously in an in-between relationship which acts as a human illumination of the processes of thought without the too-human limitations involved in the more complete historical identification with a particular period.

It was accident and luck which drove Thucydides from practical politics. It was not accident or luck which gave him the power to picture a world where the states of his day had been destroyed almost beyond a trace. But the sense of having failed even in the relatively minor practical task intrusted to him in his own lifetime and his subsequent isolation from either of the political combatants in what he saw as the supreme political contest of his day did sharpen his perception of his own historical loneliness and turned him perhaps with greater decision to speak to that unknown future world the dimensions of which could only be charted intellectually.

For other reasons Plato found himself in a similar predicament in the face of his own time. His understanding and his imagination had been enchanted by a human society which was dead and finished when he was a young man under thirty. This dead world re-created to be his life of fantasy is also that in virtue of which he is alive for us. This was the immortal part of him he left to "those who should follow in his footsteps" in what he called in the *Republic* "some barbaric region beyond our knowledge."

Acknowledgments

THIS book is the result of several years of courses in Thucydides and Plato given under the auspices of the Committee on Social Thought. To my various classes of students and my discussions with them I owe much. To one of my former students, Mr. Martin Ostwald, I am especially grateful for doing a most thorough job in editing the Thucydides part of the manuscript. To the Committee itself and to its chairman, Professor John U. Nef, I owe opportunities for work and an atmosphere favorable to it which I do not think can be duplicated in any university today.

DAVID GRENE

UNIVERSITY OF CHICAGO

Table of Contents

PART I

The Man Who Looked On

CHAPTER I

The World of Thucydides

1

IF IT is true of any historian that it was the starkness and finality of revelation afforded by his times which made him a historian, that man is Thucydides. To penetrate under the surface of his wonderfully arranged narrative and to recapture something of the impact of the raw material on the man is the indispensable prerequisite to understanding him.

The Peloponnesian War, the subject of his constant interest, broke out in 431, was briefly terminated by an inconclusive truce between Sparta and Athens in 421, and again began, formally, with the attack of the Spartans in 412 to be concluded with the complete destruction of the Athenian military power and the occupation of Athens by the Spartan army in 404. The years 421–412, during which no recognized state of war existed between Sparta and Athens, were yet marked by the Spartan-Argive conflict, the settlement of which in Argos' disfavor strengthened the position of Sparta in the Peloponnesus, and above all by the Athenian attempt to add Sicily to her empire, a venture destined by its failure drastically to weaken her material resources and pave the way for her final military collapse in 404. The whole of this great war, great in its political and psychological implications for us as well as its contemporaries, lies under the shadow of the earlier days when Athens and Sparta fought shoulder to shoulder against the Persian invader of Greece. The contrast between this war and that was inevitable for men who had lived through the one and within living memory of the other. The contrast was equally unhappy in its national implications and in its moral lessons for the

3

majority of thinking observers. Greece had lived in the secure confidence that freemen with small forces and ineffective weapons had beaten the slaves of the Persian king, though as numerous as locusts and equipped with all the resources a fifth-century militarist could desire.[1] The theme of freedom and slavery had been, for the Greeks, inevitably identified with this conflict.[2] Yet, within memory of a single man, a Greek could see the two great powers, so readily united in the cause of freedom against Persian despotism, each trying to destroy the other and acquire his empire. The revelation of such cynical realism was especially evident in the details of the conduct and consequences of this international Greek war. It drove men to ask whether the morality of the Persian Wars was a fiction, after all.

Of the two Greek partners in the struggle against the Persians, partners who had now become rivals for empire, it was Athens and the career of Athens from 478 until the opening of the Peloponnesian War which arrested men's attention. Ostensibly, at least, the Sparta of 433 stood for nothing new in Greek life and had in no sense broken with the role of leader of Greece and champion of Greek freedom which she had played in the period 490–478. It is Athens in these years which made men realize what had happened since the Persians lost their last European stronghold.

Athens has become, says Pericles in the Funeral Speech, "the school of Greece."[3] He is speaking of the openness of his city, her accessibility to foreigners, and her proud position as the object of imitation while being herself indifferent to the greatness of other states. But the lessons which her pupils learned of her were not chiefly an admiration for her particular political institutions, of which Pericles had been speaking, nor even for the manner in which she advanced so rapidly from a relatively insignificant city-state to the leadership of the League of Delos and finally to be mistress of a vast empire.

What she has taught the rest of the Greeks chiefly is to be

aware of the creation of power in the name of nothing except itself and to consider the factor of the creation of power openly and rationally. In these two respects—and they go closely together—Athens was unique in terms of past history and, it may be contended, in terms of succeeding history until our own time. The empires of the East that had preceded her were strictly monarchies—I mean, the power was conceived of as radiating from the person of the king. It is the king's enemies that are killed or subdued; it is the king's territories that are extended. The connection of the king and the religion with which he is bound up makes conquest and annexation of territory only one aspect of the absolute command exercised by ruler over subject, and there is no possibility of facing the action as a moral issue in any neutral fashion.[4] Nor do either the Roman or the British Empire later resemble Athens in the attitude of the proponents of their imperialism. Whether their expressed philosophies of empire, the concept of *Romanitas*,[5] or the superiority of British culture and rule are mere fictions with which to clothe the nakedness of greed need not be discussed here. I do not think that anyone could seriously claim that in either case the men who lived and died for these beliefs were invariably conscious or even unconscious hypocrites. The essential thing, however, is that they felt the need of explaining the brutal fact of national aggressiveness and territorial acquisition in terms of metaphysics and of justifying their conquests in terms of a morality which clearly demonstrated that it was for the good of the conquered to be subjected to their conquerors. It is not pretended that with the history of Athens, Rome, and nineteenth-century Britain one has exhausted the list of empires in the last twenty-five centuries. There are of course the Dutch, Belgian, Portuguese, French, and Spanish. All these, however, are essentially colonial in character. They involve, at least at first, the settlement of European nationals among an alien people to govern them and the manipulation of the new territory to serve the economic ends of the homeland. This is really different from the Roman attitude, which finally made Roman citizenship coterminous with the Roman Empire. It is even different from the British position in India from the nineteenth century on. The extraordinary feature of the Athenian empire is that the Athenians built it with nothing to stand between themselves and the suffering and injustice they caused; that they faced it all together, every one of them, in individual moral responsibility all the time; and that what they tried to construct as explanation of their actions was no nationalist or semireligious fiction but, as they thought of it, a rational account of the manner in which all men everywhere have acted. I have very little doubt that the quality of their philosophic explanation was clearly related to the degree of responsibility they took. The democratic assembly of Athens, in which every citizen of Athens who wished to vote, voted, debated, and decided the vital questions of war, conquest, and peace. The same men with virtually no distinction of class were governors and governed in turn. They were, with the same absence of caste, the army. Faced immediately with the actions which are the consequences of decision, and makers and un-makers of their own destiny, perhaps their speculations must sound a depth deeper than those of the soldier-governors of Rome or the British civil servants. Let us try to see how the citizens of Athens in the last quarter of the fifth century saw the sources of political life around them.

2

This can perhaps best be done by reading three passages in the *History* which, in a unique fashion, illustrate the world Thucydides surveyed and the intellectual terms in which his contemporaries discussed it. The first is part of a speech made by an Athenian delegation which happened to be at Sparta in 433 before the war's outbreak, when the Spartan allies complained to the central power of the inroads made by Athens on their particular interests. The defense proffered by the Athenians is peculiarly significant in the fashion that they, the representatives of the allegedly unjust power, chose to state their case. The second is Thucydides' observations on the struggles in the island of Corcyra, in western Greece, between the democratic and oligarchic parties early in the Peloponnesian War, 427–425. Corcyra, a microcosm of the political struggles all over Greece, was important to the two warring powers, Athens and Sparta, since she possessed a relatively large navy and was a vital factor in the trade with the West—Italy and Sicily. The third is part of the famous Melian Dialogue. In 416, that is, during the period of nominal peace between Athens and Sparta (421–412), there was a series of moves made by Athens to extend her empire at points of vantage without, as far as possible, becoming embroiled with Sparta. Of these annexations, that of the island of Melos, while relatively insignificant in size, has become notorious through the pages of Thucydides. The Athenians were particularly anxious to get absolute control of Melos because, as an island, her independence constituted a very bad example for the subjects of a maritime empire. A considerable contingent of the Athenian navy was detached to reduce the island, but before engaging in hostilities they communicated with the government of Melos and requested a conference. The passage quoted is an excerpt including about two-thirds of Thucydides' report of the speeches between the representatives of the two powers.

These three passages are cited in chronological order in order that we may see at three separate points in the war's course at once the uniformity of the tone of intellectual discussion and the gradual progression in the practical means of implementing the trends of political thought in the last quarter of the fifth century. It is assumed that the speeches are, basically at least, speeches actually delivered;[6] and in the chapter on revolution Thucydides is simply citing facts. Thus in these passages we draw as close to the actual material of the historian as it is possible to do. And as we ourselves see the scene and the man as

7

separate, we can ultimately understand the interaction of the two.

a) THE SPEECH OF THE ATHENIAN ENVOYS AT SPARTA (433/32)

"In virtue of the loyalty we displayed then [at the time of the Persian invasion], men of Sparta, in virtue of our intelligence and good sense, surely we do not deserve such extreme unpopularity among the Greeks—at least, on the grounds of our empire? For this empire we acquired by no violence of ours, but we took it only when your people refused to remain to deal with the remnants of the Persian forces and when the allies approached us and themselves requested that we should become the leaders of the confederacy. As a consequence of that action we were actually forced, first of all, to transform the confederacy step by step into what it is today, under the compulsion of fear chiefly, secondly honor, and thirdly gain. It no longer appeared to us safe policy to risk leaving the allies free, since we were now unpopular with the majority of them, some had already revolted and had been reduced to the status of subjects, and you yourselves were no longer our friends as you had been but were at variance with us, and we were suspicious—for, had we so surrendered the empire, the defections would have been to you. No one can be blamed, with matters of the greatest consequence at stake, for disposing of the risks to his own best advantage. At least, you, men of Sparta, have set up governments in the cities of the Peloponnesus to suit your own interests and maintain your leading position on that basis.[7] And if, in the days after the Persian War, you had kept your troops on the spot continuously and had become unpopular in your imperial government, as we have, we are very sure that you would have become as oppressive to the allies as we are, since you would have been compelled either to rule with a heavy hand or to risk your own position. So, you see, we too have done nothing extraordinary or uncommon, humanly speaking, in accepting an empire which we were offered and in not surrendering it, when tempted by the three greatest things, honor, fear, and gain; nor again were we the first to set such a precedent but indeed followed the established rule that the weaker has his liberty curtailed by the stronger, and we thought ourselves worthy of taking this privilege. You thought so, yourselves, until today when you make use of this argument about justice which no one has ever heeded to the disregard of his self-interest if he had a chance to obtain something by his own power. And those deserve praise who, while following the dictates of man's nature and ruling others, still prove juster than their own strength would warrant. At least, we think that if others took over our empire, they would have proved conclusively how moderate we are; yet in our case, thanks to our decent behavior, we have got a bad name rather than a good one, and this is most unreasonable."[8]

b) THE CIVIL WAR IN CORCYRA (427–425)

"To such lengths of savagery this revolution proceeded, and it seemed worse than it was because it was among the first of them: afterward the entire Greek world, one might say, was convulsed; in every separate state the fight being between the champions of democracy who wished to call in the Athenians, and the champions of oligarchy who did the same for the Spartans. In times of peace neither side had the excuse or the willingness to call in the two great powers, but when the war was on, and prospects good for damaging the opposing political party and strengthening one's own by the same act, invitations to foreign powers were very lightly made by those who wished to effect a change in government. Many terrible things befell the Greek states through these factional revolutions, things that are still happening and will continue to happen while human nature is the same, though they will vary in degrees of horror and in the forms they assume depending on the particular conjunction of circumstances which preside over their inception. In peace and good times, both governments and individuals have better judgment because they do not fall under the pressure of events too strong for will or intention: war, by filching away the day-to-day prosperity, proves a harsh taskmaster and fits the temper of most of the inhabitants to their circumstances. So the city-states were continually in a revolutionary ferment, and the outbreaks which came later profited by the knowledge of what had gone before and carried much further an extraordinary degree of innovation, both in the technical contrivance of the coups d'état and the strange horrors of their reprisals. Men changed the customary significance of words in a deliberate intent to fit the facts. An unreasoning audacity was called loyal courage, prudent hesitation specious cowardice, moderation became the excuse for unmanliness, and a general intelligence was interpreted as the same as general inactivity. A kind of frantic eagerness was assigned as man's peculiar quality, and cautious plotting against another constituted a reasonable policy of self-defense. The angry man was always believed, his opponent always suspected. A man who laid his plots and was successful was accounted shrewd, and he who suspected the plot before it happened even shrewder; but he who planned so that he would need no such measures was looked upon as one that destroyed true comradeship and was afraid of his opponents. Indeed, to forestall someone who intended you an injury was praised, as also the suggestion of an injury when there was no thought of it. So kinship became a more alien tie than party affiliation, since the latter was a readier basis for an unquestioning daring—for such associations were not formed in the spirit of the established customs of mutual help but in direct contradiction of them with the object of overreaching others, and the conspirators felt strong in their mutual pledges, not in virtue of the usual oaths by the gods but in their common complicity in crime. The honorable propositions of an enemy they received with practical defensive measures, if they had the upper hand, and never with generosity. To take revenge on another was more esteemed than avoiding the injury first of all. Whenever agreements were actually confirmed by oaths, such oaths, being only given by either party to meet a desperate situation, held good only so long as the parties had no other means of obtaining their objectives. As soon as the opportunity came the one who first had the confidence to seize the unguarded loophole had more pleasure in exacting his vengeance because of the pledges he had given than had he made an open attack, since by so doing he had put his own safety to his credit and also, by his success in the deception, had won first place in a contest of wits. And, indeed, it is easier for most scoundrels to be called clever than for most stupid men to be called good, for people take pride in the one title and are ashamed of the other. The cause of all this was the greedy and ambitious lust for political power, and from this came the violence of those who engaged in the struggle for it. The leading men in the various states heading each of the two parties with a specious slogan, the one ostensibly honoring political democracy and equality before the law, the other the moderate rule of the best elements, actually played booty with the public interests they so loudly served. In their frantic efforts to compete with and overreach one another they proceeded to the most desperate expedients and to still worse and worse measures of vengeance, not setting any limits in justice and in the advantage of the state but only in temporary party caprice. And so, becoming masters either by means of suborned votes or direct violence, they were ready to satisfy their ambitions of the moment. Therefore neither side regarded religion, but, when fair words helped men on occasion unexceptionably to attain their ends, they were thought the better of for that. The moderate elements of the citizenry were destroyed by both parties either because they refused to take sides or because their survival was resented.

"So every kind and shape of villainy befell the Greek world in this revolutionary era, and simplicity of heart, whose main ingredient is nobility, was laughed out of existence: the opposition of the two parties split the society in two, and no one trusted anyone else. There was nothing to break the deadlock, for no argument was secure and no sworn pledge was revered; but all parties having in their calculations given up as hopeless the idea of permanent security thought rather of self-defense than any sort of trust. The stupider the men, the more likely they were to survive, for fearing their own defects and their enemies' brains, fearing, that is, that in arguments they would get the worst of it and maybe be the victim of a carefully hatched plot contrived by the versatility of the others, they boldly had recourse to action. The clever men, on the other hand, thinking contemptuously that they would know in time and that, anyway, they need take no practical measures when their wits would save them, tended to be caught off their guard and destroyed."[9]

c) THE MELIAN DIALOGUE (416)

"ATHENIAN DELEGATES: On our side we will not make you long speeches—which you would not believe, anyhow—with fine phrases to the effect that our empire is a just one because we defeated the Persians or that our attack upon you now is due to wrongs suffered at your hands; and we must beg you to spare us likewise—that is to say, not to think you will convince us by saying that you did not join our side because you were colonists of the Lacedaemonians or that you have done us no injury, but let us try to get done what is practicable on the basis of the real opinions of each of our governments, each side being well aware that in human terms justice is only in question when an equal degree of compulsion exists on each side, and that in practical matters the more powerful do what they can and the weaker yield what they must.

"MELIANS: As we think, anyway, it is expedient (we are compelled to speak in such terms, since you have bidden us speak of advantage and not justice) that you should not break down what is for the common good of all—the recognition that there is decency and justice due to any man who happens to be in danger, and that he may even attain some advantage if he persuade his opponent to abate a little of his strictest rights. This is no less to your own advantage, since, if you lose your power, you would become an example to the rest of the world for the severity of the vengeance exacted on you.

"ATHENIAN DELEGATES: As far as our empire goes—we are not very downcast about the end of that, even should it fall; for it is not another imperial power, like the Lacedaemonians, that is dangerous to those they conquer—in any case, you know, our fight is not really against the Spartans—but subjects, if they should themselves attack and overthrow their rulers. However, you must let us take this risk on our own responsibility; we will try to show you that we are here to serve the advantage of our empire and to save your city, because we want to rule your people with the least trouble possible, profit our own interests, and so both find security. . . .

"MELIANS: We know—you may be quite sure of it—how hard it will be to fight against your power and good fortune, unless the terms shall be equal; yet, as far as chance goes, we trust that God will be on our side because we stand as just men against unjust, and as far as defect of earthly power goes, we trust that our alliance with Sparta will serve us, for Sparta will be compelled to come to our help, if for no other reason, because of our common race and the honorable obligations binding us. So the good heart we have is not so utterly unreasonable.

"ATHENIANS: In the matter of God's good will we think we shall have as much of a share as you; for the demands we are making or the deeds we are doing are neither outside the pale of what human beings think about the gods' doing or their settled policy toward one another. For concerning the gods we hold opinion, and concerning human beings we know very clearly that under the most natural compulsion they rule whatever they can master. We have not laid down this law nor were we the first to follow it when laid down; we but took it over, followed it, and will leave it after us, a thing already existing and destined to exist forever. We know, too, that you and many others who attain the same power will do exactly the same. That is the very reasonable ground on which we have no fear of being at a disadvantage in the favor of heaven. For the opinion you hold of the Lacedaemonians—that you can trust their sense of honor to bring them to your rescue—we must congratulate you on your inexperience of this bad world but do not envy you your unwise confidence. In domestic matters and the customs of their own land the Lacedaemonians are strict patterns of virtue, but of their conduct toward others one has a lot to say and summing it up might say it like this: That of all the people we know they most obviously think what is agreeable honorable and what is to their advantage just. Such a way of thinking is not likely to lead them to serve you as you now unreasonably assume."[10]

CHAPTER II

Our Knowledge of Thucydides

1

THE very little we know of Thucydides we know virtually altogether from himself in the course of his *History*, and, since almost no historian contemporary with the events he described has been more reticent as to his own participation in them, it is little indeed.[1] Yet what there is, is all of a piece; he insists that his really significant relation to the Peloponnesian War is that from its beginning he understood its importance and ceaselessly tried to record its course truthfully[2]—not that, thanks to the war, he was a politician who was disgraced or a general who was broken for failure. We do not know when he was born, but he was old enough to be commander of the Athenian forces in the northwest theater of operations (Thrace and its neighborhood) in 424 B.C.[3] Probably therefore we can conclude he was not less than thirty at this time and perhaps somewhat more. We also know, from his own words, that he saw the war to its end in 404.[4]

These are Thucydides' own words of himself and the war he chronicled:

"Of these years too (421–404) the same Thucydides the Athenian wrote, in order as each came by, summer by summer and winter by winter, until the Spartans and their allies deposed the Athenians from their empire and captured the Long Walls at the Peiraeus. Till this conclusion the total length of the war is twenty-seven years (431–404). If it be objected that the period of intervening years of peace (421–412) is no war, the objection is not justified. Let such a critic look at the division of the actual actions, and he will find that it is not reasonable to judge that as peace in which neither side gave back nor acquired what they had covenanted for. This apart from the fact of the Mantinean and Epidaurian conflicts and the many other mistakes committed by both sides and the continued hostility of the allies in Thrace and the Boeotian truce—of ten days' duration. So, together with the first war which lasted ten years (431–421) and the period of suspicious truce which followed it (421–412) and the war which followed after that, a man who reckons them up will find the years just about twenty-seven and a few days over. He will find, too, that for those who insisted on the value of oracles this was the only certain thing that came out right. For I myself remember that always, even in the beginning of the war right through till its end, many prophesied that it was bound to last till the years three times nine should be accomplished. I lived through it all, being of an age to observe the war and giving it all my attention so that I should know something accurately about it. It happened that I was banished from my own country for twenty years after my generalship at Amphipolis, and so I was enabled to notice things more particularly at my leisure, being present with both parties, particularly the Peloponnesians, because of my exile."[5]

2

This essay is an attempt to reconstruct the political philosophy of Thucydides, who concentrated on a true account of the events which made that philosophy and were made by it in turn. The events, as part of the totality of Thucydides, are important, but the man quite as much or more. And while Thucydides the historian intends us, however remote from him chronologically, to understand all that he can humanly convey to us about his subject, he did not intend or indeed could not conceive that we should be interested in him as the observer of the facts. No historian, perhaps, can see posterity looking at himself as a historical object.

The difficulties involved in discovering the general convictions of a historian, or the theory of political or psychological causation which he finds expressed in the particular set of facts which he treats, vary enormously. This may, of course, be due simply to differences of individual temperament on the part of the historians. Gibbon's complacence as to the moral and intellectual values of his day may be entirely a matter personal to Gibbon. Herodotus' triumphant certainty of the ultimate defeat of whip-driven slaves by liberty-loving freemen may be something peculiar to Herodotus. The ease with which we can observe the moral, ethical, and strictly political conceptions of these historians *may* be due to the coincidental development of these men's private lives. That they are also great historians may be accidental to the security of their confidence in moral values and to the readiness with which we can discover enough of their political philosophy to discuss. It may be that Thucydides is in his own person as hard, obscure, complex, and ambiguous as much of his style would indicate he was and that it is because of these things that we have such difficulty in saying of him, "He believed this or that politically"; "He is shocked by this and this."

But it may be that there is a real difficulty, quite outside his own disposition, for the historian of a time which sees the disruption or destruction of what had seemed permanent values of ethics, morality, and politics. The certainty of Herodotus and Gibbon *may* arise from being in accord with the observed trend of their own day. The patriotism of the one, the enlightened satirical understanding of the other, were in accordance with what their reading public in each case expected of the historian. The audience and the artist were at one as to the values in the light of which the facts were considered, and so there is no hidden censor to check the historian's intellect or hand from framing an implicit ethical judgment or pointing the explicit moral. But when, as in the case of Thucydides' lifetime, a man subtle and sensitive might see not only the destruction of what was great in material power—Herodotus, indeed, had the opportunity of observing that—but with it and in some inexplicable way in connection with it the progressive reduction of more and more human beings to sordid misery, the steady increase in the refinement of brutality, the unceasing abandonment of the veil of decency which had heretofore cloaked the worst actions—in the face of such a situation, perhaps the mind of the historian himself tends to focus on the only material to which he can be true in his function as historian. He can stick relentlessly to facts, to what men did and what men said. When he describes the feelings which led them to act and speak as they did, he will put an iron constraint upon himself, so that it is next to impossible in the hard objectivity of the words to discover what emotion lay behind this creation. When at appropriate moments, the death of a leading statesman or the decisive crisis of an action, it is necessary to appraise, the same hidden censor may constrain the historian to talk only of whether the qualities of the man responsible for the policy or the action were such as to be successful.

And, finally, when this historian comes to write of the great moral catastrophe of his day in general terms—and that at times he must—he will try to handle it, too, in moral abstractions related to concrete moral particulars with the same aloofness with which he may write of the relation between the symptoms of the plague at Athens and its predisposing physical factors. In such a man there may grow a blind pride in his obstinate refusal to judge or appraise as his father would have appraised. And in face of this obstinacy the reader may gropingly seek to find in the hidden nuances of the moral terms, or words uniquely employed, of the juxtaposition of speeches and actions, all too slim evidence for the political and moral convictions in the light of which the history came into being. But to seek for it is to try to reveal the evolving pessimism and despair of a very civilized man, one moreover who in all probability revised his work or most of it, so that the later verdicts come to obliterate or obscure earlier impressions. What it is important to do is to form some conception from the *History* whether Thucydides believed that the moral catastrophe of his own time revealed a decisive truth in human nature, a truth which the superficiality of the historians of past times obscured, or whether this moral catastrophe was for him a perverse aberration seen against the normalcy of past times. Such an account must, of necessity, prove only a likely story.

But since we are, in this case, trying to discover general political theory in the work of the historian of a single historical situation, we must proceed in our investigation of himself rather as he did in respect to his facts; that is, we must examine the details of his attitude toward the political parties in Athens and the major political positions of his day and proceed from this level of particularity to the more general theme with which we are concerned.

3

The sources at our disposal to establish Thucydides' political views are, in general, four:

1. Actual statements about political life in verdicts, delivered in the first person, on given political institutions or situations, e.g., the judgment on the constitution of Theramenes in Book viii,[6] and certain parts of the chapter on *stasis* in Book iii.[7] These are few but very significant.

2. Comments on political personages, whose political positions and affiliations are known to us from other sources as well as Thucydides, e.g., Themistocles, Pericles, Cleon, Hyperbolus, Antiphon, and Nicias.[8] Adverse or favorable notice of such leaders, usually in Thucydides' revealing obituary notices, are naturally very important as far as his party preferences are concerned; but they also give us extremely important clues to the kind of individual Thucydides admired or condemned.

3. Certain positive statements on the nature of man and of the general course of political development which may be identified with certain positions in the fifth century B.C., e.g., the general

observations on the nature of *stasis* and certain widely scattered remarks on the nature of the people as the source of political power (see on democracy, below).[9]

4. The speeches, which are the most important source of our information and at the same time the greatest obstacle to a plain account, for, depending on how we interpret them, either we are provided with a generous store of available material which is conveniently explicit or we are forced into a kind of interpretation which is much more difficult and perplexed.

Logically speaking, the speeches can be interpreted in one of three ways: (*a*) as free inventions of Thucydides, devised to permit the expression of his individual insight into the political actions then occurring, a sort of dramatic background imaginatively depicting the state of mind of the chief actors in the play; (*b*) as literary rewritings of actual speeches—according to this view Thucydides will never describe a speech unless one was delivered, and, while inevitably the phrases and sentences and constructions of the speech will be his own, the several points of the argument will presumably come from the original speech; and (*c*) as actual literal reports of speeches delivered. The last possibility is almost certainly to be discounted because Thucydides himself makes a differentiation between the kind of accuracy possessed by his narrative and that of his speeches[10] and because the highly schematic arrangement of the speeches does not suggest a literal version of a speech delivered but a literary production predominantly designed for reading;[11] and perhaps, also, there is a somewhat suspiciously perfect answering of point by point, with a repetition of the same antitheses, in the speeches of opposing parties.[12]

We must make a choice, then, between the first two alternatives, and, depending on our choice, there will be a certain amount of difference in the way in which we use the evidence of the speeches for the formulation of Thucydides' opinions. Part of the way we travel is the same, no matter which assumption we make. Few actual records of conferences and discussions would be kept, and so the historian would be forced to put up with a bare outline, at best, given him by his informants. What we have from him is certainly a fuller version than this, and, if he filled it out, he did so with arguments drawn from his general sense of the political and military situation applied to a particular incident. If the conference or discussion never did take place—that is, if the speeches in Thucydides are entirely fictitious—Thucydides, in attributing to the speakers the sentiments we find, must again have drawn on his general sense of the situation.

Consequently, as between the two assumptions about the speeches which have been mentioned, the only really significant difference as far as a study of Thucydides' opinions is concerned is that, according to the one theory, there must actually have been a speech at a given moment and place and Thucydides is compelled to report that, even if some of what he reports is his own invention; according to the other, the speeches are simply indications of what Thucydides is sure is in the minds of the people concerned at the time he is dealing with. This can, at times, constitute an important difference. For instance, if the Melian Dialogue[13] never occurred in fact, Thucydides, in attributing these sentiments to the Athenian officers participating in the conference, may have been using the incident of Melos to stage a debate which will point up what he thinks to be the significant attitude of the Athenian imperialists in 416 B.C. If the officers at Melos did actually employ even in outline the arguments he puts into their mouths, Thucydides has been granted by history a ready-made drama, however he may have embroidered it. In such a case we would not, for instance, be justified in finding Thucydides' sense of drama in his treatment of the Melian episode[14]—that is to say, Thucydides would not have imported any vital significance into it which is not in the rough there to compel him as a truthful historian to handle it. These differences occur frequently enough so that it is not convenient, for the purpose of this essay, to regard as immaterial which of the two alternative theories is accepted.[15]

The reasons why I am convinced that the second view is correct—that what we have are literary reworkings of actual speeches—are briefly these:

1. The inclusion of certain details of a definitely descriptive character attached to certain of the speeches would, if the speeches are not authentic, certainly furnish evidence of the historian's deliberate desire to deceive. For instance, we are told that the Athenian embassy at Sparta before the war was there not for the purpose of discussing the impending conflict but about another matter;[16] that the letter of Nicias to the assembly at Athens was read by the town clerk and that the commander had also given the messengers verbal instructions to deliver in person;[17] that there were two speeches delivered on the subject of the fate of the people of Mitylene and that two assemblies convened to listen to them.[18] In all these instances certain descriptive details or minor incidents are described in such a way as to suggest deliberately either that Thucydides was himself an eyewitness or that he received an account from eyewitnesses.

2. And this is the main point: the famous statement of Thucydides himself in the first book of the *History* leaves very little doubt as to what the historian meant us to think he did in the speeches. The key phrases are: "It was very difficult for me to remember *the exact nature of the words* that I had myself heard, and difficult too for my various informants. But I have set it down, as each of the speakers appeared to me to say roughly what was required of them in the different kinds of situation, *sticking as closely as I could to the general tenor of what was actually said.*"[19]

It is difficult to see what can possibly be the meaning of the italicized phrases except "the actual accuracy of the things said" and "sticking as closely as I could to what was actually said." If in the face of this we are to assume that the speeches are entirely fictitious, that, in fact, despite Thucydides' explicit statement to the contrary, they bear no resemblance to speeches actually delivered at that time, we are compelled to believe that Thucydides for some purpose wittingly deceived us. In this case the absolute weight of evidence against the basic authenticity of the speeches would have to be overwhelming. In fact, so far from this being the case, there is overwhelming evidence for the possibility of our speeches' representing to some degree actual speeches delivered.[20]

Furthermore, if we were to reject as deliberate deception one of the very few direct statements made by Thucydides himself and try to find some ulterior design for that deception, drawn from material which is not at our disposal, any attempt at discovering Thucydides' political and moral opinions from his *History* might as well be abandoned at the outset, since a historian who would deliberately deceive us in something so fundamental could obviously not be trusted on any other major aspect of his work.

For these reasons, then, stemming chiefly from the interpretation of the passage just quoted, the theory is to be preferred according to which Thucydides, while inventing and filling out arguments impossible of recapture through his absence from the place where the speech was delivered or the inadequacy of his information, is held never to have inserted a speech where none was delivered and in all cases to have clung as closely as he could to the available evidence of the delivered speech.

CHAPTER III

The Problem of Thucydidean Politics

1

TO DISCUSS Thucydides' theory of morals and politics is to imply, a fortiori, that he holds such a theory; but that is just what some scholars, faced with the cold objectivity of the man, have often denied. So the question of Thucydides' morals and politics is a double one: whether we can read behind the lines to some stable general view of human motives and values and, if so, to what one.

The great British classicist, R. C. Jebb, in one of his well-known statements condemns as virtually impossible the attempt to piece together a "theory of ethics or politics" in Thucydides.[1] "He has not," Jebb says, "in the sense of Plato or Aristotle a theory of ethics or politics. Thucydides groups the observed facts of practical politics but without attempting to analyze their ultimate laws. It might be possible to piece together Thucydidean texts and by filling up a few gaps to form a tolerably coherent system of doctrine; but the process would be artificial and delusive. Possibly a Shakespeare might recreate Thucydides from the fragments of his personal thought but the breath of life would be the poet's gift; the broken lights are all that really remain."[2]

The American scholar, Paul Shorey, on the other hand, has presented just such a system of ethics and politics in an early paper.[3] "This Thucydidean criticism of life," he says, "I propose to study in its two main aspects, which for convenience I will designate as (1) ethical positivism, (2) intellectualism. The fundamental assumption of this ethical positivism is that the nature and conduct of man are strictly determined by his

physical and social environment and by a few elementary appetites and desires. Around this primitive core of human nature,
society and convention have wrapped sheath upon sheath of
decorous pretence—ethical, social, religious. The naïve man is
duped by this moral drapery, he accepts the word for the deed,
the alleged motive for the true, and rarely if ever, penetrates
to the underlying realities. The wise man is not so deceived."[4]
The "intellectualism of Thucydides" Shorey defines as "his constant preoccupation with the part played in human life by the
conscious calculating reason."[5] Shorey does not go further,
however, in his essay than a general analysis of Thucydides'
philosophical position. In fact, in contrast to Jebb's position,
he produces a reasonable interpretation of Thucydides' philosophy out of the text itself.

These, then, are the two poles between which the discussion
of Thucydides as a political scientist has habitually moved—
those that affirm that Thucydides is more a historian than any
historian has ever been, that he has recorded only the concrete
facts of the situation and has no political theory as such, and
those who have fitted him into a ready-made position, rather
similar to Hobbes's, in which Thucydides is the bold proponent
of a new scientific theory of politics which disowns the morality of the past and is "tough-minded," as William James
would put it, in his contemplation of the present in the light of
his new "intellectualist" and positivistic criteria. Put more simply, if the latter view is correct, Thucydides will be seeing the
history of Athens as the supreme test of power politics and will
judge the human actions involved purely in terms of efficiency
and success.

What is interesting about each of these approaches to Thucydides is that they are both right and wrong in almost equal
parts. And what is still more striking, what is wrong in each
view is not so much the actual analysis of the historian as it is a
certain psychological color in which each analysis is invested.
It is preposterous that a scholar as great as Jebb should not have

seen the political theory in Thucydides, but his refusal so to do is due to the fact that a political theory for him is an application of a static theory of human nature to a particular body of facts, which illustrates it, and preferably an application which will indicate imperfections in the reasonable handling of these events to be remedied next time. When Jebb sees in Thucydides a man whose political convictions really grew out of the study of a particular given situation and do not lead, in overt and reasonable terms, to the exploration of better possibilities next time, he cannot call Thucydides a man "with a theory of ethics or politics." On the other hand, his real understanding of the fundamental difference in approach between Thucydides as historian and Plato and Aristotle as political scientists (in Jebb's terms) is indeed illuminating. But his desire to mark off political science from history, as such, leads him further than the difference between Thucydides and Plato and Aristotle. It leads him to such absurdities as saying that Thucydides is not concerned with the ultimate law behind the observed facts.

In the first place, it may be seriously doubted whether any man is capable of devoting almost his entire life to the study of a complicated military-political-economic situation and avowedly setting it down as exactly and truthfully as he can for the guidance of posterity confronted with a similar situation—*without* a theory of ethics or politics. But without canvassing any further the possibilities of such a thing, one must at once reject the leading evidence which Jebb cites to support his words. If there is one historian who busies himself incessantly with the "ultimate laws" which are behind the "observed facts," that historian is Thucydides. For instance, the chapters on *stasis* in Corcyra are surely full of implicit comments on the human nature that makes the *stasis* possible. And we also have an elaborate description of the effects of the loss of religion at the time of the plague.[6] The speeches of Cleon against the people of Mitylene[7] and the Melian Dialogue,[8] in whichever way they are construed, whether as Thucydides' personal exegesis of the spirit of Athenian imperialism or as the dramatic expression of speeches actually delivered, are full of evidence of a theory of "ultimate law behind the observed facts."

Shorey, on the other hand, has made an excellent formulation of the basic principles of Thucydidean history-writing when he says that Thucydides, as an ethical positivist, believes that the nature and conduct of man "are strictly determined by his physical and social environment and by a few elementary appetites and desires."[9] But a little further on we see Shorey's personal moral coloring creeping in, and the whole picture emerges as falser than Jebb's, though in point of statement it is more correct. "The *naïve* man is duped by this moral drapery," says Shorey; "the *wise* man is not so deceived."[10] These are not Thucydidean terms at all. And the proof is that Shorey, in order to inject the necessary complacency into Thucydides, has had to manhandle philologically or patronize sentimentally Thucydides' genuinely pitying comments on the elimination of the decent elements in the citizenry during the class wars, on the last speeches of Nicias in the Sicilian campaign, and, finally, on the death of Nicias himself. It is quite plain that the hard-boiled realist that Shorey pictures cannot possibly be unified with the author of these three passages.[11]

And, finally, neither the one school nor the other can make anything intelligible out of one of the very few outright and explicit moral comments made by Thucydides himself—his judgment on the orator Antiphon, who was the brains of the extreme section of the oligarchs in their revolution of 411 and who proceeded to the utmost of brutality and violence in his political actions and ultimately failed and was condemned to death by the restored democracy. About this man Thucydides says, "In respect of *virtue* (*arete*) he was second to none of his contemporaries."[12]

2

As a first step toward a more adequate view of Thucydides' political theory, let us look again at the concept of power as it developed in fifth-century Athens; that is, at the political milieu revealed in the key speeches quoted at the outset of this essay.

Because the greatness of the Athenian empire was in the eyes of its inhabitants man-made and based on its exploitation of material resources, almost exclusively, because there is no attempt to believe in a divinely imposed task or a more than human duty or the perfectibility of man, political rhetoric in fifth-century Athens develops a theory of human nature based essentially on nothing but animal desires and their satisfaction. Were there a theory of man in political dominion as a creature existing in the sight of God, or of man as in some sense perfectible in his social relations, the Athenian would not feel so sure that he had seen all that there was to see in the development of political power. But, since there was no such theory in their political consciousness, the particular expansion of Athens with its tremendously clear evidence of causation in human and material terms led inevitably to the formulation of human political aspirations in the same terms, and so for the Athenians, as for the Greeks as a whole, men in their national entities became, in the last stages of empire, the raw material on which the aspirant to political power worked. No longer geography and no longer land and no longer resources but men—in the empire, in the state, and in the family. The symbol of advancement became power, and power was finally sought just for its own sake.

Furthermore, power, rooted as it was first in the exploitation of physical and material resources and later men, and at no point growing in the framework of any metaphysical theory which took account of any world outside man's activities, makes its advances in terms of techniques. The Corinthians, in arguing with the Spartans on the relative inadequacy of Spartan institutions to meet the aggressiveness of Athens, say:

"Even had you a city like yourselves for a neighbor you would hardly obtain security, but as things stand, as we have just indicated, your institutions are old-fashioned. Successive stages of advance must always master the preceding—as in the case of technical development. If a state is to be left in peace, an unchanging code of custom is best, but a state that is compelled to face a number of different situations needs a capacity for advance in technique.[13] That is why the Athenians have made more innovations to your disadvantage—because of their larger experience."[14]

The peculiar horror of the brutality which accompanied the internal disintegration of the states is also at least partly this—that this cruelty, too, advanced technically. In the chapter on *stasis* Thucydides says: "The city-states were continually in a revolutionary ferment, and the outbreaks which came later profited by the knowledge of what had gone before and carried much further an extraordinary degree of innovation, both in the technical contrivance of the coups d'état and the strange horrors of their reprisals."[15] The procedures in dealing with other states were crystallized round essentially technical questions in the effective administration of the empire. In 427, when revolted Mitylene was to be punished and Cleon angrily urged the execution of all its men and the enslavement of its women and children, Diodotus, the speaker for the cause of mercy, won the day. But on very significant grounds: that Cleon, in introducing questions of the general justice and injustice of the Mitylenean revolt and in manifestly conceiving the situation in vindictive or personal terms, was out of order.[16] The single question is one of technical politics: Will such an act of cruelty profit our empire in its practical aspect?[17] The discussion is carried further by Diodotus into the general question of the social effectiveness of capital punishment. Sometimes the enlightened conclusions of the speaker have been admired,[18] but it has hardly been stressed enough that the basic assumptions are hardly moral at all. That is to say, the question is not whether or not certain crimes are in themselves offenses against humanity that in some invisible order of justice call for retribution but simply whether society is most effectively dealing with a social nuisance by means of capital punishment or not.

As power became largely a matter of technique, it became

more visible and tangible. The empire of Athens is represented concretely to the Greek world by the transfer of the treasury from Delos to Athens,[19] in the organization of the Athenian law courts to deal with commercial suits involving disputes between the allies and the imperial power,[20] in the technical position of the Athenian cleruchies settled in allied territory.[21] Furthermore, in private life the same scale of values is accepted as correct. Privileges of a material worth were considered by some the outward mark of the "superior" man. As Callicles in the *Gorgias* says, "The superior and more intelligent man should have more than his inferiors and be ruler over them."[22]

The staggering clarity and simplicity of this proposition only come home to us by comparison with later aspects of civilization in the Western world. The superior man in the Roman Republic or the Empire might have his personal human value expressed for the society in many different ways other than the obvious material ones. Under the Republic, the combination of humble ancestry, farming, and an ancient peasant stock remained almost to the end the proper coloring for the candidate who sought the electors' votes.[23] After 202, it was largely a sham, yet it never failed to be that which the people wanted in its rulers; and, when the people came into their own again as electors in 108, it was precisely by capitalizing on such moral assets that Marius became consul.[24] The concept of civil servant in the Roman Empire is not only not particularly associated with material advantage but especially with the exalted spiritual position of the exponent of *Romanitas*. Once Christianity is the accepted code of the Empire, the theoretical insistence on the opposition of wealth and the good of the soul opens the way to a thousand positions in which the community can see honor and distinction in terms other than material advantage.

But the significant thing is that, as the power of the Athenian empire over the rest of Greece belonged in no order of value other than materialism, and since, as a consequence, its expressions are peculiarly technical, it generates a simple theory of power politics for international relations which soon outruns its merely national applications. At first the national entity which by its coherence in spirit, institutions, and resources can impose its will on other nations is the recognized unit which figures in the nationalistic apologetics urged, for instance, by the Athenian envoys at Sparta in 432. Later a single group within a state saw that with the proper opportunities it could effectively exercise power exclusively in its own interest.[25] Here the principle of the pursuit of power as a means of advancement is the same, and it is still to some extent a communal affair, but the dimensions of the community have shrunk; it is now the rich as against the poor, or the poor against the rich. But the theory of power as the ultimate proof of superiority and the right of the superior man does not stop there. The last stage is the tyrannical man. Gradually the "natural" privileges of the superior being become psychologically attractive not only to states or to factions but to the individuals in the society. The end of the road is Alcibiades, who says, "Love of city I have not where I am wronged, but where my citizenship was secure."[26]

To see it another way, the materialism of the Athenian empire linked with the political system of Athens has the consequence that there is virtually no division, finally, between political and personal morality. Because the fusion of the individual and the state in fifth-century Athens was more complete than in the case of any other significant political community known to us, and because the nature of the empire was expressed in such clear terms for every Athenian citizen—in the buildings of the Acropolis, in the festivals, in the availability of imported goods—it was inevitable that the morality of the empire should also be the morality of the individual citizen. As the empire in its purposeful extension first, and in its repressive measures later, becomes violent and tyrannical, so the individual citizen who has personally voted on the imperialistic and repressive plans must have applied its lessons to his own life. It is important to notice that Euphemos, an Athenian pleading the cause of the Athenian alliance before the people of Camarina in Sicily, refers to "a man *or a city* which would be a tyrant."[27] And both Pericles and Cleon in their speeches before the assembly at Athens describe the rule of Athens over her empire as a "tyranny."[28] The analogy between the individual and the state is already made. It only needed the pressure of the war to bring it out. The extraordinary cynicism of some of the speeches in Thucydides, speeches before the assembly like that of Cleon on the Mityleneans, has been the occasion of surprise to a modern generation of readers. Even the most openly brutal book of our time, *Mein Kampf*, is based on some mystical faith in the destiny of Germany and its significance. But Cleon and Diodotus at Athens and Euphemos before the Sicilians, or the Athenian envoys at Sparta, speak openly of their state's imperialism and its cruelty, greed, and aggressiveness, merely claiming for all these qualities the sanction of human behavior at any time, when seriously examined.

One is inclined to wonder whether any large body of people, such as that which listened to these speeches, can have had the requisite cynicism to applaud them. The key is in the essentially democratic nature of the Athenian state and in the want of any strongly intrenched private morality to combat this exhibition of public cynicism. The dual standard of morality, one half applicable to political life and political power and the other to the individual's personal dealings, is never a very strong thing; but when, as in the last half of the fifth century, the half that belongs purely to the individual's life has no authoritarian basis, either in creed or in science, it is especially weak when confronted continuously with the necessity of acting, in a public way, counter to whatever standard of conduct is traditionally expected of the single citizen. And such necessity, there is very little doubt, lay upon every citizen who attended the Athenian assembly and voted on the measures needful to uphold the power of Athens abroad. In the man who incurred the moral responsibility of voting "Yes" to the destruction of Mitylene is the form of the possible tyrant within his own state. And since the procedures of Athens were the norm of Greek political behavior, the brutality of frankness is the rule in speeches elsewhere than at home.

It is true, of course, that the great period of tyrannies in Greece was not in the last quarter of the fifth century but in the seventh and sixth. But it is also true and deeply significant that Plato, in his study of the degenerate states, puts the tyranny as a development of the extreme democracy.[29] The earlier tyrannies and the later are not akin except in name and the acquisition of unconstitutional power. The earlier tyrannies were a means of bridging the gap between the period of feudalism and the coming plutocracy.[30] They constitute a necessary step, in political growth, and as far as political theory is concerned are quite unself-conscious. And they invariably arise from the people and not from the aristocracy which they supplant. The tyranny which haunted the minds of the fifth-century Athenians and took shape tentatively in Alcibiades and actually in Critias and his associates was a philosophically conceived monster bred of the collapse of any collective political morality but an exact replica in the tyrant himself of the dimensions and quality of the political morality of the Athenian state for nearly eighty years.

It is a cynical joke of history that this true philosophic growth, the later tyrant, had a short and insignificant success, relative to his earlier ancestor. There were tyrannies in very many states in Greece in the seventh and sixth centuries, and some lasted quite a long time—that of Athens under Peisistratos and his sons nearly fifty years.[31] But Alcibiades was only a halfway tyrant, keeping his position for but a few years, ultimately losing to a popular vote, constitutionally cast; and Critias and his associates, the so-called "Thirty Tyrants," ruled for less than a year. Yet this much must be said. The democracy of the fourth century which succeeded the last period of the Peloponnesian War and the disintegration of the imperialist democracy was never, in fact, alive, theoretically, in the way its predecessors had life.

That is abundantly clear even from its own spokesmen, Demosthenes and Isocrates. In a real historical sense Plato's sketch of the degenerate states is true: the logical end of the political process in Athens was the tyranny. It lasted a very short time and might almost be termed insignificant in its practical manifestations. Yet it is, theoretically, enormously important. It is the end of the fifth century and the Athenian political imperialism. With the imperialism the older democracy died too. What is left in the fourth century are only the dry bones clad in whatever rags and shreds of political propaganda happen to fit.

We must try, then, to find Thucydides' view of politics in the way he sees the growth of this democracy and this imperialism.

The supporting evidence from the *History* is only a series of hints which are not susceptible of certain interpretation. But it should, I think, dispel the idea that there is no moral conviction behind Thucydides' observation of the facts, and it should establish at least the nature of the political theory in the light of which he saw the facts. For understanding Thucydides is in the truest sense of the word to understand the Greece of his time, since he is one with it, in that he thoroughly comprehends the thought behind the political movements that he saw and presents it with the completeness of such absolute knowledge.

CHAPTER IV

Thucydides and the Athenian Democracy

1

THE democracy of Athens, of Thucydides' time, had been, as he says himself,[1] of about a hundred years' duration. Not, it is true, in exactly the same form, but surprisingly close to it, as we know principally from Aristotle's *Constitution of Athens* and from Plutarch's *Lives*.[2] After Cleisthenes broke up the ancestral Attic tribes in 510 and established local residence as the qualification for voting, the further changes, important though they are—universal suffrage without property restriction, universal eligibility for office, the popular courts as the final judgment on the conduct of magistrates, and payment for office-holding—only complete the model of the Cleisthenic reforms. The definitive departure from the earlier forms of government in Athens is the ending of the blood brotherhoods as the significant unit in political association.[3] The reason for this is fairly simple. So long as the blood brotherhoods and their larger organizations, the tribes, form the framework of political life, traditional associations, the antiquity of families, and the sanctity of religious ties between families and individuals are necessarily strong forces in the direction of conservatism. In certain states where no such break with the past was made as took place in Athens—in Corinth, Megara, and Sicyon, for instance—the transition from an aristocracy to an oligarchy of wealth, though punctuated by periods of dictatorship, is easily made.[4] In other states, such as Thessaly, Boeotia, and Sparta, where the traditional blood ties also remained undissolved, the aristocracy remained as a feudal landholding governing class. Only in Athens, where the traditional forces of family, blood, and religion were at a single blow deprived of political significance, did a genuine political democracy grow up out of the older organization. In the few other democratic states in Greece, the democracies had almost all come into being as the result of outside and usually Athenian pressure and consequently did not count, psychologically, in the eyes of their Greek contemporaries.[5] This is the reason why Pericles announces so proudly that his state has a constitution which does not envy that of others but is a model for them.[6] That is why Alcibiades attacks democracy, in his speech at Sparta, as "acknowledged lunacy."[7] It was a thing virtually unique and Athenian in fifth-century Greece.

2

It is idle to say that the differences between the Athenian democracy and our twentieth-century Anglo-American or Continental versions are two or three or four. The enormous size and complexity of a modern state make countless the significant differences between us. But it is probably true enough to say that a recollection of two or three remarkable political differences between the Athenians and ourselves helps a student effectively in imagining himself into their political life.

The first is a philosophical difference. The Athenians had not created their democracy in the name of the universal equality of man, as the Americans or as the French did, nor did they even acknowledge the universal applicability of democratic principles, as the British have sometimes done in the course of changes in their constitutional history. Athenian democracy remained, as Pericles said, a model for outside imitation; but the Athenians did not feel constrained to do anything about spreading it, except as an instrument of political usefulness abroad. That this last at times became an important factor we know. Diodotus, in opposing Cleon's proposition against the people of Mitylene, says that severity against the total population of a subject state in the Athenian confederacy will result in the loss of popularity for the Athenian demos among the common people of this state or other states.[8] And he himself declares that this is an important influence in maintaining Athenian control. The whole, we have noticed, is quite cynically argued. The vital thing is the preservation of the empire; the matters important to consider are the psychological aspects favorable to such preservation. It is because of this strictly nationalistic tinge to Athenian democracy that the extreme wing of the democratic party can openly argue for policies abroad which are the reverse of democratic. Indeed, as Cleon says, the peculiar qualities of Athenian democracy, the freedom of political association and speech, are extremely unfavorable to a stable and uniform conduct of imperial affairs.[9] His conclusion is certainly not that there is something wrong with democracy at home. It is simply that the Athenians should firmly resolve not to be democratic abroad.

While we keep this fact in mind, that no one in Athens would seriously accuse Cleon of a fatal inconsistency in this policy, it is interesting to note that some approaches to democracy were perhaps unwillingly and perhaps hypocritically made by the Athenian democrats who administered the Athenian empire. Matters in dispute between Athens and her subject states, matters concerning mercantile contracts and commercial rights, were settled by the Athenian courts; but the notable thing is that they were settled by law courts and not by the Athenian army, a thing Cleon bitterly criticizes.[10] Moreover, the shadow of local autonomy was preserved in the states; they were governed by men professing democratic principles and administering a democratic organization, and, although we have enough evidence from the pages of Thucydides that those democratic governments came into being at the dictation of Athens and that no other kind suited, there were no Athenian armies kept on the spot to back the local government.[11] And we should remember that, when Sparta took over the empire in 404, Spartan garrisons with military governors were an indispensable condition to even the brief existence of the oligarchic governments which she created throughout Greece.

The second difference between the Athenian and later democracies is a mechanical one—the often discussed lack of a representative system in the Athenian democracy. As a result of this lack, the will of the people was expressed in the assembly by whatever number of citizens happened to be on the spot. Admitting that at times there were periods of apathetic attendance,[12] for the most part, matters of public policy, the general's account of his campaign, and the decisions affecting peace or war (as in 432) were submitted to a body of laymen numbering thousands and completely without individual responsibility to a larger public. It is only in our own day, the day of fireside chats aimed directly at the electorate and over the heads of their representatives, of Gallup polls and multiple-signed telegrams and letters sent to administrative officers and members of Congress, that we find again so direct a pressure of the mass of the people, or organized blocs of the mass of the people, upon those who govern them. The will of the people of Attica, which in terms of attendance normally meant the will of the people of Athens, struck their elected governors with an immediate impact and, except in rare cases such as Pericles, superseded the judgment of the government as to the long-term good and ill of its constituents.

When there is added to this the short life of the Athenian administration—one year only—the fact that officials when they turned in their books faced immediate trial for unsatisfactory conduct before the popular courts, and the almost total want of a permanent civil service, one sees a democracy operating literally on the immediate and day-to-day will of the people. The intense caution of a man like Nicias, who made his political fortune largely by doing nothing and passing all real issues on to the opposite party or the administration who succeeded him; the demagogic vulgarity of Cleon, who made *his* political fortune by letting neither decency, mercy, nor honesty stand in the way of giving the largest number of people the largest amount of material goods and prestige from one moment to the next, thus earning his political sobriquet "the watchdog of the people";[13] the extraordinary tricks, tergiversations, and popular coups, now successful and now abortive, of an Alcibiades, that brilliant personage who played the democratic game when he had to, though he was later to describe it, with heartfelt conviction, as acknowledged lunacy; above all, the real uniqueness and power of the lonely Pericles, who could lead the people and not flatter them—all become comprehensible when put in the setting of this very direct democracy.

A third point of comparison—we will call it that, since the difference from the practice of our times is much less great than in the two former cases—is the Athenian system of party government with relation to the administration. The archons, nine in number and nominally the "governing ones," were by the middle of the fifth century quite insignificant. They were selected by lot from the entire people,[14] and not even the Athenians with their fanatical insistence on universal rights for the citizenry desired an administration chosen in such a haphazard way. The archons administered the religious festivals and certain of the public formalities. The real administrative power was vested in the Board of Ten Generals, who were elected and worked with the Council of Five Hundred, which was chosen by a mixed procedure of election and lot as a committee of the assembly with the duty of framing resolutions in proper form for submission to the larger body and as a permanent governing body for the immediate political needs of Athens.[15] Apparently, though our records are not complete enough to be satisfactory, one of these generals was given a position of pre-eminence.[16] He corresponds with a combination of president and active commander-in-chief in the United States or prime minister and active commander-in-chief in Britain or France. The other generals were presumably deputed to minor administrative jobs.[17] Pericles held this leading position, with a few upsets, from 459 to 429; apparently at times such conservative

democrats as Nicias were associated with him in the administration.[18]

The administration in the person of the ten generals embodied
something which we could call party administration. That is to
say, we have on the confession of Thucydides, Plato, Aristotle,
and Plutarch the statement that through the last three quarters
of the fifth century there are two leading parties—that representing the many, who are variously called the demos, the many,
or the poor, and that representing the few, who are variously
called the best, the few, or the rich. The issues of empire, international commerce, trade as opposed to agriculture, universal
as opposed to limited franchise, split these two parties like a
knife. For a long time the rift remained merely a party difference, compatible with a unified co-operation in the framework
of the state. This was probably due partly to the possibilities of
expansionism in the imperial program from 478 to 432. Though
morally the oligarchs had strong views on the undesirability of
imperialism, their moral views were not really translated into a
desire to abandon the empire; and the empire and Athens with it
were prospering. It was also partly due to the person of Pericles.
Pericles was the aristocrat of aristocrats; his family was one of
the oldest in Attica and with a distinguished record of public
service. That he and his family had always led the democratic
party was looked upon as a kind of foible. We have it on the
authority of Aristotle that the people of property only became
seriously worried when the party of no property found leaders
no longer among the aristocracy but in tradesmen and work
people.[19]

3

Such, then, in brief outline, was the Athenian democracy in
Thucydides' day. In terms of formal adhesion to the principles
of one of the two parties—that of the many or of the few—it
looks as if Thucydides' affiliations would be easy to describe.
His views on the merits of the two parties seem at first sight

quite clear. He avows himself openly in favor of a moderate oligarchy when he praises the conservative constitution of Theramenes, which was briefly in effect in 411[20] He lists the shortcomings of the democracy as the guiding force in his country's destiny: explicitly when he speaks of their fickleness and unsteadiness toward Pericles[21] and after the debacle of the Syracusan expedition,[22] where the failure of the expedition is attributed to the democracy; implicitly in the letter of Nicias to his home government: "Your natures, you see, are difficult to rule";[23] and: "Because, too, I know your natures—that you want to hear the pleasantest things, but find fault afterward if you find that the outcome of them is not equally pleasant—I decided that the safer course was to give you a clear account of the truth."[24] And again: "The enemy's relief coming from the Peloponnesus will be slower, it is true, but if you do not watch carefully, you will overlook the one *as you did before*, and he will be too quick for you with the other."[25]

Implicitly, again, the undesirability of control by the larger masses of people is conveyed in the verdict on Pericles himself: "The reason [for his success] was that to *him* the people, though free, were subjects, and that he led them himself rather than was led by them";[26] or when he says in praise of Alcibiades: "At that moment there was no other single person except Alcibiades who could hold the mob under control."[27]

Summing up, we could say that he regarded the Athenian democracy as one of the main reasons for the city's failure to win the war, that he favored some form of change of government that would vest the power in the hands of a select and presumably more intelligent few than the greedy and stupid mob which was the source of authority from the death of Pericles until the revolt of the Four Hundred, and that he discovers the big difference between the Periclean democracy and that of later days only in the supreme and able control vested in the hands of Pericles himself: "In name it was a democracy; but in fact it was ruled by its first citizen."[28]

Furthermore, the point of view here described—a philosophical distrust for a radical democracy, a practical preference for some fairly strict limitation of the franchise, and a distinction between the Periclean democracy and the "demagogic" democracy—is well known as the mildly oligarchical middle-of-the-road position clearly set forth in Aristotle's *Constitution of Athens*, where the historical processes of the fifth century which would support it are so obligingly described. There is no doubt that there is much truth in seeing in Thucydides an anticipation of the later oligarchic philosophy.[29]

CHAPTER V

Thucydides and the Athenian Empire

1

BUT to say of Thucydides that, in the last quarter of the fifth century B.C., he is an oligarch, only scratches the surface as far as our deeper interest in the political situation goes. For the real issue which was dividing political affiliation internationally and domestically was the moral position on the subject of power, and in Athens this was symbolized by the issue of the empire. And this issue does not clearly divide oligarchs from democrats.

By what right had Athens virtually obliterated the external autonomy of the various states which had originally joined her League of Delos against the menace of a recurrent Persian invasion? This was the outspoken question or indignant charge put by every state outside the Athenian sphere of influence. We can hear these charges in the mouths of the Spartan allies at the conference at Sparta before the war and again in the grim accusations of the Plataeans by the Thebans after the capture of Plataea in 427.[1] There is no doubt that, in exercising control over the external affairs of her confederate allies, Athens was outraging the accepted code of international Greek morality as it had existed from before the Persian Wars.

But it is significant to notice that in the pages of Thucydides the accusers of Athens by no means invariably assail Athens on this moral ground. The Corinthians openly declare to the Spartans that they blame not the Athenians for seizing whatever power they can acquire but the Spartans for the neglect of their own and their allies' interests in permitting such a thing to happen.[2] And later in the war Hermocrates, in defending a

"Monroe Doctrine" for Sicily, also sums up the situation by the naked statement that the Athenians are in no way blameworthy for following the dictates of human nature but only the Sicilian states for being so blind as not to see what was afoot and defend themselves.[3] We can thus see that even abroad the success of the Athenian empire was having its effect. That is to say, many of the enemies of Athens were *not* fighting her on moral grounds but only on grounds of national survival, while explicitly affirming, in intimate diplomatic talks, that the cries of injustice raised against Athens were really only a façade.

But this façade was, at least, put up, as we can see, in the claims of Sparta to fight the war against Athens as the champion of the autonomy of the smaller states.[4] And it is in the name of freedom that Brasidas won his extraordinary diplomatic victories in the northwest between 424 and 422.[5] We have, therefore, a moral issue being posed in international terms, by the Athenian empire, even at the particular moment when the most advanced political thinkers on both sides, both in the ranks of the Lacedaemonian confederacy and at Athens, cynically declared that morality was not the issue at all but the naked question: Who should, as the Greeks put it, have the hegemony of Greece?

This confused situation in the Greek states outside Athens is mirrored in the domestic policies of Athens herself. Here, too, we find a certain attempt on the part of some of the conservatives to oppose the empire on moral grounds and at least publicly to make this the slogan of the party. And consequently such conservatives are more favorably disposed to Sparta than to Athens, which openly avowed the cause of imperialism. Because of this they are loath to fight the war with any degree of energy and are really always hoping that the end will be an "arranged" peace so that Greece may again be administered diplomatically by a friendly understanding between the two original partners in the Greco-Persian Wars, Athens and Sparta. But by the time that the conservative party had become determined enough to destroy the democratic constitution and reform it on the basis of a limited franchise, it, too, was permeated by the new "realism" in morality and would surrender the empire only if this were the sole means of purchasing peace with Sparta and a reactionary settlement in Athens herself.

This ambivalence in attitude in the conservative party is perhaps not wholly the result of a change in moral position. It may, to some extent, be due to the fact that many of the early heroes of the conservatives had actually helped to build the empire when it was not yet quite clear that it was ceasing to be the League and becoming the empire. To study some significant details, it is particularly in the twenty-five years before 450 that we have indications that oligarchical preferences and a willingness to expand the area subject to direct Athenian control could go hand in hand. For instance, it was Aristeides who first promoted the confederacy of Delos, which, palpably, from the very start bore in it the seeds of a greater Athens, and he is cited in the *Constitution of Athens* as the leader of the conservative faction.[6] To take a more significant example, it was Cimon, himself an aristocrat and labeled by Aristotle as the leader of the aristocratic party,[7] who made the first definite annexations to the Athenian empire, as distinct from the voluntary inclusion of allies.

But there are fairly convincing proofs after 450 of a steadily growing aversion to the empire on the part of the conservative section of the Athenian electorate.[8] The first and strongest voice raised against the systematic exploitation of the allies, a voice raised not long after the formal transference of the treasury from Delos to Athens, was that of Thucydides, son of Melesias, whom we know to have been the leader of the oligarchical party against Pericles.[9] The statement, "It seems to us that this is a vile piece of insolence against the dignity of Greece and that which is clearly tyranny is being exercised over her. For she sees us gilding our city with the tribute which we force from the rest of Greece for the war; sees us in fact glorifying Athens like a courtesan hung about with precious stones and statues and

ships of a thousand talents' burden," is no doubt his.[10] There-
after the policy of the conservative parties in Athens—and it is
safer to speak of "conservative parties" than oligarchs, since we
have no real evidence of their desire to replace the democratic
by an oligarchic constitution prior to 411—appears to be steadily
opposed first to the extension of the empire, and then, when
the war presses them hard, they are a little more than ready to
abandon the empire in exchange for security at home, the security being inseparable from the limitation of the franchise
to such people as the conservatives were tolerably sure would
vote their way.

The anti-imperialist position of the conservative wing is more
or less forced upon them, irrespective of their moral convictions, since a termination of the war and friendship with Sparta
are essential if they are to check the extremes of democracy
at home, and such friendship with Sparta is only purchasable
in exchange for the abandonment of the empire, or at least a
considerable part of it. Thus there is a clearly discernible inclination on the part of the conservatives to regard the war as a
nuisance of democratic contrivance and an increasing willingness to see in Sparta not an enemy but the preserver of oligarchic privilege throughout Greece. Hence we find an alignment in the conservative camp of antidemocratic, anti-imperialist, antiwar, and, finally, pro-Spartan elements.

The mixture, of course, takes a long time to solidify. For instance, there is no reason to suppose that Nicias had not deserved his reputation for loyalty and safety in his various gen-
eralships down to 421. And yet, surely, Nicias did make a peace
with Sparta in that year at a moment not very propitious to
Athenian imperial interests and certainly at a moment which
delivered Sparta from various difficulties. Athens still held the
prisoners of Sphacteria, and Sparta was as anxious to obtain
them as she had been in 424. The Spartan treaty with Argos
was due to lapse in 420, and the position of Sparta, with a hostile
Argos to face in the Peloponnesus and the Athenian fleet to

oppose her at sea, was most unenviable.[11] A resolutely anti-Spartan policy might have then implemented with far greater success the schemes of Alcibiades, halfheartedly carried through in 418. The Nicias-Pleistoanax peace was a stall for time, and Sparta should not have been granted time at this juncture.

Again in the debates on the Sicilian expedition in 415, we find Nicias opposed to the audacious project of conquest there submitted for discussion.[12] It is quite true that this opposition may have proceeded from Nicias' personal caution. No doubt, he still had in his head the advice of Pericles at the beginning of the war: you will be safe if you do not extend the empire.[13] But it must be remembered that Thucydides' own appraisal of the Sicilian expedition is of a project fundamentally sound and practical in its conception and only marred by the incompetence of the political administration at home.[14] When the expedition is beaten and the defeat completed, Nicias surrenders to the Spartan Gylippus, "for his trust in him was greater than in the Syracusans."[15] And his death is due not to Spartan but to Sicilian agency.[16]

The policy of the oligarchic party installed by the coup d'état of 411 is a further advance in the direction of abandonment of the war and friendship with Sparta. It is true that the movement toward the oligarchic change comes from Alcibiades, who was the former leader of the democratic party, and that the arguments he uses are to the effect that a shift from democracy to oligarchy will win the Great King's friendship and that the Great King's friendship will win the war for Athens.[17] But, as soon as the oligarchs get near the objective of abolishing the democratic constitution, the policy of ending the war by negotiation is at once mooted. Almost the first act of the new oligarchic regime was to make peace feelers to the Spartan king Agis, and it was only the political naïveté of the latter which prevented their acceptance.[18] As the pressure on the oligarchs increases, their willingness to accept Sparta almost as protector becomes obvious—and this is 411, not 404. Thucydides himself records his opinion as follows: "They wanted, most of all, to rule the allies too, but if they could not do that, they wanted independence with their fleet and fortifications intact, and if they were debarred even from that, they wanted at all costs to avoid their own liquidation at the hands of a restored democracy, and, rather than this, were ready to bring in the enemy, come to an agreement abandoning ships and fortifications to him, and letting him have control of the city, providing they could buy their own personal safety therewith."[19] It is unnecessary to carry the story further, except to notice that what Critias did in 404, in accepting a Spartan garrison and governor and ruling with their aid, is already clearly foreshadowed in the conduct of the leaders of the Revolution of the Four Hundred in 411.

In surveying the development of conservative foreign policy at Athens from 450 to 404, we may, perhaps, find the clue to the shift from conservative democracy to oligarchy and from honest acquiescence in a democratically voted war policy to the final surrender of their country to its enemy in the domestic effects of Athenian imperialism. Here we must be content with other than first-rate proofs, but, such as they are, they are not inconclusive. The *Old Oligarch* indulges in tirades against the mass of foreigners in Athens and the insolence of the vast citizen body no longer held in check by their sense of aristocratic privilege or subservience to wealth.[20] In the *Laws* Plato discusses the undesirability of foreign trade because it introduces into the city a horde of foreigners, unacquainted with its traditional customs, and too numerous to be absorbed easily.[21] The sneers directed at the manners of speech and deportment of Cleon and his associates by such oligarchically inclined writers as Aristophanes and Aristotle point the same moral.[22] As the empire increased in wealth and extent, the population of the capital became one where the traditional privileges of the well-born or wealthy met with no traditional acceptance. Athens ceased to be governed by gentlemen. The wealth acquired by trade was for the most part in the hands of the metics, or resident foreigners. The financial resources of the typical oligarch were drawn either from landed estates, which were destroyed by the Spartan invasion,[23] or from investment in the mines,[24] likewise destroyed by Spartan occupation in 413,[25] or from professional skill, such as the law, where the people's dislike of cleverness, education, or sophistication was a constant stumbling block.[26] With all these factors increasing in force, it was very likely that the conservative democrat of the 420's should become the reactionary oligarch of 404.

2

Thucydides' own attitude to the imperialism he saw develop and expand in his lifetime can be defined to some small extent by positive statements in the *History* and much more completely by negative inferences. Let us take, first, what positive evidence there is.

In his *Archaeology*[27] Thucydides gives an account of the development of Greece from the earliest times down to the League of Delos, and this together with his version of events during the fifty years from 478 to the beginning of the war is for him the raising of the curtain to the great event he is about to chronicle. In this entire story we are made aware of what one can only call a "natural" or inevitable development, that is, a compulsion exerted upon individual states in terms of geographic and economic necessities which when united with a certain temperament in the inhabitants lead to certain "natural" results.[28] Money, commerce, naval power, and large-scale centralization are the necessary steps on the road which leads from a condition of simple barbarism to the developed and sophisticated empire of Athens.

This prehistory proper and pre–Peloponnesian War history lead straight on to Thucydides' own expressed opinion of the cause of the war. This was, we are told, the Spartan fear of the growing power of Athens.[29] Directly contrasted with this, the real cause of the war, we are told about what was most *said* to be the cause[30] at the time of the outbreak, the Corcyraean affair and the attack on Potidaea.

We are at once reminded of a series of oppositions which dot the pages of the *Archaeology* and the *Fifty Years*. There we hear often of the real, always materialistic causes which Thucydides discovers as opposed to various fanciful and romantic accounts given by poets like Homer or historians like Herodotus.[31] These "real" factors in the development of history are certainly not confined to geography and resources; they take in the whole psychology of the human beings concerned. For instance, it is Sparta's fear of Athens that is important, not merely the fact of Athens' power. It is the Corinthians' impression of the Athenian character that matters, not merely the existence of that character and temperament.

On the other hand, the issue of freedom or slavery as such, with the moral connotations of either, is never explicitly commented on by Thucydides in person. This theme occurs in the mouths of the representatives of various peoples,[32] as important factors in their eyes, or on their lips, at any rate; but nowhere does Thucydides vouch for the actual existence of a genuine power in the moral issues themselves.

It may be that Thucydides' sense of the dimness of these moral issues in any given political situation is virtually forced upon him by the historical situation. The practical question of justice or injustice in international procedure in his day almost always fell back to claims as to what this country or that did against the Persians in the wars of 490 and 480. And it is exactly the association of the theme of freedom and slavery with the Persian Wars which renders it suspect in the eyes of Thucydides. It was in the conflict with the Persians that the Greeks achieved their first superficial unity, in what was for the fifth century "modern" times. The Trojan War, with all its historical verity for them, *did* belong to a very remote past. This was the first time, within practically verifiable recollection, that the various Greek states had, even temporarily, yielded some of their local independence in the undertaking of a common plan—the defeat of the Persians. Freedom meant for a Greek prior to 480 just the right of his own community to manage its own affairs, irrespective of the form of government which his community favored. And, in order to make even the temporary surrender of such autonomy acceptable, the entire conflict between the Greek world and the Persian had to be represented as a community issue of freedom against slavery.

It is therefore significant that in the eighth book of Herodotus the direct appeal of the Persian spokesman, Alexander of Macedon, is made to the Athenians in the name of the local autonomy which, the Macedonian declares, the Persian king is willing to concede to Athens.[33] That this was extremely effective propaganda is evidenced by the concern of the Spartans lest Athens should accept.[34] And the ringing answer of the Athenians, their championship of the Greek world, alike in blood, language, and custom, is, in a genuine way, a new thing.[35] The formation of the League of Delos in 478 was on the side of the allies a consequence of their realization of the effectiveness of the centralized control exercised by Athens and Sparta during the Persian Wars and constituted an effort to continue the last phases of the war, after the departure of the Persians from Greek soil, on the same basis.

There is, I think, no evidence that the allied Greek states ever thought of the League as a permanent feature of their national life. The assumption presumably was that after the satisfactory liquidation of the remains of the Persian power in Europe, and after the recouping of the damages inflicted by the Persians, the League would dissolve. That is the implication, at least, in the indignant speeches of such people as the Theban spokesmen against the Plataeans:

"The Plataeans claim that when the Persians came against Greece they were the only ones of the Boeotians who did not take the Persians' side. That is the principal source of their pride in themselves and their insults against us. But we, for our part, say that they did not join the Persians then because the Athenians did not do so either, but that, by the same token, when later the Athenians assaulted the rest of the Greeks, they, the Plataeans, were the only Boeotians that took the Athenian side."[36]

Thus the idea of justice or injustice in international procedure resolved itself into the issue of freedom or slavery, and this was very simply understood as the sole right of a given community to live as it pleased in terms of its legislative, administrative, and judicial procedures.

This immediate and direct local autonomy is challenged in the pages of Thucydides' *History* by the other concept of a relatively centralized government. It is significant that we see that for Thucydides the process is continuous, that is, extending from the *Archaeology* through his own days. Sicily in the 420's is going through the same development that continental Greece had experienced earlier, and, just as in continental Greece in the thirteenth and twelfth centuries the fear of pirates and the increase in trade led to the formation of all larger units of government, so, faced with the menace of Athens and Sparta, Hermocrates advised the Sicilians to band together under the leadership of Syracuse.[37] As he points out, such temporary surrender of their particular advantages to the larger advantage of the larger unity is the only way that even the particular Sicilian states will survive without direct subjection to an outside power. The same point is made again, several times, against the Spartans.[38] They manage *their* allies by seeing to it that no state in their sphere of influence has a form of government which is unsuitable to them; that is, all Spartan-controlled states are governed by oligarchies. Where Athens is not already in a position to impose her will directly on another state, she works hard to see that an allegedly "democratic" machine is in charge of the government.

Thus for Thucydides and many of his most penetrating contemporaries the issue of freedom and slavery is old-fashioned and insignificant. The subjection of weaker to stronger states in some form is the necessary trend of the times. It is only the form which is important. And so, too, international justice consists not in the older simple rule that each state should manage its own affairs but in the kind of interference the ruling power practiced. It is actually at this point that the descent to atrocity starts—not from the earlier principle of the rights of small states. And it is in the light of this realization—that neither Athens, Sparta, nor Syracuse, later, proposed to leave their associate states "free" in the old sense—that Thucydides describes the gradations in which the ruling city first maintains a wavering sense of some extraneous "justice" or balance or fairness in her treatment of her subjects but is gradually forced by circumstance to treat the subject people purely as a means to an end, practicing only such decency as is completely inexpensive.

Thucydides' contention throughout both the *Archaeology* and the *Fifty Years* is that all previous wars, in point of view of scale and significance,[39] are dwarfed by comparison with the Peloponnesian War. The Persian Wars belong to the past, and their moral issue, freedom or slavery, fades into insignificance before what those same Greeks did to one another when they attained the height of their power. As if to mark the deadness of the entire Greek-barbarian issue, Thucydides is careful to record in the first book the willingness of Sparta to enlist Persian help[40]—and Athens accepted back Alcibiades to win Persian help.[41] Thucydides himself, in his estimate of Pericles' judgment in the war, is at pains to point out that Persian help was one of the decisive factors in the ultimate victory of Sparta.[42] We know that Greece was haunted by the ghosts of the warriors of Marathon[43] and that the issues of the Persian Wars seemed to the contemporary critical "moderns" of the last half of the fifth century old-fashioned and meaningless. It is hard not to feel that Thucydides is in agreement with the Thebans in their contention against the people of Plataea that what they did in the

Persian Wars has no bearing on their political position in the contemporary world.[44]

Of course it is theoretically possible with a historian as austerely bent upon refraining from comment as Thucydides to assume that the absence of a direct moral censure of the empire may still carry with it an unspoken censure on the part of the historian. Yet a close survey of the *History* will hardly bear this out. He does actually comment favorably and unfavorably on some institutions and on many men throughout this war. He passes judgment, contemptuously and bitterly, on the institution of democracy, not once but many times.[45] He openly declares that the best government Athens had in his time was the oligarchic regime of Theramenes.[46] He speaks of the "vulgarity" of Hyperbolus.[47] He gives us the views of "sensible" men on Cleon,[48] which is fair evidence that he thinks the judgment "sensible" himself. He says that the crime against the children of Mycalessus was "the most terrible" in the war.[49] He says that Nicias "deserved least to die as he did."[50] And, above all, in his chapters on *stasis*[51] he bears indisputable testimony to his belief in the meaningfulness of moral epithets. No Greek can speak of a decency and nobility, etc., without indicating that he thinks there are such qualities as decency and nobility. The old values are overthrown in times of revolution, but he writes as a man who knew they had existed and did in some sense exist, even if human beings no longer paid them their former homage. In view of all these direct comments on individuals as moral creatures and on moral changes in the community, it is only reasonable to assume that the absence of any moral censure of the empire, the like of which he visited on the democracy, on its leaders, and on individual acts and men, must mean that he did not consider such a moral rebuke in order.

We have, then, come to the conclusion that the point of view from which the *History* is written is not that of a democrat or perhaps even that of an oligarch of the ordinary party affiliation. Not democrat because, quite apart from Thucydides' numerous unfavorable criticisms of democracy in action, he has gone on record in favor of the constitution of Theramenes, which replaced the older democratic constitution, and specifically rejected the notion of an unlimited franchise, which is the keystone of the democratic position. Yet he is not the older kind of oligarch certainly, since he has no moral censure for the empire or, in general, for the violation of the old-fashioned autonomy of the various states. In describing Thucydides as neither a party democrat nor an old-line oligarch, I do not mean to emphasize the want of a direct party affiliation. When he held his generalship in the northwest in 422, he did so presumably in conjunction with a conservative democratic administration. He was not in Athens at the time of Theramenes' revolution, which he praises. But, leaving out of account his party adherence, he is against the avowed principles of the democrats or the oligarchs in rejecting the rule of the many and refusing to criticize the rule of one state over another. What we are looking for, then, is not a third-party affiliation into which the historian fits but a third theoretical position politically.

My contention is that this position consisted in seeing that the aspiration toward power, both in the individual and the nation, is the most basic of human qualities and the quality in the light of which the historian should judge all political actions but that within this framework of a new political theory, widely current in the fifth century, Thucydides exhibits two personal deviations—an understanding pity for the victims of chance in the game of political power and a unique political value, assigned to the thing created by the aspiration toward power and the relation between it and the man or men who created it.

CHAPTER VI

Historical Necessity

1

IT IS worth while to notice again how Thucydides in his survey of past history—the history of ancient times and the fifty years—stresses the interaction of the psychological and materialistic factors and how he takes issue with the poets and logographers of the past for their distortion of the emphasis on each. The scope of these chapters is concerned with the need of proving that no other war before Thucydides' time can have been as important or as large as the Peloponnesian War. And, though the stress on this point is perhaps somewhat subtler, no other historian before his time has handled the material as a serious historian ought to have handled it. Therefore he has chosen to examine these two great wars of the past, the Trojan and the Persian conflicts, in the parade of past history and in his own terms to point out the hidden significance of events which the vainglory of the poets and the unscrupulous popularizing of the chroniclers have obscured.

The prolonged siege of Troy, for instance, is due not to the tenacity and courage of the Trojans but to the ineffectuality of the Greek arms, and this is owing to their inability to bring sufficient provision with them to maintain the siege with all their force.[1] The war, then, is, in this particular and in others, revealed as an insignificant affair in fact as opposed to its repute, which it owes to the poets.[2] Agamemnon's power over the suitors is due not to the oath that bound them to him—a fanciful tale—but to his wealth, in which he excelled the princes of his time.[3] And Homer's evidence concerning the Arcadians confirms the extent of Agamemnon's power, though Thucydides even here permits himself to sneer at his authority.[4]

But his whole account is far more than an attack upon the older poets and chroniclers. It is asserting that, for a man who wants to know the truth about the past, an honest search into that past will indicate that Greece's weakness until the early fifth century and her strength since then is a matter of money, commerce, naval power, and large-scale combination and centralization.[5] Therefore, what the poets and chroniclers have to say is only cited as indirect evidence of a truth which they consciously or unconsciously try to conceal.

As we look at the factors of sea power, centralization, commerce, and money, we are impressed by the close parallels in this, Thucydidies' own account of the growth of Greek civilization, with the account of the Athenian envoys, quoted at the outset of this essay, of how they came by their empire: in virtue, namely, of men's fear, honor, and greed.[6] In the establishment of larger cities and the growth of commerce, we are told in Book i, "the weaker, being eager for gain, submitted to the slavery of the mightier, and the more powerful, having a surplus at their disposal, compelled the lesser cities to be their subjects."[7] Here surely are fear and gain. And the omission of the great events due to honor is, I think, deliberate. The time for honor is, as we shall see, the time of the great days; and the great days are not yet. They are still to come in the Athens of Pericles.

We must always remember in reading the *History* of Thucydides that it is a book about a war. This war is not for the author mainly a matter of military or strategic interest, though both aspects are of course important in the description of it. It is in Thucydides' terms the culmination of a long historical process which started back in 479, when the Persians retired from Greece and when Athens at the request of the allies assumed the leadership of those who still thought of a Persian menace to Greece. In the year following (478), Athens founded the confederacy of Delos, initially a league of free states against

57

Persia; within thirty years it became a highly organized empire designed solely to serve Athenian interests. This is the true background of the war for Thucydides, and the war is then the moment of crisis which reveals by its demands the true nature of the state and the men in it, destroying all that is inessential inherited from the tradition of the past.

Yet important as the *Fifty Years* are as the background of the Peloponnesian War, behind the story of the *Fifty Years* itself is the story of Greece back to the days of the Minoans, and this story, told by Thucydides in the first eighteen chapters of Book i as the *Archaeology*, together with the *Fifty Years* itself, all belongs together as a prelude to the war. Not simply a prelude in the chronological sense of the word. This is a tale of the process which leads to a war, not *the* war but a war. This war was of interest because it is the biggest the Greek world had ever known, and Thucydides, too, was able to see it personally—give it his attention "so that he would know something accurately about it."[8] But it is still a story of a war, not just this war. War is the final step in social development for Thucydides, the final somber act of every historical drama.

To see this with Thucydides' eyes we must look not only at what he says directly about this war and its antecedents in Book i but what is said in the speech of Diodotus on behalf of the people of Mitylene in 427.[9] This Diodotus is pleading the case of revolted Mitylene before the Athenian assembly, which the day before had determined to execute all adult males and sell the women and children into slavery. Diodotus is anxious to make quite clear that he is not interested in discussing the justice or injustice of the sentence—only its expediency. To his mind severity in the repression of acts of aggression either within or without the national unit, either exercised against the individual criminal or the rebelling state, never is profitable because of the constitution of human nature. His own words follow: "Poverty with its goad of necessity supplies daring, and abundance, with its pride and insolence, greed, and all the other conditions, as each is possessed by a particular human temper, drives man into danger under the stress of something irremediable and greater than himself. And in every case there is hope and there is passion, the one leading and the other following, the one thinking out the plan of attack, the other suggesting the fulness of luck. These are what do the most damage and though they are unseen are mightier than the dangers seen. Besides these there is chance itself, which no less contributes to encouragement; for sometimes it stands by a man past all expectation and leads him on to run a risk though his resources are inferior. This is also true of states inasmuch as for them the stakes are of the greatest—freedom or the empire over others. With all these things each man judges himself unreasonably a match for something greater. So it is just impossible and a mark of great simplicity of thought to imagine that by means of the strength of law or other terror one can devise a way of turning men aside from their goal when their human nature would earnestly have them achieve it."[10]

The drift of Diodotus is toward the assertion of a perpetual aggressiveness in both individuals and the state. This is regarded as the natural condition of man, singly and politically, and it is the underlying elements in this natural condition that Diodotus exposes. Consequently, war between political societies, *stasis* in a single society, and anarchic war of the individual against his particular society are the natural potentialities of man's life.

Diodotus had equated the position of the criminal in society and the rebellious state in the confederation, and that is the point to bear in mind as we turn to the *Archaeology*. Diodotus had also indicated the "greatest stakes" for cities, and these again are equated—freedom or empire over others. Thus you cannot prevent the criminal from crime by the fear of death, and you cannot prevent Mitylene from rebelling to save her freedom, by any terror of death individual or collective. The story of the *Archaeology* is, rather dreadfully, the same. It is the story of an entire nation of small states moving inevitably to the great moment of war.

True, this is obscured because in the *Archaeology* the inventions of technical significance are treated as the peculiar human reaction to the material circumstances; in other words, instead of the weight of the narrator's interest bearing on why it is impossible to prevent men committing the crimes of rebellion and war, it is centered on the positive results, in technological terms, of their response to their circumstances. Thus we learn of the building of fleets, the fortification of towns, the extension of trade, the growth of *stasis*, the formation of tyrannies, and the coming of the great centralized leagues as the direct human answer to the earlier poverty, born of piracy, and the potential wealth resident in the access to the sea and the large potential market in the growing population. Yet undeniably the direction of all the *Archaeology* is toward the war: the steady growth of material prosperity is matched by the corresponding passions in the cities and the men, and the result is bound to be war, sooner or later.

There is in Thucydides' narrative no possible other solution, either philosophically or practically, because there is for him no static concept of a balanced harmony of justice or any embodiment of it in a given power or combination of powers. The restless movement which carried Greece from the early defenseless nomads whose poverty forced them to trading, cities, and the sea to the two great leagues embattled in their last desperate struggle is to continue indefinitely in endless cycles with roughly the same beginning and end as this one. It is with this in mind that he writes of his history as an account of what happened and will happen again "according to what is human,"[11] in the same or similar forms, amplified by his statement about *stasis*, where he speaks of "things of this sort which are happening now and will again while human nature is the same, but more or less violent in form depending on the particular conjunction of circumstance which presides over their inception."[12]

And there is no doubt that Thucydides phrased with especial bitterness the words of the Athenian envoys at Sparta before

the war: "If you should destroy us and assume the empire yourselves, you would soon lose the good will that you have now
because men are afraid of us."[13] The immediate hatred turned
against Sparta following the Peace of Nicias in 421,[14] and the
formation of new leagues against her power in the Peloponnesus
and of course the much more violent reaction to the new Spartan
empire of 403, must have been in Thucydides' mind as living
proofs of the truth of his theory that the Peloponnesian War
would settle no ultimate problem of power and tyranny; it
merely removed one tyrant power and substituted another. The
circumstances compelled the concentration of power, and the
human reaction to this intensified the consequences of such concentration. The war of one state against another, and of one
class against another within the state at the favorable opportunity, and the individual and anarchic war of one man against
his society, when poverty or plenty drive him by "constraint"
or by "pride and insolence" (e.g., the career of Alcibiades), are
parts of the entire chain of necessity with which everyone and
every state is fettered.

2

Let us look at some outside evidence on the current political
discussion in the fifth century. Plato has given us two figures,
Thrasymachus in the *Republic* and Callicles in the *Gorgias*, of
especial interest to readers of Thucydides. Callicles is apparently a democrat; Thrasymachus takes a position which is not necessarily either that of a democrat or an oligarch but will vary,
according to considerations of personal gain, with the government of whichever state he happens to be a citizen.[15] Both of
them, however, under pressure reveal that they regard the current moral conventions, including most of those on which a
democracy is based, as artificial constraints imposed on the
stronger by the weaker for their own preservation inside a
society, and these constraints the truly wise man will ignore if

he gets the chance. Both of them, at least until refuted by Socrates, affirm that the life of the tyrant is the happiest one.

Thus we find in these two character sketches a philosophy of politics and personal morals which actually transcends any particular political party alignment in the last quarter of the fifth century. A Thrasymachus or a Callicles might be a democrat; he very likely would, since the democratic party was more likely to be on top in Athens, and on its platform he would most probably gain power. He might, however, be an oligarch. Critias was such, and there is no reason, on the basis of his conduct, to regard him as other than a historical version of the successful man portrayed by Thrasymachus in the first book of the *Republic*. But whichever he was, or whatever medial position he assumed, the philosophical basis for his conduct would be one which transcended the immediate political party loyalties. He is one who has found that the gratification of self-interest, and therefore the acquisition of power, is the supreme object of his life. And when expressed in international terms this means that a nation, like an individual, granted the opportunity, should exercise its power to the fullest extent for its own national satisfaction.

It is perhaps not unimportant to notice in both Thucydides and Plato the same halfway houses and the same conclusions. The ambassadors of Athens at Sparta still urge some inappropriate "moral" arguments amid their "natural" utilitarian reasons. They say, for instance: "Those deserve praise who, while following the dictates of man's nature and ruling others, still prove juster than their own strength would warrant"[16]—whereas, of course, if the implications of their whole argument are sound (the Athenian officers at Melos interpret them rigidly), the justice, natural justice, of Athens would be exhibited in going as far as she could, and consequently she needs no defense on moral grounds. In the case of Thrasymachus in the *Republic*, Book i, the initial stages of his argument again rest, or appear to rest, on certain conventional moral assumptions. It is only in the

Melian Dialogue in Thucydides (Book v) and in the last stage of Thrasymachus' discussion that the naked doctrine of force and self-aggrandizement is cited as the new *natural* justice. And, significantly, in both cases, it is brought forward with some hesitation and seeming backwardness and, at last, only on the plea that the speakers are being asked for their real reasons and that no uninitiates are present.[17]

The psychological approach of a Thrasymachus or a Callicles or of the Athenian ambassadors at Sparta is in Thucydides united with his own theory of materialistic causation in history, and it is on the interaction of the psychological and materialistic factors that he bases his hope of whatever future usefulness his work may have. At least three times in the *History*—on the war, the plague, and *stasis*—he calls our attention to the fact that his accurate reporting of the facts of certain tremendous catastrophes may be of help when they occur again; and in two cases—*stasis* and the plague—he asserts that they undoubtedly will recur.[18]

In respect to *stasis*, moreover, he has left us in no doubt as to what that time is. Revolution, of this particular domestic variety, with its attendant moral debacle, comes in conjunction with a great war, because this war "removes the security of men's daily lives."[19] Similarly, one notices, the moral catastrophe which afflicted Athens at the time of the plague was due to the removal of any confidence in men's minds that they would be alive tomorrow. Hence they did whatever they pleased today in defiance of the outer constraint of law or the inner of conscience.[20]

And is it going too far, then, to see the application of the recurrence "according to what is human" of the great wars to Thucydides' own account of the *Archaeology* and the *Fifty Years?* Surely what is being indicated in his introductory account of Greek history to his own time is that as nations grow wealthier, and commerce and communication increase, the cumulation of factors, some material and some psychological, makes for the great centralized empires. When this happens, such an empire is bound to clash with whatever neighbors or combination of neighbors its power appears to threaten, and, in this light, we can see that he is correct, according to his theory, in seeing the fear of Athenian power as the basic reason for the Peloponnesian War. He does not indulge in moral criticism of the empire or the empire-makers because it would be as out of place so to criticize them as to blame the Athenians for the onset of the plague. The crowding of the population into the city was certainly a major cause of the plague, but the compulsion of necessity enforced the crowding.[21] The empire was certainly a major cause of the murder and devastation of the war—but the compulsion of historical necessity, according to Thucydides, enforced the empire.

3

This compulsion must be remembered, too, when one interprets the famous sentence in which Thucydides differentiates himself from his predecessors in the following terms: "Perhaps the nonfictional quality of my narrative may seem a trifle austere to some, but if those judge it *useful* who want to know the clear truth of what happened and what will happen again in the same or similar form according to what is human, it will be enough for me."[22] But there is no explicit expansion of the nature of the useful, and an analysis of causation in the history leaves us exceedingly doubtful that Thucydides conceived of any particular work antecedent to the particular event as useful to the extent of obviating the roots of the catastrophe.

This point of view is, indeed, almost inevitable in the context of his insistence on the historian's truth to the uniqueness of historical events. The recurrence of the pattern is there, of course, otherwise history would afford no interest whatever to the historical observer of the present. But the uniqueness of the particular set of circumstances involving the pattern is also there. The emphasis lies on the permanent recurrence of certain human factors producing certain results and on the difference of the outward form of the recurrence on each occasion.[23]

Now a man of today, or of any day after Thucydides' time, reading this historian *may* find a certain usefulness in it, even to the point of dealing more competently with existent disaster. But the wisdom acquired by reading Thucydides is not to be directed to the elimination of the *causes* of future catastrophes. He is not saying that by understanding the truth of what happened in the last quarter of the fifth century you will know how to prevent men from re-creating the same havoc and ruin. Far from it—for the motives which produced the havoc and ruin will still be there. But perhaps, if you understand the particular set of circumstances in all their particularity and uniqueness, you will acquire something of the skill necessary for handling the next contingency created by the same motives.

An inner true comprehension of one historical event like the Peloponnesian War, with the necessary matching of one's understanding of the permanent in man's desires and the temporary and unique form they have assumed, may lead to the only valuable quality in the political observer of the future, the shrewd guess and the intuitive insight into men's political doings. It is in just this spirit that he says of the plague, the great physical catastrophe which parallels the moral and political disasters: "Let each man speak about it as he knows, doctor and layman, as to what is likely to have caused it, and the grounds which he thinks powerful enough to have motivated such a change. But I will tell you how it was, and will indicate such symptoms as a man observing, should it happen again, will have the best foreknowledge against ignorance. For I fell sick of it myself and saw other sufferers."[24]

4

Now if the factors of historical change are, in Thucydides' eyes, virtually fixed, it follows that we should find that the rudimentary value of statesmanship is foresight. If the extremes of poverty and wealth produce definable reactions in men, and the emotions of men that can be separated from their material conditions can be summed up as passion and hope, the statesman, to be a statesman at all, must have good judgment in fitting these general concepts to the particular circumstances of his time, and this quality is what is called "foresight." To try to break the chain of necessity is folly; with a correct understanding of the degree of determinism forced on man by his circumstances, and his basic unconditional aggressiveness, a statesman may still be ineffectual for a number of other reasons. But without the understanding of such determinism he cannot be a statesman at all. Since, too, the moment of crisis for the society and the man, in Thucydides' terms, is war, it is there that the statesman's talent is put to its ultimate test. And that in various ways. For he may be unable to devise technical military expedients to win the war and consequently lose the position of dominance for his society; or he may be unable to control the psychological reactions to the war within his own society; or he may himself fall a victim to the disease of individual aggression which war as it removes the luxuries of unnecessary sentiment provokes in a pathological degree. All these dangers for the statesmanship of Athens can be seen described in the pages of Thucydides, and the more extended notice of three statesmen whose peculiar function it was to face the three dangers mentioned is our best evidence of the real coincidence of Thucydides' theory of historical causation and that of Diodotus. The three men are Themistocles, Pericles, and Alcibiades.

In all three cases there is a marked emphasis on their foresight. Themistocles is the shrewdest guesser at the course of the future and the most brilliant improviser in dealing with difficulties as they arise.[25] Pericles' estimate of the holding power of Athens in the war and the course the war itself would take was so carefully made that even with the injection of two or three unknown factors his judgment comes out correctly.[26] Alcibiades is less especially praised for this in explicit terms, but, implicitly, his plans for the unification of the enemies of Sparta in the Peloponnese, his judgment of the chances in the Sicilian campaign, his skill in gauging the opportunities of victory after 413, including his brilliant and terribly effective advice to the Spartans to establish a permanent occupation post at Deceleia, show the same wisdom in assessing the future.[27]

This quality of the Thucydidean statesman—his foresight—is integrally connected with the factors of political change in Diodotus' list. All three statesmen are possessed of the proper understanding of the necessary link between the force of material circumstance and the temper it engenders in human beings affected by it, though the role which history demanded of each of them in the light of their understanding of necessity is different.

Themistocles' peculiar contribution is the invention of technical means to satisfy the needs of political power at a comparatively early stage of its development. In the case of Athens this means the long walls and the fleet. The talent here is mostly one of sheer technical invention; that is to say, the need for both forms of defense was relatively obvious to the people whom the statesman must persuade. There was some difficulty, it is true, in persuading the Athenians initially to forego the communal distribution of funds which were necessary for the creation of the fleet, but we do not gather that they were very hard to persuade.[28] Again, in dealing with the Spartans, who, to be successful in the historical game, ought to have interfered decisively with Athens' plans at this point, Themistocles shows his cleverness in "improvisation," but the stratagems are relatively easy to carry out.[29] It is the technical inventiveness which the necessity of history calls for here, and this Themistocles possessed.

In the time of Pericles the demands on an Athenian stateman are not so much directed to the elaboration of technical means of dealing with war prospective or actual. It is rather to the understanding of how to control the psychological response to war in his own people and correctly to interpret and forecast the temper of the enemy. Here again we notice that this is just what Thucydides stresses about Pericles. He is the man who can "lead the people of Athens and not be led by them"; he can "control them, yet in a spirit of freedom."[30] And his judgment of the manner in which the Spartans will react is proved continuously correct throughout the first book.

The point to notice is that the pattern of necessity has shifted; the condition which must be met in political terms is no longer chiefly the construction of plans or engines of defense or aggression. It is now almost altogether a grasp of the necessary psychological consequences of a given position and the evolution of successful means of dealing with them. Pericles' advice to the Athenians on the moment for the declaration of war and the implications of the war and the plans for its successful continuation and conclusion are based altogether on an accurate vision of his own people's feelings and those of the enemy.[31] This is why the plague, being the incalculable factor injected by chance, injures the plans almost to the point of wrecking them. Almost, but not quite. For even here, with the full force of the irrational hatred of the people beating on him, Pericles is able to convince them that they must see the plague for what it really is—the work of chance and not as evidence of a politician's incompetence or as a good reason for changing leadership or direction.[32]

It is in the case of Alcibiades, however, that we can see that a statesman may possess in the highest degree the qualities of technical invention necessary to deal with a given material condition, and an accurate understanding of the psychological response of human beings to circumstances, and still fail. Alcibiades' technical plans are excellent, whether made on behalf of Athens or against her.[33] Furthermore, he is capable of gauging the psychological reaction to his proposition with all the skill of Pericles. He can persuade the Athenians to the Argive alliance and the Sicilian expedition; he can persuade the Spartans of the soundness of his advice, though he appears before them as a traitor to his own country.[34] Neither in the invention of devices nor in the understanding of human feeling is he deficient. And, as it were to mark how near Alcibiades is to being the statesman required by the moment, Thucydides ventures on one of his extremely rare hypothetical statements: The excesses of Alcibiades, he says, by causing the people to distrust him, contributed "not least" to the ruin of the Athenian state. The implication of this is clearly that, had they placed their confidence in him, he might have saved them.[35] Yet the explanation of what is missing is furnished by Thucydides himself in the speech of Pericles in Book ii. He is discussing three kinds of statesmen who will prove worthless to the city:

"The man who knows what is necessary and has failed to give a clear exposition of it to the people is as valuable as if he never had had the thought at all; the man who knows and can speak clearly but who is no good friend of the city will still not speak with truly personal feeling; but though he have this besides and is a slave to money yet shall all of the commonalty be sold for the sake of this one."[36]

In Alcibiades it is not the love of money but ambition; and the dangers of ambition were peculiarly, almost irrationally, felt by the Athenians, as Thucydides points out in his account of their historical romance elaborated round the destruction of the tyrants.[37] There are kinds of personal moral defects which render a statesman suspect in the eyes of his electorate, and then even his true perception of the necessities of history will not save him from ineffectiveness on the stage of historical action.

CHAPTER VII

Chance and Pity

1

EVERYBODY who reads Thucydides has been struck by the sparseness of any personal moral comment on the men and the happenings which he describes. But few seem to have noticed how curiously the moral comment, such as it is, has been directed. There are, in particular, three passages of this kind, each embodying some personal judgment of the historian and at first sight quite separated in the nature and variety of comment, yet which on closer scrutiny show a similar kind of detached humanity.[1]

a) The first is the story of the destruction of the Boeotian town of Mycalessus.[2] Mycalessus was far inland, its walls ineffective and in parts dilapidated; it was quite remote from the war or any concern in it. Unfortunately it happened that the Athenians had hired a body of Thracian mercenaries who were supposed to go with Demosthenes to Sicily. They came too late to join the expedition and proved too expensive to keep on foot without a specifically allocated military task. So the Athenians ordered them sent home and put them, for their return journey, under the command of an Athenian officer. Since the state was paying them a drachma a day per man, as long as they were under Athenian orders, and the journey home by land would take a considerable time, Deitrephes, their general, was instructed to employ them to do all possible harm to the enemy on the way back.[3] It was under these circumstances that they marched through part of Boeotia and made their foray on this sleepy little country town of Mycalessus. Then Thucydides says: "They stormed Mycalessus and sacked its houses and its temples, killing every human being. They spared neither young nor old but killed everyone they met, women and children alike and even the pack animals and every living thing they saw. For these Thracians, like most other barbarians, are most bloodthirsty when they are confident. There was there, then, a terrible confusion and every form of death: in particular, they attacked a school—the largest in the town—where the children had just come in and butchered every one of them. This whole city suffered a catastrophe second to no other in its unexpectedness and horror."[4] At the end of the passage he writes: "This is what happened to Mycalessus, a thing which is as much worth our tears as anything that occurred in this war, considering the small size of the town."[5]

b) At the end of the Sicilian campaign Nicias surrendered to the Sicilian troops, though, as Thucydides tells us, because he trusted their Spartan general, Gylippus, rather than the Sicilians themselves.[6] He and the other Athenian general, Demosthenes, were held for a while by the Sicilians at the request of Gylippus, but eventually they were both executed. According to Thucydides, the Syracusans among the Sicilians were afraid to spare Nicias lest under torture he should reveal the names of the considerable party within Syracuse itself which had tried to open negotiations with the Athenians. The total failure of the expedition and the loss of close to forty thousand men, killed, wounded, and prisoners,[7] is very largely attributable to the stupidity, timidity, and incompetence of Nicias. Demosthenes had repeatedly tried to save the army, and his plans for this end were sound and their success probable. Nicias consistently balked them. These facts are vouched for by Thucydides himself in the seventh book. His comment on the end of Nicias is as follows: "On this charge, then, or one like it, Nicias died, being the least worthy of all the Greeks of my time to come to such a depth of misfortune, since he had lived all his life in accordance with what is popularly called virtue."[8] Of Demosthenes he says nothing.

c) In 412–411 the democracy of Athens was overthrown by a conspiracy of oligarchs who had long been discontented with the prospects both of war and of peace if Athens remained democratic. The hope of enlisting Alcibiades and with him perhaps the help of Persia, which he was reputed to be able to deliver, weighed with some of this party. But the roots of the oligarchic attitude to the war, the democracy, and Sparta go back much further, as we saw in an earlier chapter. There were two wings of the oligarchic clique—a violent faction whose aim was a strong administration of a very few and a moderate constitutional party who wanted a restriction of the franchise and a remodeling of the constitution to bring it nearer to what Aristotle later calls a *politeia,* a mixture of democratic and oligarchic elements. The chief planner among the extreme oligarchs was a man named Antiphon; that of the moderates, Theramenes.

The extremists made the initial moves in the revolution and administered the city for a while by secret-police methods when, as Thucydides puts it, "no one of the rest of the citizens spoke against these measures, being afraid and seeing the size of the conspiracy; and if anyone did he was immediately killed in some convenient manner, and there was no search for the doers of the deed or justice to be had against them if suspected, but the multitude kept quiet and were so terror-stricken that each man who had no violence done him, even though he kept his mouth shut, thought it a gain."[9] The terror did not last long, and the moderates among the oligarchs took control and drafted a new constitution which was to limit the franchise to five thousand. The extreme oligarchs had already formally suggested this, but, according to Thucydides, this was a mere pretense to make the transition from the democracy easier; they had no intention of making the five thousand a working political unity. Theramenes, however, the leader of the moderates, wanted the five thousand in good faith, and of the constitution set up in the name of the five thousand Thucydides says: "For now for the first time in my lifetime the Athenians seem to have enjoyed an excellent government; for there was a blend in it of the few and the many, and this was the first thing which lifted the city out of its ill condition."[10]

2

Now if we look at these passages, first in their contexts and then in conjunction with one another, something of their strangeness becomes apparent. In the first place, none of the three constitutes what one might call remarkably merited comment—on a comparative basis. Is it not strange that the man who records the total destruction of Melos conducted in the most cold-blooded fashion, and the almost complete destruction of the city of Mitylene, and the execution of the Plataeans who surrendered after the siege should have had not one word of pity for the victims or blame for the executioners and reserve this pity and blame for the murder of a few hundred villagers and a schoolhouse of children in Boeotia? Is it not strange that the man who notes the end of Antiphon (described as "second to none among his day in virtue")[11] and the end of Demosthenes, who had won the Pylos campaign so brilliantly, who had even almost rescued the Sicilian expedition from the failure to which Nicias' leadership doomed it, without even a single phrase or comment, should have delivered so complete and comprehensive a verdict of praise on Nicias, who had lost the decisive battles of the war? And is it not strange that the man who had seen Periclean Athens and acknowledged its enormous power, resilience, and vitality should have reserved his praise of the "best government" for the rather dim academic experiment of Theramenes, which lasted a couple of months and was really hardly ever alive, as a functioning unit, at all?

One way to remove the sense of strangeness in these comments is to explain them individually and piecemeal. Each of them is, of course, susceptible of an individual explanation. We can say that, after all, Thucydides is human, like any other man; that the devastated village and the murdered school children appealed to his sense of pity as greater and more terrible events had somehow failed to do. Or we might force ourselves to see the emphasis on the size of Mycalessus as the important matter. Other cities greater than this had fallen but none more completely, considering its smallness. And we can explain away the comment on Nicias by assuming a personal friendship between Thucydides and Nicias and a personal hostility between Thucydides and Demosthenes. And we can explain away the statement on the constitution of Theramenes by saying that, after all, Thucydides is a moderate oligarch, by preference, that he has never approved of the democratic empire, and that his word of praise for the polity of Theramenes is his personal voice as a fifth-century politician. The common thread which runs through all such individual explanations is a separation of Thucydides the historian and Thucydides the man. We picture to ourselves a Thucydides austerely bent on his task of recording the Peloponnesian War yet at times revealing a sort of private humanity which he shares with all of us.

When a historian is primarily a philosopher of history and secondly a historian, as in the case of Hegel or Spengler, such a bifurcation of the professional and the personal is conceivable. Because the pattern is conceived first, born of the impact of some set of facts on the individual artist before the set of facts has taken artistic form. When this takes place, the particular foibles of the philosopher-historian can, at moments, crack the mold he has created. But when, as is true of Thucydides, the concrete particular, in its completeness, is both the form and the totality of the philosophy, the personal cannot intrude. What he has seen, detail by detail, is the story, and the story has major implications; but the implications spring from the story, not the story from a theory. The personal, in such a case, enters only when the historian selects his subject in the first place; it does not appear as an addendum or an interruption in the treatment of the subject.

3

More than this. If we look again at the three passages quoted, we *can* see a common link in the moral comment. All three passages deal with men or events which are peculiarly within the realm of chance rather than in that of necessity.

In the case of Mycalessus, Thucydides stresses this. The soldiers who did the deed were mercenaries who came late for the operation to which they were assigned; it was a mere casual chance that they were sent back by way of Boeotia and that the instructions they received—to do all the harm to the enemy that they could en route—led them in the most accidental way upon this wretched Boeotian village.[12] Mycalessus itself, witness its fallen and crumbling walls and its sense of utter security, was a place in no sense suited to play a role in this war. Melos might and naturally did become a bone of contention between Athens and Sparta; an island inhabited by Dorians siding with neither Athens nor Sparta is bound in terms of the logic of the war to suffer. But Mycalessus need not have, as far as this same logic went, and it is for that reason that Thucydides pities it.

The same sort of pattern is discernible in the story of Nicias and his relation to the Sicilian expedition. He did not want such an expedition at all and least of all wanted to command it, as we learn from Book vi.[13] Being, in spite of his own intentions, elected general, he is, then, in a purely fortuitous way, deprived of the two assistants who could have made it a success: of Lamachus by death and of Alcibiades by desertion.[14] He makes another desperate effort to get rid of the command following on his first failure, when he demands reinforcements so large that he assumes the Athenians will refuse and a successor to himself because of his incapacitation through illness. He succeeds in neither request.[15] Fatally, the Athenians sent another army so large that he had no excuse left for failure; and they affirm their confidence in him by insisting on his retention of office.[16] Finally, when beaten in the battle in the harbor, he might still have withdrawn his forces relatively intact, but the eclipse of the moon intervening found his superstitious weak spot, and the result of his enforced delay is the complete destruction of the army and himself.[17]

The peculiar poignancy of Nicias' position is further emphasized when we bear in mind that he was, in his own esteem and in that of the Athenians, a very lucky general. He comes before us time and again with his uneasy reliance upon good fortune. Thucydides tells us that he was especially anxious to negotiate the peace of 421 which bears his name, because so far his good luck in generalship had been unbroken and he wished to have the record of a general never defeated.[18] He had "lived all his life in accordance with what is popularly considered virtue"[19] and with the timid caution of one who has been lucky and knows that luck can change. And the result of his "popular virtue" and his caution about luck is to be involved himself and involve his country in the most prodigious catastrophe she had ever experienced.

There is, I believe, in these two passages the sense of Thucydides' awe in the face of chance. Thucydides was not a superstitious man; he plainly did not believe that chance was our name for God's contrivances or that the area which Diodotus labeled "chance" is really the pattern of destiny. But, I think, the peculiar ironies of chance inspired him with a kind of horror, and in these two instances, that of a well-meaning, decent, and incompetent man, meaninglessly enmeshed in a task demanding enormous skill, and the simple little country town with its men and women, children and animals, senselessly slaughtered by a hired mercenary army for no conceivable military purpose, the disproportion between the people and their fate awakened a human pity which is nonetheless explicable according to his own theory of history and its development.

The last instance—that of the comment on the Constitution of the Five Thousand—is much harder to place. The Constitution of the Five Thousand is certainly not peculiarly the product of chance, nor does chance in connection with it exhibit the irony which is remarkable in the case of Nicias and the village of Mycalessus. On the other hand, there is perhaps another way of seeing the Constitution of the Five Thousand as a thing not directly growing out of the necessity of history—thus explaining Thucydides' comment on it. In the chapter on *stasis* Thucydides says: "In peace and good times both states and individuals show better judgment because they do not fall into necessities which are too strong for will or intention."[20] The "better" here probably indicates the same kind of moral comment as the "best" applied to the government of the Five Thousand: that is to say, in both cases "better" and "best" refer to some sort of moral excellence which is no longer possible when the stress of circumstances "likens the temper of most men to their circumstances."

This is further supported if we seek for a definition of "better" in the chapters on *stasis* and for "best" in that section dealing with the Constitution of the Five Thousand. The gist of the chapter on *stasis* is that the proper qualities of man in a state of normalcy—courage, caution, decency, and intelligence—become superseded by peculiar distortions in fact, such as insensate daring, ruthlessness, and universal suspicion, and that the use of the moral terms also changes. The distorted extremes received the moral titles due to their normal counterparts. In the chapter on the Constitution of the Five Thousand, Thucydides *cannot* mean that the "best government" is best in the sense that it will help Athens win the war, for the first actions of this government are directed toward a peace with Sparta. The reason he gives himself for the attribution of "best" is true and significant. "For it was a blend of the few and the many, and this was the first thing that lifted the city out of its ill condition."[21] The conflict of the few and the many is the basis of *stasis*, and *stasis* Thucydides stamps as the peculiar internal condition resulting from external war.

In other words, allowing for the basic drives of human nature which lead to the potentiality of war between states and the potentialities of war within the society between the few who have and the many who have not, the actualization of human aggressiveness in war and in faction represents the hysterical condition at which point moral comment is no longer significant, since man's capacity is now entirely limited by circumstances, and neither his will nor his intention has any free play. At such a time the art of politics finds its proper exercise, since it is pre-eminently the art of understanding necessity and operating within the possibilities afforded by necessity. But the area where *moral* comment is in order is only that in which human beings can be regarded as in some sense operating with freedom to choose between one alternative and another without the direct force of necessity constraining them.

This latter is the case with the Constitution of the Five Thousand. It was, in a way, an academic experiment, since it tried to cure, in a root-and-branch fashion, the basic disease of the Athenian state, the conflict of the few and the many. It did this in preference to setting the winning of the war first, as the democrats would have it, or the establishment of a stable government, by fiat, as the extreme oligarchs wanted. It belongs in one of the rare breathing spaces between the compulsive assaults of necessity and embodies an effort by men consciously and freely to choose, theoretically, a better state. And it is in this spirit that Thucydides comments on it.

Summing up the three passages, we can state the result like this. Thucydides saw a struggle between good and bad in an individual man or a situation as worthy of comment only when the man or the situation belongs in the region which lies outside the direct control of necessity. Thus the chance destruction of Mycalessus and the chance which carried Nicias to be commander of the disastrous Sicilian expedition show, briefly, a piece of history which might have been different. In the light of its hypothetical difference the historian may and will comment morally. Again when an action can actually be consummated with the true possibility of choice—that is, when it proceeds from men's freedom of decision rather than the compulsion of necessity—a moral comment can be significant. But moral comment is out of place in the discussion of the war and the empire, for here are only the final and natural responses to a continuous process of circumstances, and what men ought to do in regard to the war and the empire *should* be dictated only by the necessity of coping with the existing situation.

CHAPTER VIII

Beyond Necessity

1

THOUGH the comments we have last discussed are probably to be integrated in this theory of history as I have shown, they do not reveal the most significant attitude of Thucydides as a historian. In a sense this is quite evident in the light of the manner in which they have been traditionally explained. Had there not existed a very marked contradiction between these passages and the general spirit of the rest of the narrative, so many scholars would not have tried to see them as sentimental inserts or taken them at their face value as sarcastic comment.[1] The analysis we have pursued so far does in fact show why there is this discrepancy of tone. In the passages on Nicias, Mycalessus, and the Constitution of the Five Thousand, Thucydides is remarking on phenomena which in a special way belong outside the realm of necessity. The *Archaeology* and the *Fifty Years* combined with certain of the speeches indicate to us what he considered the necessity of history to be and the qualities required by statesmen who would be true statesmen in the light of this necessity. What we must try to do now is to discuss where within this area—the necessity of history—the highest praise is given—to statesman and to state. When men's free will is effectually curbed by circumstances, and when chance does not obviously confuse the issue—in other words, in the true domain of politics—where does Thucydides find his highest value?

2

We can start from a passage which is puzzling enough in itself, unless we find the explanation we are seeking. Antiphon, according to Thucydides, was the intellect that dominated the extreme party of the oligarchs, the party, that is, that installed and maintained the reign of terror in 411.[2] Here are the historian's own words: "The man who brought forward the proposal and to all outward appearance was the most energetic in destroying the democracy was Peisander; but the one who engineered the whole business and the manner in which it was brought to this pass and had thought most deeply about its contrivance was Antiphon, a man among the Athenians of his day second to none in virtue."[3]

The word "virtue," unqualified, stands in the sharpest contrast to that in the verdict on Nicias, "what is considered virtue."[4] A little research into the deeds chronicled of each figure amplifies what our conception of the two virtues should be. The violence of the oligarchs of Antiphon's party is quite clearly noted by Thucydides. There was a reign of terror in which order was maintained by judiciously selected secret executions. Thucydides' cool words of this demand attention: "And they killed certain men, though not very many, *who seemed to be suitable ones to remove*, and threw others into prison and banished others."[5] In a sense, the whole record of Nicias, with his hesitation and irresolution and general tendency not to do the effective and ruthless thing, stands in the strongest contrast to this; but it is capped, as it were, by the pathetic note in his last speech to his soldiers: "I am in the same danger and hazard as the lowliest of you; I am no stronger than any of you—indeed you can see how my sickness prostrates me. Yet in my private life and otherwise I think my good fortune has previously been second to none. I have lived with much devotion to the gods and much justice in the sight of men and have merited no man's grudge."[6]

It is hazardous, of course, to take a man's own judgment on himself as the historian's, but when the narrative, the historian's verdict, and the general's own speech all jibe, there can be little reason for rejecting the total portrait of Nicias as the presentation of a well-meaning incompetence, just as surely as Thucydides' comments on Antiphon and his party lead us to form a picture of ruthless efficiency. In other words, "conventional virtue" and the virtue of the statesman according to necessity are at opposite poles. We might notice too that the phrase in the general description of Antiphon, "the ablest in forming conceptions and in giving them voice," recalls another similar passage. This is Pericles' description of the duties of statesmen,[7] in which the emphasis falls exactly on these two qualities with the same words: the need for forming conceptions and being able to express them. We might remember also the passage on Themistocles:

"Themistocles was a man who showed most certainly the strength of a native talent and for this is more worth our admiration than any other. By virtue of his peculiar understanding, without previous study to better or supplement it, he was the shrewdest judge of those crises that admit of virtually no deliberation and the best guesser at the future to its utmost limit. *That which he had in hand he was always able to give an account of* and was not incompetent to judge sufficiently well even that of which he was inexperienced. The future he foresaw, both for better and worse, to a remarkable extent. In a word, by brilliant natural gifts with the minimum of application he was the ablest man at improvising necessary measures."[8]

The negative part of an inference from the use of "virtue" in the Antiphon passage is thus established. It is clear that the virtue Thucydides is praising in Antiphon has essentially nothing to do with mercy or humanity. We can also be sure of this in regard to Pericles, whose words on the empire we would do well to remember: "To acquire the empire may have been unjust: it is dangerous to let it go. You must remember that you hold a tyrant power."[9] Is there any other attribute which can be exercised from the blanket definition of Antiphon's virtue which will help us to understand Thucydides' comment in a more general way?

Yes. Surely, according to Thucydides, the virtue of the statesman need not carry with it success. Neither Themistocles, Pericles, nor Antiphon was successful—personally successful, at least. That is to say, each of them achieved an enormous political task, the one the building of the long walls and the fleet to make the new empire, the second the extension of the empire and its preparation for the war, and the third the destruction of the democracy. But, in each case, the judgment of the multitude at some point intervened to wreck the purely personal satisfaction in achievement. Themistocles died in exile, a guest of the Persian king he had helped to defeat;[10] Pericles at the end of his life was disgraced by the democracy he had led so long, even though in the last few months of his life he was reinstated;[11] Antiphon was finally tried and executed by the people.[12] Yet Thucydides tells us that Themistocles was "more worthy of our admiration than any other man in history,"[13] that Pericles was a single statesman of unique caliber in Athens' record,[14] and that Antiphon was second to none of the Athenians in his day in virtue.[15] Personal success, then, cannot be a necessary factor in the attributes of greatness, according to Thucydides. This is the more noteworthy, since, for him, foresight and efficiency are the prerequisites of a good statesman.

3

What do we find, then, positively, on the side of the statesman who commands Thucydides' admiration and the attribution of admiration? The achievement of a deed notable in terms of his own *History*, be that deed good or bad according to conventional Greek morality. More than that. The achievement must rise to the stature of uniqueness. As Thucydides felt that the historical significance of his time with its clash of these two great empires was unique, so uniqueness is for him, in a way, a guaranty of the importance of a given event. The fleet and the long walls; Athens' extraordinary endurance in the war; the destruction of the Athenian liberties of a hundred years' duration—all these have, for Thucydides, the stamp of singleness and the stamp of greatness. This is perhaps the very key to the personal failure of the statesmen, for the multitude cannot be taken along as a willing partner in the achievement of unique greatness. They constitute the difficulties to be overcome, the barrier that tests the strength of the assailant. And so, when the task is done, the many and the one relapse into their natural condition of antagonism, and, when the conflict becomes personal, the one must be beaten. But in the strange impersonality of self-sacrifice, in the desperate power and will to create something greater than the reach of a single man's ambition or benevolence, Thucydides found that which he called "virtue."

The life of nations for Thucydides is all of a piece in the early stages: the struggle for existence and then the struggle for supremacy. The object of interest for the nation in its historical development is *dynamis*, power, and this means dominion over others. Fear and greed are the driving motives on the road to imperialism, and there is no turning back. Yet in the course of the development there is a moment when these two factors are not the only ones. There is, as the Athenian envoys state it, honor. In the greatness of the thing created, the empire, there is a quality different from the qualities which created it; it is great in itself and for itself, and honor is its due from all.

The historical moment cannot, perhaps, last long; yet its greatness and dignity is the magnet of the historian's attention, and its decline the most penetrating exhibition of political motives, failures, and successes that can be offered him. Here is the significant recurring thing for Thucydides. That men struggle to live and then to dominate one another individually and nationally is a recurrent theme but does not attain any precision of form until their concerted and collective efforts have built a great monument to their individual greed and fear. In the hour that they honor that monument not only as the source of their own material well-being but as something apart from them, greater than them and worthy of their sacrifice, the greatest development of man, as Thucydides saw him, greatest politically and socially, has been attained. And, correspondingly, as the moment has called forth the most subtle and sophisticated sentiments of man living in a political society, its balance is rare and precarious. Overnight it dissolves again into an association of men, fearful and greedy.

History would be, then, for Thucydides, a series of significant mountains, the peaks rising at intervals in the endless chain. And, for the historian, the greatness and symmetrical proportions of the great thing that was made became valuable for their own sake, though, of course, the very appreciation of the greatness and the proportions implies a historian's emphasis. It is not hard to put this aspect of Thucydides' study together with his avoidance of conventional moral judgments, both on men and on the corporate political entities which they constitute and, more important still, with the inclusion of the few rather strange judgments we possess. The conventional moral judgment is, from his point of view, a failure on the level of significance. The ordinarily denominated virtues of man are not significant, in Thucydides' eyes, since they are not for him the genuinely predisposing factor in the creation of power; and only in power, in the building of something bigger than himself, is the peculiar excellence of the pressure of truly compulsive forces, fear and greed and their occasions—and the ability to transcend them within limits.

Yet the transcendence has no object; it must be its own object. This will hold good for the statesman and the state and the historian alike. The great statesman is the man who governs, not for his own advantage or necessarily for the good of the governed (which would be the classical statement), but for the continued dignity and survival of the state which in Athens has its characteristic expression in power, wealth, and extent. The great state, like Athens, will seek no models but in itself be the object of imitation, living in the radiance of its own beauty and magnitude. The greatness of the history is in its truth and its significance; that it serves no man's delight or vanity or affiliation;

that thus the events were and thus they will be again, since they are truly described and of the order that will recur.

4

Among statesmen a unique position in the history is occupied by Pericles, and it is to Pericles and Periclean Athens that we must look for the most significant expression of Thucydides' admiration.

There are only three speeches of Pericles reported in the *History*. They are the speech in which he advocates the declaration of war,[16] the famous Funeral Speech, delivered over those that had fallen,[17] and the speech in which he defends himself against the people's dissatisfaction with his conduct of the war.[18] These three speeches peculiarly express the spirit of the city of Athens as she entered on her long struggle, and, apart from their significance inside Thucydides' *History*, they probably constitute the most extraordinary document we possess revealing the relation between the leading statesman and his people in a naked and unqualified democracy.

The first aspect of all three speeches that may surprise us is their frankness. It is not often that before a democratic electorate a politician can reveal his hopes and fears almost exactly as they must appear to himself, though perhaps in this there are signs of what Thucydides describes as Pericles' odd attitude to the people: "He dominated them, but in a spirit of freedom."[19] For instance, in the first speech—that in which he urges the declaration of war—he warns the assembly that they may be inclined to feel quite different about the war when they are in it than when they are contemplating it as a future possibility. This, he tells us, is the wrong thing to do. "For it is possible for the outcome of events to proceed no less stupidly than the plans of men: that is why we are used to blame chance for whatever happens to us unexpectedly."[20]

In the last speech in the *History*, where Pericles is forced to defend himself against unjust resentment in the early years of the war, he unhesitatingly lays the blame where it belongs: on the plague and the people's suffering under it which makes them unfair in their estimate of himself. He then proceeds to try to make them realize the true possibilities of success temporarily concealed from them by their immediate defection. Yet, as he does so, he cheerfully reveals to them that there is a *secret* in mastering them; that he is not handling them as man to man.

"As to your fears of your sufferings in this war, lest it grow so great that we can no longer surmount it—let suffice for you what I have told you before on the many occasions when I proved that your suspicions about the war were incorrect: yet I will add this one further matter on the greatness of your empire, something I am sure you have not thought of before yourselves nor have I made mention of it in my former speeches to you. Even now I would not have introduced this thing; for its presentation is somewhat too imposing—but that I see that you are unreasonably depressed. You think that your empire is over the allies alone; but I will show you this: there are two elements of the world for use, land and sea, and of the one you are total masters for as far as you now exercise that mastery and further if you please. No one, neither the Great King nor any other people on earth at present, will successfully repel you if you sail against them with the fleet you have now."[21]

Here we are not concerned for the moment with the calm arrogance of the speech—that will be important later—but with the frankness it exhibits toward his audience. There is so clearly the implication that he is managing them, as of right of character and talent; that he knows the correct parts of the case to put now and at another time. And he tells them just this: *I would not have thought it advisable to produce an argument that is so arrogant in fact but that I see you irrationally depressed, and so I find that a little more of the naked truth than usual is necessary to restore you to a sensible frame of mind.* Here is the note of complete personal responsibility, without the blessing of divine sanction or hereditary legitimacy; and here is equally the undeviating openness of one who informs those whom he controls that his judgment is better than theirs and that only exceptional circumstances such as the present make it necessary for him to show them the deepest factors in his calculations.

But the frankness of these speeches is only one side of their basic character, and that may be summed up by saying that they are concerned with man and nothing but man. It is extraordinary in such speeches as these—one contemplating the city's engagement in a long war, one spoken in praise of the dead, one defending a leader suspected because of what was accidental mischance—that, with the exception of one insignificant and quite colorless reference,[22] there should be no mention of divine guidance, divine blessing, or even, in a merely sentimental allusion, fatherland's gods.

That this is no general Greek practice, if we need convincing on the matter, we can see from Thucydides' own observations on the last speech of Nicias to his troops before their final battles in Sicily: "He said other things which men in such a contingency are apt to say, not guarding against appearing to anyone to talk platitudes, about women and children and gods of our country, things continually brought forward in the same form on behalf of all causes, yet in the presence of an existing emergency men judge them useful and urge them."[23] But Pericles even in crisis will guard against seeming to talk platitudes. He shares with his hearers—knows it and draws his power from it—the knowledge that he and they are not like those of another age or another state who will bolster their hopes or their fears or even their sorrow by reference to beliefs outworn and dead. The city which is committed to the war, the city whose lovers the dead were over whom Pericles made his speech, was a man-made thing and existed only by the will and sacrifice of its men.

Here is the explanation of the strength of the materialistic appeal of Pericles to the citizens of Athens. They enjoy the products of the ends of the earth as natively as those of Attica.[24] They may live their lives as they please, and no one may interfere.[25] They are not harried by the demands of a harsh and continuous military service.[26] Because, in a certain sense, the city is theirs and from beginning to end exhibits the immediate choice of its inhabitants, not the influence of tradition or sanctions imposed from outside. And in his final assessment of the city's chances against Sparta, Pericles, in the spirit of his city, describes the world as something essentially *for use:* earth and sea are for use, either in war or peace. In such a statement there is nothing of a reverence or an awe before something greater than man or even merely alien to him; nor is there any hesitation involved in balancing various intricate factors, some subject to human control and some not, which can go to the resolution of a military dilemma. There is the starkly bare statement of basic determining areas of conflict and power. Athens is master, absolute master, of one element. She is therefore virtually bound to win the war, in a land like Greece where in war or in peace the sea is the source of power. These speeches are exceedingly direct, and man is the center of the universe in the mouth of the speaker and the minds of the hearers.

Yet there is a very remarkable impersonality in the man-made object, the city for which the human sacrifice is demanded. The fathers and mothers who have lost their sons are urged to have more children: "For as far as you are concerned as individuals the children that are successors to those that are gone shall be a forgetfulness of these, and, for the state, this will profit her doubly, since she will not be left empty of men and shall be safer besides; for there is no giving of just or even counsel on the part of those who risk their children on the consequences of their advice and those who do not: these two parties are not on the same footing."[27] Here we see that the reason for new children is largely at least to preserve the city and not only in respect to numbers but, subtly, because only those who have their most precious human possessions to lose will take sufficient thought for the considerations of state policy! The more one thinks of this, the more one sees that the city, "the praises of which, as I have spoken of them, are such in virtue of the fair deeds of her sons,"[28] is not only man-made; she has attained an independent existence such that her preservation means more than the happiness or misery of all her inhabitants.

This position is still considerably removed from the forms of state worship we have come to know later, because, in the first place, it is a state the total scope of which is itself—it does not, for Pericles, embody an ideal that is greater than it; and, in the second place, he contemplates its destruction at some future day, when the glory of it will be the only thing left.

"You must realize that your city has the greatest renown among all mankind for not yielding to misfortune, that it has spent more men's bodies and pains on war than any other, and that it has obtained the greatest power that the world has yet seen up to now. Even if we shall one day in this time come to disaster—and this we may, for everything that is born decays too—the memory of that power shall be everlasting: that we were Greeks and ruled more Greeks than any others had; that in the greatest wars we held our own against them all and individually; and that our city was the greatest and the most abundant in everything."[29] You must disregard the hatred of your subjects, he says, for "hatred does not abide for long, but the brilliance you have now and the repute hereafter are all that are left for everlasting memory."[30]

The bareness of this, in all its abstractness, is terrible enough. Glory is all that remains, yet the glory is not of the victory of a principle, a faith, or a civilization; it is glory that attaches ultimately to defeat as well as to victory, a memory held in awe, in which the blackest deeds against Greek morality have their place as truly as the love of beauty and wisdom, the story of a city whose greatness is lovely and untouchable, created by man but not responsible to him, knowing no God and no life beyond itself.

And Thucydides' conception of his own worth as a writer is closely linked with the value he saw in the war and its political setting. Slowly and painfully he left behind the values of the poets and the logographers. He did not want to entertain nor did he wish to record great and glorious events, "that their memory might not be lost from among men . . . or fail of their due distinction."[31] That which is true and that which is permanent are what he wanted to record, and what was true and permanent in the nature of man reflected in the deeds of fifth-century Greece was rarely entertaining and hardly ever glorious. Harsh, brutal, and bloody as the deeds were, he must face them with no comforting possibility of moralizing them away against a prospect of a necessarily brighter future or a universal good design of divine origin. To realize them in their true meaning, to divest himself of hope of things different and of unmeaning resentment at things as they were, to cling bitterly and doggedly to explaining the cold-bloodedness and brutality in terms that could at least be verified after the fashion of his world, became the whole duty of the historian. As his work attained its peculiar austere perfection, perhaps Thucydides felt a kinship with Pericles, who sought no glory and no reward except in the creation of something greater than himself, yet a something rooted in the brutal truths of the life around him.

Pericles is great because, though he rose on the fear and greed of his countrymen, though the empire he built was built on fear and greed, he and perhaps it transcended this fear and greed. He feared nothing and was greedy for nothing. He cowed the people when they were overconfident and heartened them when they were downcast. Everyone knew that money could not tempt him. And it is because of this that he stood above all his fellows, and it is through the defect of this quality of disinterestedness that his successors reduced all again to the level of their fears and greeds and ruined both the state and themselves.[32]

And the city of Athens, the national equivalent of Pericles among individuals? Is she not the school of Greece? However she may have robbed the allies to build the Parthenon and robbed the Greek city-states of the freedom they treasured, she had become, as the Funeral Speech indicates, something greater than all this. She had become a model of human society, tolerant and gracious, now that the days of conquering were over. In the Athens of Pericles Thucydides saw something great and admirable which compelled his intellectual homage and his emotional acceptance as nothing else did. If one believed that the history of man politically is a story of greed, strife, and fear, and their working in the society created by them, there was still a time when these passions had for a historical moment been immobilized in a balanced beauty and strength, and Periclean Athens was this historical moment. The enormous wealth which the commercial democracy alone could create—as Thucydides so well knew—was here to set off dramatically the symbols of Athenian rule: The Athenian can eat at his table the fruits of the ends of the earth as commonly as the olives of neighboring Attica.

Yet the democracy whose dynamic was greed and fear and whose might was the offspring of that greed and fear was held in check by a single autocrat whose rule it accepted because he was not as other men were. In this voluntary acquiescence of the vulgar, in this submission to the statesman who neither flattered nor feared them but who put heart into them or made them tremble with the witchcraft of his own aloof certainty, Thucydides may have seen the transcendence of the materialism in which he believed. Here was power as it truthfully was, based on fear, pride, and greed, yet it touched something too magical for measurement.

PART II

The Man in the Duststorm

CHAPTER IX

The Word and the Deed

1

PLATO'S life is framed by a single continuous intellectual relation which dominates his thought. This is the connection between the multiplicity of concrete detail, of the actions and implications of the world around him, and an immutable and single existence behind them. I do not intend this as a restatement of the familiar philosophic position attributed to Plato—the division between the ideas or eternal forms and the world of becoming. It is more than this, for this philosophical doctrine itself is one manifestation only of the intellectual drive which animated the man in his teaching, his writing, and his political ventures. There can be no complete separation between any of these parts of his life; and, since within Plato's thought itself everything is interdependent, any kind of division of subject matter ultimately proves inconclusive and unsatisfactory. An isolation of one aspect of his thought—and I propose in a certain way to isolate his politics—can only be attained, if at all, when the whole man is imaginatively understood. The important thing to understand about him is, first, the central theme rather than the several manifestations of it in their differences. And this theme is the sustained passion to hold together a sense of the reality of what man can see, hear, smell, and touch—what he can love, hate, and feel inclination to or revulsion from—to hold together these and an assurance of something beyond such reality that will not render this world trivial but will satisfy an appetite for design, completion, and beauty.

It is the togetherness of the multiplex and the single, of the concrete and the abstract, that matters to him most. He cannot endure the thought of an invisible order of reality which does not simultaneously inform all that is around him; that the moment of union is a mystery expressible only in myths and parables does not mean that it is not the central concern of his intellectual and emotional life. And accordingly the true development in Plato's life is clear when we notice the change in position and significance of the two worlds.

For until Plato is well over sixty the force of his written work —and in a different way of his teaching and statesmanship, too— bears on the actual creation in art or life of an approximation of the order and design he believed lay hidden in and behind the world he saw. The dramatic details of the dialogues and the painstaking building-up of character in the interlocutors; the founding of the Academy and its emphasis on the training of future legislators and statesmen; above all, the two painful failures actually to train the philosophic monarch in the person of Dionysius II of Syracuse—all point the same way. At this time the relation between the detailed and observable present and the transcendent for Plato was one where he struggled to see the two in such balance that action in this world had significance and meaning. In the last stage of his long life, between his sixtieth and eightieth years, this has changed decisively. He has no less concern than before with the identification of his two worlds, but the impulse comes now from the other side—from the need for certainty in respect to the forms, and ultimately from the calm which that certainty gives him. There is no room here for the energy and effort necessary to change things in the world around him. It is understanding he is seeking—for himself and to a much lesser degree for other men—rather than action or creation. And the understanding is of no ordinary kind, for it must treat the knowledge of all objects and even the processes of knowledge themselves as only instrumental to the act of apprehension of what is beyond them. The life of man or citizen or state, man's body, the anatomy of the universe itself, are only analogical expressions of what is true beyond them and beyond the reach of any ordinary means of communication. The work of the later years—the sketch of the sophist and the statesman, the map of the "good life" of the *Philebus*, the physical research of the *Timaeus*, or the plans for a future good state in the *Laws*—though appearing in various aspects to be concerned with our human world, lies under the spell at once of a detachment which vitiates its ostensible practical purpose and of a terrifying profundity and insight which has no discernible human application.

2

Plato was born in 427, four years after the commencement of the Peloponnesian War, which Thucydides observed so closely that "he might be able to know something accurately about it." He was a young man of twenty-three when the war ended and the democracy at Athens fell in 404, and he was just twenty-eight when the restored democratic administration executed his friend Socrates in 399.[1] Directly following the latter date he left Athens and traveled in Greece and elsewhere until 387, and, when he returned to Athens in that year, he founded the Academy for the training of philosophers, statesmen, and lawgivers. The first twenty-eight years of his life, lived in Athens, and presumably the last ten or twelve of these years in close association with Socrates, constitute a unit apart from everything else. The Athens of the Peloponnesian War and Socrates are for Plato the compressed experience of a lifetime. Though he lived to be an old man of eighty and though close to forty years of that life (387–347), except for the two brief visits to Sicily, were passed in fourth-century Athens, almost nothing of that fourth-century Athens comes to us in his writings.[2]

We know quite a lot about this period, both about Athens and other Greek cities, from the writings of Isocrates, Demosthenes, Aeschines, and the other orators. We have much detailed and precise knowledge about the diplomatic and military successes of Philip and the gradual decay of the Greek city-states before

the coming of the Macedonian monarchy. But of the fourth
century with its various interesting political experiments hardly
an echo exists in the works of Plato. For him there are the years
in Athens when he was a boy and a young man, when what he
later came to consider the vital political issues found their dramatic climax, and it is this world and these issues which the
early and middle dialogues re-create. It is of course true that if
the *Gorgias, Protagoras, Republic,* and *Phaedrus* are in a sense
extensive commentaries on fifth-century political life, the later
dialogues, such as the *Statesman, Critias,* and *Laws,* are political
works in a vein and on subjects far removed from the fifth century. Yet the questions of these later works are also not fourth-
century questions. They had attained a new kind of abstraction
and generalization. It is possible to show a connection between
the political position of the early works and the later while admitting the difference between the two in tone and significance.
But it is not possible to connect in any important way the political content of the later dialogues with the political happenings which actually surrounded them in time.

It is very hard to date the dialogues decisively.[3] The efforts
to do so have predominantly followed two main lines. The one
of these depends on the investigation of stylistic evidence and
the interpretation of Plato's use of particular datable events; the
second, on the emergence and development of philosophic doctrines. Of these methods, the first at its broadest appears fairly
useful.[4] Anyone can see a real change in the manner of writing
between the *Republic* and the *Laws,* and the canons of style fixed
by these two points, the location of which we know roughly
at least, are probably sound enough. These canons of style en-
able us to date blocks of dialogues with some degree of certainty—to say, for instance, that the *Gorgias, Protagoras,* and *Phaedo*
belong in one group and within a space of fifteen or twenty
years—but they do not settle the question of the priority or
posteriority of the dialogues mentioned.[5] The second kind of
scholarly work, concerned with dating the dialogues with refer-

ence to their philosophic content, is less satisfactory,[6] because, in the first place, by Plato's own admission, doctrines, in the strict sense of the word, are not to be found in his dialogues.[7] That is to say, one has no right to assume that the changes in philosophic position between one dialogue and another are due to Plato's development of a thesis; they may be due entirely to a desire for one dramatic emphasis in one place and another later. In the second place, even those scholars who have admitted this but have tried to date the dialogues in terms of the prominence or disappearance of certain doctrines have achieved very little that is constructive and have met with some decisive failures. For instance, they have thought that one can show that the theory of forms occurs first here, that it is given less importance there, and does not occur after such a place. And then they would use these points in a chronological sequence.[8] But the theory of forms itself, which is the main peg on which all such treatments depend, can be shown to be implicit in dialogues written long after it should have vanished if this thesis were correct.[9]

Roughly, then, the early and middle periods—from the year 399, when Socrates was executed, to 362, when Plato returned from his last visit to Sicily—are represented by the following list of dialogues: *Crito, Apology, Euthyphro, Laches, Lysis, Charmides, Phaedo, Gorgias, Meno, Protagoras, Republic, Phaedrus,* and *Symposium.* Within this list no really certain sequence of dates can be established.[10] Nor perhaps does this matter unduly. What does matter is that we have in broad outline a sense of the development of Plato both as an artist and as a man, and this is not the same as a knowledge of a shift in philosophic doctrines. It would be, for my part, impossible to conceive of the *Republic* as postdating the *Statesman;* it does not matter much, and I cannot feel certain, whether the *Symposium* was written before the *Phaedrus.*

These years between 399 and 362 are the time in Plato's life when he was concerned with constructing something in political life at its broadest which would be significant as an imitation of the permanent and invisible world of forms. The dialogues here represented are closely related to this effort of construction both in their objective artistic presentation of political problems and, in so far as they have teaching value, in the way that they indicate indirectly the approach to the good life for man and citizen. Some of them fulfilled the latter purpose more completely than others. The *Republic,* for instance, in its two halves came as near as Plato ever was to do to charting the shape of the best state on earth, while the *Gorgias, Protagoras,* and *Phaedrus* are rather animated studies of the complex human factors involved in considering political life at all. The work at the Academy, though we know regrettably little about it, seems to have been designed to furnish to such Greek states as demanded them lawgivers and statesmen.[11] And in his two efforts to change the government in Sicily, in 367 and 362,[12] Plato bears witness to the sincerity of his convictions that the philosopher who does not care to try to alter the course of contemporary events, when the occasion presents itself, brings disgrace upon the fair name of philosophy.[13]

In the last period of his life, from 362, when he came back to Athens, to his death in 347, Plato confined himself to his teaching at the Academy and to his writing. He had nothing further to do with active political life, and when about 352 the factional quarrels in Sicily had been fought to a standstill and certain of those concerned appealed to the old man, now close to eighty, to help them once more establish a new form of state, he wrote the letter of tentative refusal which we know as the *Seventh Letter.* In it there sounds unmistakably the voice of someone who would never again enter the world of politics himself and yet was anxious to set forth the course of events which had guided his whole life toward unsuccessful political experiment. This is a document which, as we shall see later, is revealing in more ways than one.[14]

During these later years he wrote the *Theaetetus, Parmenides,*[15] *Philebus,* and also certain dialogues which were to have fitted into a series; but the series is, in neither case where he undertook it, complete. Thus the *Sophist* and the *Statesman* were to have had another dialogue added dealing with the Philosopher (which was never written), and the series beginning with the *Timaeus* was to have been continued by the *Critias* and the *Hermocrates*. Of these, the *Critias* breaks off in the middle and the *Hermocrates* was not written. Last of all is the *Laws*, the sketch of the good state of the future.

This essay will be concerned with presenting what I conceive to have been a kind of development in Plato's work with relation to the whole man, though I have chosen for particular discussion what he says and what he did about politics. For my interpretation of this development, Plato's gradually declining interest in all practical activities and the emergence of a new and almost entirely mystical conception of intellectual work are vital. This view is in direct opposition to the conventional position which would have Plato emerge from a kind of artistic chrysalis of the early and middle period into something like a scientist and even perhaps a practical man of politics at the last. In this common view, the *Sophist* and the *Statesman*, among his later dialogues, mark his pedagogic concern with new logical methods,[16] the *Timaeus* his interest in physics;[17] the *Philebus* is a kind of textbook summary of his ethical theory[18] and the *Laws* a new and improved practical version of the *Republic* for immediate application.[19]

If at times the picture of Plato's development which I shall draw should seem esoteric and perverse, the reader would do well to remember one aspect of the Platonic problem which constitutes a decisive objection to the easier and common interpretation which I have just outlined. Those who hold the latter theory have always leaned heavily on the works of Plato's old age and on the evidence of Aristotle, who of course only knew Plato personally when he was already sixty. This, the conventional view of a Plato who steadily approached closer and closer to the scientist, the scientific teacher, and the practical political planner, was based on alleged Platonic "doctrines" found in

Aristotle and not obtainable from the dialogues, on accounts of alleged Platonic "lectures on philosophy,"[20] and on ingenious interpretations of the *Sophist* and *Statesman* and equally ingenious dismissals of the *Timaeus*.[21] The early and middle dialogues with their strong dramatic tone were difficult to associate with particular philosophic doctrines, though even this had been tried.[22] But when in the later dialogues the outline grew barer and the arguments more interesting metaphysically the commentators have assumed that this is the moment when Plato becomes a serious philosopher. And, since this is the time of his life when Aristotle knew him, the "Platonic doctrines" in the latter's works and the "lectures" all fell into place. It was felt that, if anywhere there is a Plato who speaks his mind as a philosopher should, it is the old Plato, and there is a kind of textbook quality about the *Philebus*, *Sophist*, and *Statesman* which made it look as if Plato were becoming refreshingly practical. The *Timaeus* was dropped out of the discussion as a strange fantasy of the old man.

But the fact seems to be that Plato never taught anyone his own philosophy in any more explicit way than we can understand it from the dialogues. He has assured us himself in the *Seventh Letter* that his philosophy has never been put into writing and never will be.[23] Moreover, a recent brilliant and painstaking study has proved conclusively that Aristotle had no sources to draw on for Plato's doctrine except the dialogues which we possess.[24] A strong case is made for the view that the Academy concerned itself almost exclusively with geometry and mathematics, these being conceived of purely as propaedeutic studies of philosophy,[25] and that there is little or no evidence of formal instruction in philosophy by Plato himself or of an official doctrine for the Academy[26]—witness the fact that Plato's two successors in the direction of the Academy, Speusippus and Xenocrates, actually abandoned the theory of ideas, which, in some form, is certainly central to whatever was Plato's philosophy.[27]

That in fact the conventional view is the exact antithesis of what may be learned from reading the last dialogues imaginatively I hope to show.[28] In the effort to understand Plato we must never lose sight of the figure of the director of the Academy at the end of his life lacking almost all significant intellectual contact with those around him. Aristotle in his discussion of Platonic doctrine continually asks what Plato really meant, and the same difficulties are raised by his successors, who had known him well.[29] If these men did not understand what evidence they had—and that is apparently the body of the dialogues, for they cite virtually nothing else—they could have asked Plato himself. Probably they did and probably they got no answer. Certainly they *had* no answer, and come before us as the first of a long series of students puzzled by the paradox of an abundance of philosophic material with no adequate clue to its interpretation as to the position and doctrine of its author.

In its most superficial form, the puzzle is simply to disentangle Socrates and Plato. Since Socrates is the spokesman for the winning side, philosophically, in almost all the dialogues, the easiest solution is to equate Socrates and Plato and treat Socrates as the champion of the Platonic position[30] or, alternately, to separate them entirely and count the Socratic dialogues as literally Socratic.[31] Both these interpretations, however, are very unsatisfactory. The first leaves unexplained the disappearance of Socrates as a dramatic figure in the later dialogues, and both leave unexplained the emphatic statement by Plato himself in the *Seventh Letter* that no book containing his philosophy had been written.[32] Above all, the inconclusive nature of many of the dialogues themselves leaves one wondering what, if any, position is being maintained by this Plato-Socrates.

3

"Not only in shape but in everything else too," says Meno to Socrates, "you are exactly like that flat sea fish, the sting ray. It, too, numbs with its shock whoever comes near it and touches

it; and that is just what you have done to me now, I think."[33]
"When I hear him," says Alcibiades, "my heart leaps in me
more than that of the Corybantes; my tears flow at his words,
and I see many others that feel just as I do. . . . And with this
man alone I have an experience which no one would believe was
possible for me—the sense of shame. He is the only one that provokes it. For I know in my own heart that I cannot gainsay that
I ought to do as he bids me and that when I leave him it is my
vice to yield to the favors of the many. . . . Often I would be
glad if I should not see him again in this world, but if this should
happen I know well that I should be more miserable than ever;
the truth is, I do not know what to do with him."[34] In words
like these several speakers in the dialogues testify to the
extraordinary personal impact of Socrates on all that met and
loved him. The strange effect of his conversation was, of course,
partly due to the physical peculiarities of the man. Intensely
ugly with his bulging eyes and apelike face and his rolling gait,
indifferent to heat or cold and food and drink, he was a kind of
prodigy.[35] Indeed, the Oracle at Delphi, which for some reason
and in some context unknown to us pronounced him the wisest
of mankind though he was himself aware, as he said, that he
knew nothing, seemed to mark him out as a prodigy.[36] When
Alcibiades in the *Symposium* describes him in a parable, he
speaks of the image of the Satyr Marsyas, the demon of sensuality. This figure, he says, is in its ugly exterior the very picture
of Socrates, yet, when the statue is opened by some mechanism,
it is full of golden images; and so of Socrates, behind the ugliness and sensuality, you cannot believe how full of chastity
he is: "He spends his life in ironical jest with his fellow-men,
and as to those images that are within him when he is serious and
the statue is open—I do not know if anyone has seen them. But
there was a day once when I saw them, and they seemed to me
so divine and golden, so beautiful and so marvelous, that I had
simply to do what Socrates bade me."[37]

Plato is no artist in fiction in the ordinary sense of the word

and his Socrates no creation of an artist in fiction. The latter
may, it is true, put together a man out of remembered fragments
of many men, out of the way this man said certain words or that
one's face looked or the other walked. A composite picture
emerges which in its completeness bears a symbiotic relation
to its creator and at the same time is independent both of him
and of the fragments of real life out of which it is composed.
But for Plato the start was made with a whole figure imitated,
for it was the existence of the unique Socrates which drove him
to write. Without the historical, physical assurance that Socrates existed there is no beginning to the dialogues. For Plato
there must have been a Socrates of flesh and blood, sensuality
and ugliness and ignorance, yet pointing beyond to the immaterial soul, spiritual, beautiful, and wise and fusing the oppo-
sites in one indissoluble person.[38] This historical character is for
Plato one which had moved in a city and a time that he knew
well or of which he could recover knowledge. And the death
of Socrates, executed by the restored Athenian democratic government, "for impiety and corrupting our young men,"[39] meant
much to Plato and in many ways. It meant, as he tells us when
many years later he wrote the *Seventh Letter*, the ultimate proof
of the worthlessness of political life as it was organized in
Greece and the need for a root-and-branch change in which political power would not be acquired and employed haphazardly
but with a sense of a true community with a meaning to it.[40]
It meant, too, that in his unhappiness he left Athens for nearly
twelve years, and, when he came back, his first act was to found
the Academy to be *his* place and *his* means for training philosophers who would be capable of changing political life de-
finitively. All this Socrates' death meant to Plato, and all this is
part of Plato's response to his friend's death.

But within his life as a philosopher and writer the death of
Socrates meant something different and something more difficult for us to see and convey accurately. Socrates had been in a
physical and personal fashion for Plato the awakening of a vision

of the world. The significance of this vision, theoretically, was probably not yet understood by Plato when Socrates died. He was a young man still, and in the early dialogues in which he has chosen to dramatize the death there is only a sense of Socrates as a human being almost monstrous in the combination of the outer man and his inner life; the sense of one whose whole being expressed a truth single and uniform as other men's bodies and words did not; the sense of a riddling, jesting spirit which was the necessary concomitant of the inner truth which the man could not reveal. What Plato has given us as the image of Socrates' death and his last hours dramatically points up all the intellectual implications of his life, personal and political. This image is in the *Apology* and *Crito* and *Phaedo*—and we cannot go behind the drama to the facts that inspired it. But it is true to say that the feeling of these dialogues is historical—that is, their entire effect is to recapture as exactly as can be the impact on others of the end of Socrates' life. I do not mean that every detail happened as has been written in these dialogues but that in them, as distinct from others written within ten years, their force does not reside in the intellectual contest with Socrates as chief contestant. In these dialogues a few hours of a man's life epitomize dramatically the meaning of that life. Thus the *Apology* as the philosopher's defense, the *Crito* as his argument on the duties of a citizen, and the *Phaedo* as his understanding of this world in the shadow of the next are not illustrations of the philosophic position. They *are* that position dramatically.

Yet the dramatic form in which Plato cast the events of Socrates' trial and condemnation was in a certain way to die with them. The end of Socrates' life was recognized and expressed by Plato as an end not merely accidental but perfect. It is of the order of things that must, as well as that did, happen. And so, as the years went by, the image of Socrates became both remote and fixed in that attitude which Plato felt was ultimately the true Socrates, true to what was deepest and most hidden in him. A living Socrates contemporaneous with the dialogues about him is inconceivable, for his natural decline and decay would have destroyed Plato's picture. In the *Second Letter* Plato himself or one of his pupils wrote: "None of the dialogues are mine; they are all Socrates', but a Socrates grown young and handsome."[41] I think that what is meant is that the dialogues take one back from the figure of the old man, as in age and ugliness and triumph he faced his accusers in 399, to the continuous revelation in scene after scene of the golden images within the figure of Marsyas the Satyr. Here, as the writer of the *Letter* saw it, there is true youth and beauty, and age and the changes of this world cannot touch them.

This Socrates, who cannot grow old, is the static figure of inquiry in the dialogues, forever sifting the issues with a human knowingness, yet only allowed to partake of humanity himself in the small personal touches of his physical form and habits—the demon that arrested him when he was about to do something wrong, his bare feet, his bulging eyes, his odd oaths, and his preoccupation with homely examples.[42] These are the touches out of which a novelist would have created a living and therefore necessarily changing character. Plato has done the unexampled thing. He has created a figure with the human attributes which bring him to physical life before us; he has shaped the conversations he holds and the people he meets so that our minds are prepared for action and development—not necessarily action or development in the dramatic sense but an intellectual action and a development which might leave us feeling different about Socrates at the end of the tale than at the beginning—and yet we do not. The intellectual ramifications of the dialogue bred of the incessant probing of the impersonal figure at the center leave us with only one sensation, the magnetism of Socrates.

Both the humanity and the impersonality of the figure are simultaneously achieved because we are not asked to contemplate any change in *him;* only to see him in a certain attitude, to listen to his words in the context of other words, to note the contrast of his mood with that of others. We grasp the particularity of the other speakers differently from that of Socrates. We can imagine *them* briefly and uncertainly—for it is only a passing thought we are inclined to give them—doing things and living their lives like ordinary people. But in the dialogue they are being drawn always into the circle of Socrates' magic, the bare impersonal country where their words and their thoughts will stand naked before his analysis, and where he acts not as a living person, changing in his acts, but as a touchstone himself unchanged.

Seen this way, we understand why for Plato in the earlier part of his life—or more truly for all his life until the last fifteen years —the function of Socrates in the dialogues is ultimately to embody the union of a deeper truth and a seeming contradiction within a single figure. The image of Marsyas the Satyr which is Socrates, according to Alcibiades, has all the outward appearance of sensuality, but, when it is opened, we find inside images of gold of divine beauty. "The carving of his outside is indeed the casing of a Silenus, but when opened up you cannot think how full of chastity he is."[43] The paradox lies in the person of Socrates, but the inner truth involves a supersession of the untrue first impression.

And even as we grasp Alcibiades' meaning in this likeness we must not lose the thread of the argument in the *Symposium*, of which this is the culminating point. Before the entrance of Alcibiades and the talk of Socrates as Marsyas, Diotima, the fictional prophetess invoked by Socrates in his speech, had told of the ladder of love. In this we learn of man's progress from his knowledge of the world of becoming to that of true being. First he shall love among the multiplicity of beautiful bodies one single body that is beautiful and then discover the community of this with all other bodies that are beautiful, and he shall then love bodily beauty in all of them rather than in one. And next he shall find the beauty of soul rather than of body and shall love the beautiful soul though it be lodged in a body inferior in beauty or even ugly. And, lastly, he shall find the beauty of soul which is common to all beautiful souls and shall contemplate, in so far as a man can, true beauty.[44]

There is a progression here in which each step carries one away from the prior step, in which each advance renders insignificant the stage we have left behind. And this process is epitomized in the person of Socrates, who, ugly and sensual in appearance and speaking the language of sensuality and with all the magnetism of sensuality, is now utterly removed from sensuality itself. His power over Alcibiades is, in fact, that he wins the young man to try to trade the possession of his bodily beauty for a glimpse of the brightness of the all-gold images. And, in so doing, Alcibiades discovers that he has nothing to give Socrates, and so Socrates retains his power over him. For Socrates, lust has no meaning any more; it is only, like his irony, a kind of tantalizing mask concealing a truth different from the mask's face.

When Plato grew to be very old, this image of Socrates ceased to express the truest way of seeing reality. Then there was for him no truth which is grasped apart from the world of becoming. There was not a process in which the earlier steps on the road are left behind. There was no beginning and no end, no first and last stages. There was a continuous fusion of the one and the many, an indissoluble fusion of individual body and soul, and world body and world soul, and meditation on this fusion constituted the true way to understand what is beyond it and beyond the complete grasp of man's vision. The union of man's body and soul was the representation of the inner truth—the way his limbs act and his brain controls them, the thousand hidden clues to divine workmanship which man's body and man's world afford.

This is not Socrates' way, and Socrates could not remain in the dialogues. As history had put him there, doubly significant historically and philosophically, Plato could not change or twist him. For the original he had too much reverence. But he had ceased to care for him, as a painter will cease to care for a style in which he has once painted while he can retain his satisfaction in what he has painted in that style. There may even be a hint in the *Theaetetus* of the fashion in which Plato himself saw the abandonment of Socrates as a symbol.[45] He is the son of a mid-wife, Socrates tells us there, and his intellectual work is like the physical work of a midwife. The class of midwives consists, he says, of those who have done with childbearing themselves and now can only assist birth in others. So he cannot achieve wisdom himself; he can only bring it to birth in others. This is again the uniqueness of Socrates and the meaning of the unique figure historically. Yet Plato had perhaps come in his old age to seek rather for some philosophical expression of life itself. It could no longer be confined within the necessary limits of a single human figure, however great, and especially when even the greatness of this figure carried with it a certain sterility, a certain removal from the processes of life. For Plato in his last days, if life could not be seen as a process, as the momentary union of the one and the many, it could not be truly seen, and, if not truly seen, the vision of what was beyond the union could not come either. So Socrates is left behind and with him the vividness and life which Plato had once loved to re-create. It was a new kind of life and a new kind of vividness he needed in his last days and one no longer expressible in human terms.

4

But the problem of the relation of Plato and Socrates by no means exhausts the ambiguity inherent in Plato's work. The major difficulty is in the interpretation of the written work itself. For the dialogues are a living contradiction; a contradiction between the perfection of their form and the expressed contempt of their author for them; a contradiction between their dramatic character and Plato's expressed hatred and fear of drama; a contradiction between their philosophic meaning and Plato's denial that they are philosophy. These are the tensions within which Plato wrote. Against the expressed denial there is ranged the silent opposition of the act of creation itself, the fruit of which is the body of the dialogues: the dialogues, quasi-historical, mimetic, philosophic, halfway between thought and the outcome of thought in men's lives.

Let us see in what words Plato himself denies that his dialogues represent his philosophy. The first statement comes from the *Seventh Letter*.

"But this much I can say about all of those who have written and will write saying that they *know* the nature of the subject which is my most serious interest, either as having been students of mine or others or as original discoverers on their own—in my opinion it is impossible for any of these people to know anything about the matter. For there is *no* treatise of mine on these things nor will there ever be, for it is not a matter communicable in words like other studies, but a thing which comes from constant association with the subject itself and constant living with it; it is like a light which is kindled from a leaping flame in the soul of the knower and then supports itself. Yet this much I know, too, that had these things been written or spoken, they would have been best spoken by me, and, written ill, would have grieved me most. But, if I had thought that it could be written and spoken adequately for the multitude, what finer thing could I have done in my life than write this great blessing for mankind and set true nature in the light for all to see? But, actually, I do not think that even the so-called attempt in that direction is good for all men, but a few only are capable of finding what they seek themselves with little help. As for the others, some of them instruction will fill, incorrectly, with a most unsuitable contempt and others with a high and vain hope as men who have learned a strange and solemn matter."[46]

The piece that follows this is hardly less important:

"In the case of every existing object there are three things whereby knowledge of that object must be acquired: the fourth is knowledge itself; a fifth one must postulate to be the object itself which is cognizable and true. Now these are, respectively: the first, the name, the second, the definition, the third, the image, the fourth, knowledge. To understand what I mean let us take a single example for all. There is a thing called a circle the name of which is what I have just said—'circle.' The definition of it is a sentence composed of names and verbs: so 'that which is everywhere equidistant from the extremities to the center' will be the definition of that which has for its name 'round,' 'spherical,' and 'circle.' The third thing, i.e., the image is that which is in the course of being described and wiped away, of being formed by a lathe or being destroyed. All of these things are related to the circle itself, but the circle itself does not go through any of these processes, for it is something totally different from them. The fourth thing we mentioned was knowledge, intelligence, and true opinion on these matters, and these we must assume to be a single whole which dwells not in words or in the outline of bodies but in the soul. And this is clearly different, both from the three we mentioned before (name, definition, image) and from the nature of the circle itself. Of these intelligence in point of similarity and kinship is nearest to the fifth and the others are farther removed.

"The same is true of the straight and of the spherical form, and of color, and of the good, the fair, and the just, and of all bodies artificial and natural, of fire, water, and all such things, of every living thing and of all moral acts or passions in souls. If a man does not, somehow or other, gain the four, he will never become a perfect partaker in knowledge of the fifth. Moreover these four, by reason of the weakness of language, try to express the quality of each object no less than its essence; and that is why no man of sense will ever try to commit to language his thoughts: particularly is this true of language which is unalterable, as in the case of writing."[47]

It must be remembered that this comes from the last days of Plato's life, at a time when he had quite abandoned the truly dramatic dialogue. But I think that his view of what can be conveyed about a subject matter was not substantially different somewhat earlier. The name, the definition, and the image are, in the middle dialogues, less analytically distinct. They are fused in the personalities of the protagonists in such dialogues as the *Gorgias* and the *Protagoras*. They come to life in less separate but nonetheless clear phases of illustration and argument in the *Republic*. But it is always the problem of relation that is dramatically illustrated—the name, or how men call what they recognize but must fashion a name for; the definition, as they seek to describe the function and character of the form they see—a definition which will vary as one aspect or another of the form is imperfectly understood; the image, as they try to identify its shifting likeness in the world of becoming.

Probably written ten to a dozen years earlier than the *Seventh Letter* is the passage in the *Phaedrus* containing a series of speeches put into the mouth of Socrates. Plato is almost indubitably speaking of his own dialogues, the only record of his work which we possess. His curious slighting detachment is very marked.

SOCRATES: So, the man who leaves, and the man who takes up, a treatise in writing, as a thing that will be clear and certain from the writing, would be a very simple fellow and would really be ignorant of the oracle of Ammon, imagining that written words are something more than a means for recalling his memory to a man who already knows what is written there.

PHAEDRUS: Quite right.

SOCRATES: For, you know, Phaedrus, there is this curious property of writing which it has in common with painting. The children of the art of painting, too, stand there as though alive, but if you ask them something they preserve a very solemn silence. It is the same with arguments. You would think that they could talk as though they knew something themselves, but if you ask them, wishing to learn something of what was said, they just say the one thing and the same thing always. Every argument, once it is written down, rolls about everywhere both in the minds of those who understand and those who should have nothing to do with it, and it doesn't know to whom to talk and to whom not to talk. But being insulted and unjustly reviled it continually needs its father to help it; for it cannot defend or succor itself.

PHAEDRUS: That, too, is quite right.

SOCRATES: Very well. Let us look at the other kind of argument, the true brother of the one we have just discussed, and see how it arises and how much better and more capable it is in its growth.

PHAEDRUS: What is it, and how, according to you, does it come into being?

SOCRATES: It is written with knowledge in the soul of the student and can succor itself and knows how both to speak and be silent to the proper listeners.

PHAEDRUS: You mean the living and ensouled argument of the man who knows, whereof the written one may justly be called an image.

SOCRATES: Just that. Tell me this: Would a wise farmer dealing with seeds that he cared for and wanted to be fruitful seriously plough and plant them in summertime in the Gardens of Adonis, and watch them with delight coming up in a week in all their beauty, or would he do this, when he did it at all, only for amusement and a kind of holiday? And in the case of those he was serious about, would he not use all his farmer's craft and sow them at the right time and be satisfied if they came to fruition after seven months?

PHAEDRUS: Yes, Socrates, the one will be his serious proceeding and the other in quite another vein, as you say.

SOCRATES: Are we to think that one who possesses knowledge of the just, the beautiful, and the good has less sense in regard to his seeds than a farmer?

PHAEDRUS: No.

SOCRATES: Then he will *not* seriously sow them with black water through a pen in conjunction with words which cannot help themselves and are incapable of teaching the truth adequately.

PHAEDRUS: In all probability, not.

SOCRATES: No. But these literary gardens, it seems, he will sow and write, when he writes them, for amusement, and for himself to lay up a treasury of memories against the coming of old age and its forgetfulness and for any other who treads in his footsteps; and so he will have his pleasure in seeing their tender growth, and when others enjoy other forms of amusement—dinner parties and other similar relaxations—then he, it seems, will pass his time with the amusements I mention instead of these.[48]

5

What, then, if in some sense they are not philosophy, have the dialogues to communicate to us? We can answer this question only if we consider not alone Plato the philosopher who mistrusts the expression of philosophy, not alone Plato the writer who mistrusts the written word, but Plato the artist who dreads the power of art. For they are in fact one: the lover of the ineffable forms who yet feels he must bring those forms to life through the distortions of definition and of image; the passionate lover of life who yet feels that life contaminates the invisible and intangible forms which alone are really real. The elusiveness, the ambiguity, and the richness of the dialogues lie in their expression of this single central tension.

At the beginning of Plato's career as a writer his two first works, the *Apology* and the *Crito*, belong by themselves. They are very nearly pure history, although there are a conscious centering of interest and a dramatic theme which overstep history. The works which directly followed them are slight if charming exercises—the *Euthyphro, Laches, Lysis, Charmides*. They differ from the *Apology* and *Crito* in Plato's development in that it is no longer only the great moment of Socrates' life—his trial and condemnation and the last days in prison—which is his concern. He has started to build up the Socratic world in a series of conversations. This is a greater shift than is at first apparent. The death of Socrates—how it came about in moral and social terms, and how he bore himself in the face of it—is a great theme rooted in a single moment. It actually is, in a certain way, Plato's greatest theme in its broadest aspect—the composition and dissolution of the thing that is a man; the part that reason can play in arming him against the abstract turn of death; the indications that exist of the unity of man and his world, so that we can argue for the destiny of the soul.[49] All these subjects he is to treat later in his greatest dialogues, yet they are hidden in the historical happenings of Socrates' trial and death as he has put them into the *Crito* and *Apology*. When he turns from this theme to the dialogues which follow them, he is starting back on the road. He has no longer the magic of the great moment to guide him and is casting about for what in a dramatist would be plots for his plays. For Plato they are intellectual topics which can be transformed or destroyed, as topics, when conceived of in a human situation. Thus, in the *Euthyphro*, the clear definitions of piety and moral duty become blurred and obscure when seen in the context of the relations between Euthyphro and his father; in the conversations with Laches, in the dialogue named for him, the evils of cowardice and the virtues of bravery become uncomfortably mixed up; and so on. And from the start Socrates has already been given his role—that of inquirer and destroyer—which he is to hold as long as he is a significant figure in the dialogues at all. The peculiarly static quality of his part is already there. But the depth of the understanding of character which we find in the later dialogues is wanting. These early sketches have a kind of sharp simplicity which is very unlike the later Plato. It is the dialogues of the years of Plato's middle age that fully embody his ambiguity as a writer and a man. And the problem of the ambiguity centers in the relation of art and thought to reality.

In the great dialogues of the middle period Plato sees, on the one hand, all the multiplicity of experience as partial and fragmentary imitation of a remoter reality. In the *Republic* the political thinker in the guise of a painter is challenged because he cannot prove that any human being as beautiful as his rendering of the human form could ever exist.[50] Socrates answers that it does not matter whether the beautiful picture ever comes to life in a beautiful human being. It is, in itself, his statement seems to imply, a more or less true rendering of the Beautiful whose pattern is elsewhere than in the world of becoming. So in one sense Plato is concerned to obviate the difference between act and word and thought—in so far as the action and the word and thought were alike imperfect copies of a perfect original.

True beauty is for him, probably, most directly reflected in the magic of the right lines, patterns, and colors. But even these purest existent harmonies are themselves reflections; they instinctively clothe themselves in attributes bodily and therefore mortal and therefore subject to change and imperfect—and so do they when they become realized, not in wood or paint or metal, but in a human mind. Similarly, but necessarily in a more complicated way, the pattern of justice becomes contaminated.[51] Probably the pattern of justice in so far as it can be expressed is more akin to a mathematical formula than anything else we can conceive of.[52] But even the mathematical formula is not abstract enough to prevent distortion. How much more the notions of a balanced society, the harmony of classes, the economic co-ordination of interests. All these cannot be conceived without their human clothing, and this carries with it change, death, and imperfection.

There is between the thought of justice in the mind of a thinker, and the form of the thought in words, and the transformation of the expressed thought into action a relatively small difference for Plato theoretically. If any significant difference exists, the approach to perfection is closer in the thought that still dwells in the mind without formulation by the thinker. Plato must have been aware that such thoughts are, in part, the product of words from others and that they never ultimately emancipate themselves from the verbal formulation; but he also believes that as long as the thought remains unexpressed, and particularly unexpressed in writing, by the man in whose mind it has been formed, it is somehow safer from the violation of the world of becoming.[53] This holds a fortiori for the world of action. Hence he finds it necessary in the *Republic* to make explicit the inevitable discrepancy between a plan conceived and a plan carried out.[54] But within the framework of his theory all these, the thought, the word, and the act, are imitations, are man's response to the understanding of abstraction which lies hidden in him and gives him not only his sense of classes or genera, which enables him to group particulars together, but his only assurance of objective truth.[55]

Thus Plato can say that it does not matter whether the ideal painting has a counterpart in the world of becoming or ever did have, or whether the ideal state ever will come into being or ever has; from one point of view the apprehension of the form, however imperfect, is all that matters. In the *Republic* Socrates says: "I understand. . . . You are speaking of the city we were founding, the city that lives in our argument, for I think she is nowhere on earth. But . . . there is a pattern laid up in heaven for anyone who wishes to see and so doing to make himself its citizen. It makes no difference whether it exists now or ever will, for the politics of this heavenly city will be his, and those of none other."[56]

Yet, for all that, there is the intense perception of life which is peculiarly Plato's. We can glimpse it in the absorption in detail observable everywhere in the dialogues—in the absurdities of Protagoras' pacing back and forth in the courtyard and thereby discomfiting his respectful disciples who are always in danger of getting in front of the master; in the feeling for the appropriateness of the early dawn, when the young man visits Socrates, and in the glimpse of the slave hunt carelessly alluded to in his first words; in the last moments of the *Symposium* with Socrates, Aristophanes, and Agathon the only guests still left at the table; in the mannerisms and uncouthness of Thrasymachus in the first book of the *Republic*. This passionate sense of life, which had originally made Plato respond to the physical appearance of Socrates, to the paradox of ugliness and beauty, entirely denied, in his middle age, what his theory would have asserted: that there is no significant difference between the thought in the mind, the thought in word, and the thought in act—that it does not matter whether the statue can come to life or the imagined state find its fulfilment in the physical existence of country, men, and women that should compose it. These things Plato sought intensely with one side of his being. He wanted as much as any man ever wanted to see the city of his dreams, to see the state where the citizens were like to himself in an inner acceptance of what he valued; and so, again in the *Republic*, he can say that, if the ideal state is incapable of being realized, "we here should justly be laughed at as people who are idly uttering things akin only to wishes and prayers."[57]

But this passionate sense of life which yet strove to find a form which would arrest the flow of sensation and fix it in a mold beautiful and imperishable was hardly the driving force of a statesman. It turned, much more readily, to the mysterious world of imagination and fiction, both in thought and in character, where the material is less immalleable and the ugliness of disorder can be more effectually banished. Plato longed deeply for a bodily garment for the creations of his mind—yet he distrusted his capacity to create it. Ultimately he fell back on his conviction that the other life, which he knew behind the passing world of becoming, remained immutable and unmoved. Yet the sense of conventional reality, the men and women you could see and know and hear, who would have made up his city if he could have founded her, haunted him as beings of whom he must take account. Once in his life, later, he was to face this conventional reality, halfheartedly and full of misgivings. In the meantime he was no less in the grip of his intensely Greek conviction that the end of thought is action and of ethic *praxis*. Somehow, at least, he must *see* the men and women, must hear the words and grasp the implications which gave immediate meaning to his speculation.

Nor was it enough to create them purely out of his own imagination. He distrusted his own love of drama so that he must have some assurance that the men and women were real, that he was not entirely a manipulator of puppets. And it is the historical authenticity of the basis of the dialogues which gives him this assurance. The memory of the dead living past with Socrates as its center ebbed imperceptibly into the present of Plato's living thought and questions, and the power of history's actuality became for him the guarantor of truth for his own imaginings, a truth not yet put to the test of a living experiment. The dialogues of the middle period, embracing some of his greatest achievements, are just this—a shadow world between philosophy as pure speculation and action in the form of teaching and politics.[58]

6

Yet Plato was not capable of resting satisfied with this shadow world. It gradually dissipates before the assault of the two driving forces of his life when these separated one from another. On the one hand, the tendency which led him to desire the historicity of Socrates as the basis of the earlier dialogues led him further to the experiment in Sicily, where living beings and a living state would test the truth of his dreams, and, finally, when he turned again to literature, to the strange fancies of the *Timaeus,* where the participation in the forms is embodied in the person of the universe and the explanation in the parable that the Demiurge made the universe by persuading Necessity to combine in his design. On the other, the passionate belief in the forms led him to distrust his own imaginative skill in the representation of human beings and their life, for there lay the greatest of dangers—that his mind would contrive and his tongue utter "the thing that is not." This thing-that-is-not is most commonly the patchwork of images, of fragments of images from this world, which are used as disguises to deceive and to conceal the emptiness beneath; and it is most commonly the artist who works through such deceit. So we find in Plato's theory of art both a further illumination of the nature of his own dramatic dialogues and the reason why they could not be for him more than a temporary and tentative escape from his own dilemma, a way station on the road to the Plato of the *Timaeus* and the *Laws.*

The invisible, intelligible forms are communicable to man, in so far as they are communicable at all, in subjects which are intelligible and by means of concepts rationally apprehensible as wholes.[59] Thus the true image of a man is in part, but only in part, the fictional man created by a writer. His externals and his habits of speech and thought are indeed an imitation, but an imitation at the most superficial level. If the writer should actually cling to the imitation of a single man, and that a man who had actually existed, he would be less apt to be led astray himself or mislead others. For the coming into being of this man and his existence must actually have had a real relation to the form, or he would not have been. Such a writer would be an imitator at the third degree of reality, like the painter who painted the chair which the craftsman had made. But he would still be a harmless imitator in so far as he was honest and clung to the simple imitative description of the man and what was positively known of his words and acts.

In fact, however, as Plato well knew, there are very few writers of this order. Much commoner is the writer who has tried to convey an image of the whole man, for much of whom no actual knowledge of what he was or did is available. To supply this, the writer must draw on his imagination and knowledge of all men. It is Plato's conviction that at this point the desire to imitate in order to persuade and convince others leads him to an easy fragmentation of the wholeness of the form which should stand behind the created image in its entirety, as definitely as in the case of an object or a man that has actual existence in life. This is why all art must be discussed by Plato as mimetic art and why, when he chooses some salient example, it is most often to the theater that he goes to find it.[60]

Let us take the example of a man mourning for his dead friend as this may be treated by a writer or a playwright. Since the mourner does not truly know what awaits him or his friend after death, he may passionately bewail his own impending death or the death of his friend; at another time, when there is no compulsion of circumstances upon him, he may rationally discuss the possibilities of survival, and his reason or belief in tradition will assert the superior likelihood of survival. Now the true pattern of the qualities of the soul for Plato, like the true pattern of the circle, admits of no contradiction, in which the soul at one moment knows this, at another feels that. But the perpetual seesaw of doubt and hesitation, with its accompanying passionate manifestations, is an inevitable feature of any man's life in this world. And it is precisely this condition of hesitation that attracts the imitator and which he copies to the inner delight of his readers and auditors. The mimetic artist does not care whether he is imitating what is insignificant when he imitates the man mourning his friend, since for him there is neither significance nor insignificance behind the immediate passion which possesses the man, or whether he is imbuing those who hear or read him with a true notion of value, since for him there is no value except the communication to his audience of what in this case is true here and now and what his inner artistic instinct tells him is common to himself, his created object, and his listeners. The mainspring of the mimetic artist's attraction is the artistic representation—and exploitation—of the moments of man's extreme joy and sorrow, exactly when his world is transformed or destroyed, and where no unified conception of life, admitting of both joy and sorrow, is clearly present. And it is only such a unified conception of life, admitting both joy and sorrow, and the subordination of both to something higher, which in Plato's view is a proper representation of the form.

The evil effect of the artist on others is, moreover, that, although he conveys no truly unified view of the form he supposedly imitates, he often appears to do so, so skilful is his fragmentation and recomposition of the form by images. Oedipus' self-discovery seems to be not only a representation of a unique figure, Sophocles' Oedipus. It seems also a picture of the dilemma of every man in the world. But it is a presentation of that dilemma alone. It does not extend itself so that the horror of Oedipus may be harmonized with the other events of his life and a unified picture of the man, with all that would mean for all men, may be seen in it. It is exactly the art of the dramatist or the painter that the single scene they have created shall in its intrinsic power blot out the conception of the other scenes in the context of which this scene becomes a part of a whole life.

try to avoid a falsity of emphasis such that, for instance, we are led to identify Plato superficially with certain modern political doctrines because specific parts of his total picture recall them.[3] There are very few individual items of belief in a political philosophy which in themselves justify the drawing of similitudes and comparisons with that of another; it is only the totality of the intellectual picture which can be so likened or compared. We must not distort the emphasis in that total picture.

2

The dominant feature of Plato's political theory at all stages of its life is the root-and-branch character of the change it advocates in existing Greek institutions. Almost from the moment when he began to observe political life and certainly since he began to write of it, he did not want any piecemeal renovation of an existing structure or even any series of four or five central reforms but a transformation of the state in the light of an entirely new concept. This concept was a new philosophical formulation of the objectives of man's existence and the state as the expression of such objectives.

To form a state entirely on a theoretical and philosophical foundation or to remake the constitution of an existing state in a similar way was more frequent in the political experience of Greece than that of later Western civilization. Aristotle in his *Politics* says that in deciding on the nature of the best state he must take account not only of such well-governed states as exist but also of such theoretical structures as men have created from time to time in their search for the best form of political community.[4] Earlier than Plato's days apparently both Sparta and Crete had adopted "planned" constitutions which to a greater or lesser extent continued to exhibit the main features of their authors' original plans.[5] And within Plato's own lifetime, not only do we find Plato himself trying to create the Sicilian state anew,[6] but it seems that the Academy was treated as a sort of political workshop to which at times the Greek city-states applied for lawgivers or constitution-framers.[7]

This tendency is something that we can readily understand, but we have not seen many instances of it in later European history. The work of the American Constitution-makers and the founders of the French Republic is perhaps closest. Yet in both these cases there does appear to be a lesser, or at least a derived, emphasis on philosophical speculation about the nature of the state and a closer relation to a given historical situation. The eyes of both the Frenchmen and the Americans concerned are on the defects and merits of existing governments; their theories spring from such observation and never completely abandon it. The American concept of liberty brought forth on this continent a new nation; their belief in liberty implied an opposition to, a rejection of, the systems of the Old World and shows this in its formulation.

The fifth-century Greek, on the other hand, was strikingly unhistorical in his attitude politically. Apparently he tended to view political experiment as a series of explorations of logical possibility within the framework of a fixed human nature. If he had gone wrong with one possibility, he would try a new and entirely different one without an awareness of traditional links binding him to the past. He would, in fact, start all over again. This is not true of all Greece, or at all times. The progress of the Athenian democracy from the beginning of the sixth to the end of the fifth century does follow an observable pattern in which certain steps are taken gradually, and the transformations within the democracy are made as slowly and with as little violence as we are accustomed to in America and Britain. But in many states, notably rich commercial states, like Corcyra and the cities of the Ionian seaboard, and in Athens herself by the end of the fifth century, there are frequent examples of abrupt changes from one kind of government to another, with new constitutions and new theories of political life continually appearing. It may be that

the fact of the internal strife between the rich and poor sharp-
ened the theoretical faculty in the body politic. A change from
democratic to oligarchic or oligarchic to democratic government could not be made gradually. It must come with violence,
and the violence brought with it a demand for a new theory of
government, not just an emended version of what was wrong
before, but a new view of the meaning of the state as the instrument of man's desires.

It is against such a background that we must see Plato as a political theorist. He, too, felt the struggle between rich and poor
as the chief disease of the states of his day.[8] But whereas the
sharp changes in political fortune drove others to formulate constitutions which would more effectively serve the interests of
their class or the external advantage of their country, the observation of the same factors made him see the state as an expression
of what was wrong with man himself. Plato's theoretical states,
then, are nothing less than the projection of a new consummation for what is truly human in the best meaning of human, as
he understood it. It therefore involves a radical readjustment
of teaching and education; it involves a reconsideration of the
meaning of justice until it takes in the whole significance of
human nature. This is why the discussion of the state, in the
Republic, is only introduced as an annex of the argument about
justice in the individual, as an example where the dimensions of
the quality would be larger and more discernible than in the
single man.[9]

3

Let us see how Plato tells the story of his own approach to
politics in the *Seventh Letter*. He was, of course, an old man
when he wrote the following words, but I believe he probably
is not misinterpreting this younger self who comes before him
as he writes:

"When I was a young man," he says, "I felt as many young
men do: I thought that the very moment I attained my majority

I should engage in public affairs, and there came my way an opportune turn of political events that I will tell you of. The democratic constitution, then loudly decried by many people, was abolished, and the leaders of the revolution set themselves up as a government of fifty-one men—eleven in charge of Athens proper, ten in charge of the Peiraeus, each of these commissions to handle matters of administration in the market at Athens and the surrounding villages; and over all, with supreme authority, there was set up a government of thirty. Some of these men, you must understand, were relatives of my own and well known to me, and, what is more, they actually invited me at once to join them, as though politics and I were a fit match. I was very young then, and it is not surprising that I felt as I did: I thought that the city was then living a kind of life which was unjust and that they would bend it to a just one and so administer it; so I eagerly watched to see what they would do. And, you must know, as I looked, I saw those men in a short time make the former democratic government seem like a golden age. I will say nothing of their other crimes but of one only: my old friend Socrates, whom I would not hesitate to call the justest man of that day, they sent along with others to arrest a certain citizen then abroad and bring him home to his death; they did this simply in order to involve Socrates, willingly or otherwise, in their actions. He refused, however, and risked the final punishment rather than share their crimes. All of this I saw, I tell you, and much else that was not slight, and my blood boiled at it. So I refused to have anything to do with what was going on.

"Some time afterward the government of the Thirty fell and with it their whole constitution. The urge to public service and political ambition drew me slower now, but it drew me still. There were at this time, too, many offensive things happening, as was inevitable at such a moment of confusion, and it would not have been surprising in the revolution if some crueler revenge had been wreaked on many by their opponents. Yet the returned democrats actually showed considerable leniency. But by some chance it was again my friend Socrates who got into trouble; some of those who were in high places threw him into jail on the vilest of charges and one least fitting Socrates. For they indicted him of impiety, condemned him, and executed him—this man who had refused to share in the arrest of one of their own friends when he was a fugitive and when *they* were the political party in trouble and in exile, because this arrest was unjust. I looked at this, you see, and at the men who were in politics, at the laws and the customs; and the more I looked and the older I grew, the more difficult it seemed to me to administer political affairs rightly. For you cannot do so without friends and comrades you can trust and such existing it was not easy to find, for our city no longer lived in the fashion and ways of our fathers, and it was impossible to get new friends with any degree of facility, as the corruption of both law and traditional behavior went on apace and increased extraordinarily; finally, eager though I had been at first to go into politics, as I looked at these things and saw everything taking any course at all with no direction or management, I ended by feeling dizzy. I did not abandon my interest in watching political life to discover how it might be bettered in other respects and especially in the whole matter of constitutional government, and I was perpetually waiting my opportunity. But at last I saw that as far as all states now existing are concerned, they are all badly governed. For the condition of their laws is bad almost past cure, except for some miraculous accident. So I was compelled to say, in praising true philosophy, that it was from it alone that one was able to discern all true justice, public and private. And so I said that the nations of men will never cease from trouble until either the true and genuine breed of philosophers shall come to political office or until that of the rulers in the states shall by some divine ordinance take to the true pursuit of philosophy."[10]

Here we have in Plato's own words the way he saw his interest in politics, viewed from the very end of his life. It is the attempt of the Thirty to enmesh his friend and the execution of that friend by the restored democracy which colored all Plato's further speculations on political life. In seeing the attempt to entrap Socrates as an accomplice in crime, in seeing him condemned and executed, Plato not only saw an innocent man condemned unjustly, but the pain he experienced in his friend's suffering was no ordinary wound.

Socrates was, I say again, for Plato a kind of portent, a revelation of a truth that could only be brought to life, in all its ambiguity, in Socrates. As the combination of his outer ugliness and his inner beauty is full of hidden meaning, so are his life and the end of that life. I can imagine that at this time when Plato was still a very young man the paradox of Socrates' ugly beauty had only been felt as a kind of repulsive magnetism, a puzzle which was to yield its full meaning later. But the facts of the end of Socrates' life, the paradox of the man's quality and its reward, politically and socially, were clear. Because the conduct of Socrates was constantly dictated by an inner knowledge and an inner rightness which was not part of the external political world, there was an irreconcilable conflict between him and Athens, the most flexible and sensitive and consequently changeable of existing states. Thus he falls foul first of an oligarchic and then of a democratic government. The conclusion which impressed itself on Plato's mind and which later experience hardened into dogmatic conviction is that all existing states were ordered with no conscious relation to the pattern of justice. If it seems that this was a hasty and unwarranted judgment, that Plato had no reasonable ground for generalizing from the conduct of two successive governments in Athens toward a single person to the nature of all governments everywhere, the answer lies in the person of Socrates and Plato's relation to him. A great deal of understanding can be compressed into a single experience if the event is rich and the observer sensitive enough. That an administration composed of extreme oligarchs who cared nothing for public opinion and another composed of democrats who lived by giving the people exactly what they

wanted should both have tried to remove from his unique position of difference this strange man was what Plato saw and
noted. When in later years the young man's conviction of Socrates' innocence and justice was deepened into the understanding of what such justice was, the last years of Socrates' life and
his treatment by the two successive governments became more
significant than ever.

Yet it would be quite false to interchange the role of Socrates
in the earlier dialogues and the context of his political observations with the political position or views of Plato himself.
If we do that, we miss entirely the peculiar value which the
figure of Socrates has for Plato in his political setting. The dialogues as they represent the old philosopher's life and conversations again and again stress the difference of this life from the
social organization which surrounded it. Socrates is the most
just and wisest of men in a society which felt his justice and
wisdom as a thing alien and at last eliminated it. Socrates as he
is dramatized by Plato is the individual in the light of whose
virtues the true state should be founded. Paradoxically, such a
new state would automatically remove the need for or the
occurrence of Socrates, as he actually lived in this world. For
it is his sense of difference from others which is not the least
potent influence in making him what he was. But Socrates as
Plato wrote of him proved in lifelike dimensions *why* the existing states could not admit of the just man or be transformed
readily by ordinary political means into just states. Plato is
always the man who from outside Socrates' society saw in that
society the evidence of the necessity of an order of political life
completely different, and the political discussions of Socrates
and his friends and enemies are, in their harmony and opposition, the arguments for the necessity of that change.

There are two aspects of Socrates, in the early dialogues,
which perhaps reveal Plato's keenest interest in the historical
figure. In the first place, Socrates was entirely indifferent, intellectually and morally, to the complexities of the world of be-

coming and completely true to his vision and understanding of
the world of being. In other words, unlike Plato himself, he
did not try to change the times in which he lived in the light of
his inner vision. When his vision and the existing political necessity conflicted—as in the case of Leon of Salamis[11]—he unhesitatingly followed his vision. Thus the destruction of the
destructible part of Socrates in this political world is for Plato
an all-significant illustration of the ultimate incompatibility of
such "justice, wisdom, and goodness" with the ordinary social
life of a Greek state. Socrates, as far as they would let him, did
not meddle in politics and tried to "save his own soul." But in
the Greek society of his time the conflict between his standards
and theirs must necessarily become explicit.

Yet despite his vision Socrates, without trying to change his
political and social world, implicitly admitted its rights over
him, however painful this exercise might be.[12] This is what
makes the *Crito* one of the most important early dialogues of
Plato. Socrates, faced with the injustice of his judges in this
world, will compromise on nothing in his intellectual discussion
with them; but he will not escape from the consequences of
their verdict because he is a citizen and they represent the laws
of his state, and this is the natural relation of man in this world.
However corrupted or defaced, this is the basic pattern of justice. This acceptance by Socrates of moral obligations which he
regards as truly conceived, amid an intellectual structure which
he rejects, is to be the keynote of Plato's thought for a long time.

4

In the study of Plato's political theory the *Republic* has a
unique place. It is the one dialogue of the middle period in
which he systematically gives us an account of the state that
should be built, the state so unlike the one that surrounded him
as a young and middle-aged man, and he also indicates in this dialogue what are the smallest changes in an existing state which
would bring it closer to the state as it should be. The *Republic*

must be considered by itself and in some detail. Let us look first at two other dialogues of this period, the *Gorgias* and the *Phaedrus*, which deal with rhetoric—a political subject matter for the fifth century—and so have a direct bearing on politics.

These dialogues are in their political aspect analytical. That is, they reveal both by their arguments in themselves and by their arguments taken in conjunction with the persons who bring them forward the main sources of political action, as Plato saw them. Thus they constitute a sketch of actual political life in the fifth century with the implications of that life for an understanding of what political life should be. They do not, as the *Republic* does, actually show in detail the shape of the state as Plato would have it. In so far as they are concerned with politics, they present us with two very important aspects of Plato's views. These are the "natural" relation of governor and governed within a city and the role of persuasion in bringing about the union of the two.

There is, in the *Gorgias,* a striking image with which Socrates dismisses the merits of Themistocles and Pericles as great statesmen. You can hardly call these men great statesmen, he says, since they failed to make the people "better and gentler"— witness the fact that at the end of the career of each of them the people disgraced them.[13] The key to this is the notion that in the natural relation of governor and governed, where the interests of the whole community are the decisive factor,[14] the people must realize that their governors are governors not for their own enjoyment but for the good of the society. If this realization does not exist, something is wrong with the "naturally good" relation of the statesman and those he governs.[15] If the people are ungrateful, it is a sure sign that the government has not achieved its end, and therefore the statesman is not a good statesman. If, Socrates says, a teamster undertook to train a team of horses and ended by having the horses run away and throw him from the carriage, you would not call him a good teamster.[16] The analogy is important, for it helps us to realize how pointedly true this seeming paradox is for Plato. The natural functional relation of driver and team, in which an initial unwillingness has given place to a regular co-operation based on a recognition of a "stronger" whose strength is not mere power, is the way Plato would see the true relation of governor and governed. If the governor-teamster cannot control his subject-horses, he is no true governor or teamster. Since for Plato the truth and basic justice of the relationship *must* force its way to the consciousness of the subjects no less in the one case than in the other, a failure can be explained only by the defect of the superior element in the partnership.

Yet even the relationship of the horses and the teamster does not come about spontaneously. Some kind of action on the part of the superior element is necessary to produce the ultimate co-operation of the two. As Plato looked at the Greece of his boyhood and his middle age, he saw that this cement of political association was as defective as the character of the governors. For the two common means of maintaining the government were force or a certain kind of debased persuasion. The first was typical of the tyranny and the second of the Athenian democracy. All Plato's natural inclination was against the tyranny as a permanent form of government. When he accepts it as a starting point, practically in Sicily and theoretically in a brief passage in the *Laws*, it is always with the end of transforming it into a monarchy according to the laws.[17] The position of the tyrant morally and of his subjects politically is for Plato detestable, as the *Gorgias* and the *Republic* show us.[18] For if there is not finally a degree of willingness in the subjects, if in this sense there is not freedom, the relation is vitiated completely. But the freedom of choice of the Athenian demos, swayed by one bribe or another and flattered, frightened, and cajoled, is hardly less contemptible. In a later passage in the *Gorgias* Socrates answers his interlocutor's question whether he does not think Pericles and Themistocles were greater statesmen than their modern followers. No, he says, they were only more effective in giving the people what they wanted. Pericles filled the city with "harbors and dockyards and walls and tribute and such trash."[19]

5

The most important question which Plato wishes to animate dramatically in his political dialogues of these middle years is the value or significance of rhetoric, or the power of persuasion exercised by the statesman. In the Greek city-states like Athens and most of the Ionian seaboard cities where an immediate and direct democracy was the form of government, the capacity to persuade one's fellow-citizens was the most valuable asset a man could wish for if he wanted to be in politics, and everyone who lived in these cities was in a sense in politics. It is clear from what we know of the last half of the fifth century that in Athens, at least, real political success was almost entirely a matter of knowing how to persuade the popular assemblies. In modern parliamentary systems the rhetoric addressed to the audience cannot have as its unequivocal purpose the persuasion of the men sitting before the speaker to the adoption of one special measure. It must remind them of their responsibility to their constituents, and in the weeks of protracted delay involved in the discussion before the final vote not a little of the speaker's rhetoric is directed over the heads of the audience to the people whom they represent in order to apply indirect pressure to the audience actually seen. Thus always the rhetoric of a modern democratic statesman tends to the creation of a general attitude on the part of very large numbers of people. A political atmosphere must be produced in which a measure can then be forced through Congress or Parliament with general approval behind it and a number of special political "deals" facilitating its passage past particular obstacles.

Your Greek politician talked directly to the people who were going to vote, not in three weeks or three months, but usually within the course of the day in which they listened to the rival speakers. And they were going to vote on one measure, often containing tremendous implications for the future of their city or its policy for many years to come. The act of voting did not even involve the labor or difficulty of writing to their congressman or M.P. It was attended by considerably less disagreeable notoriety than attends the action of a congressman or M.P. whose vote cuts across party lines, since there was a large attendance which varied from day to day, and the party machine was probably not nearly so well organized as in a modern democracy. Under these circumstances it is little wonder that the pages of Thucydides are full of complaints by statesmen who declare that the attitude of the assembly listening to two proponents of different measures was not very different from that of almost the same people listening to two competing plays and that their vote at the conclusion of each performance was hardly more the fruit of heart-searching and reflection in the one case than in the other.[20] It is this that colors the bitter reflections of Socrates in the *Republic* when he speaks of the teacher of political theory of his day and the democratic statesman:

"Each of these private teachers who teach for pay, whom the politicians call sophists and regard as their rivals, really teach nothing except the opinions of the many when they are gathered in their assemblies. *That* is what they call wisdom. It is as if a man were keeping a great strong beast and should learn very thoroughly all the moods and passions of the creature, and how to approach him and how to touch him and when he is most savage and when most gentle and what makes him the one and the other and the sounds that he makes to express each and again what sort of words of someone else's uttering calms him or makes him furious—it is as if a man were to learn all of this through keeping company with the creature for a long time and finally call his knowledge wisdom and should construct it as a system or an art."[21]

To this empty show—the politician bidding for the people's support with bribes and the people casually assuming responsibility which they later ignore—Plato opposes a picture of a deeply functional relationship and a kind of rhetoric closely related to the real difference between the speaker's and the audience's capacity to understand.

6

It is, I believe, a mistake to discuss Plato's view of rhetoric purely in terms of his political beliefs or, epistemologically, by contrasting rhetoric and philosophy and the relation of both to knowledge. In this as in so much else in Plato there is an area of vital illumination. Once this is understood, in a fashion comparable with that in which he understood it himself, the other aspects of rhetoric fall into place. For Plato neither analogy nor a separation of the various sides of life has any real importance. The truths that he discovered came to him in a single moment of illumination—in an aspect of human relationship or physical existence. From this there is a progress in which the illumination spreads to all the rest of life. It is the peculiar value of the dialogues that they constitute the artistic re-creation of the moments of illumination—in conversation, in chance happenings, and, as it were, in particular intellectual silhouettes. They are not philosophy, as philosophy has since been understood, but the artistic correlative of the experience that makes philosophy. It is when we realize this, the nature of illumination in Plato, that we can understand why, in the case of rhetoric, its deepest meaning for Plato is expressed in conjunction with love.

His main dialogue on rhetoric juxtaposes the two themes in what appears a puzzling conjunction. Phaedrus reads to Socrates a discourse of Lysias purporting to be a plea urging the beloved to yield to a nonlover rather than a lover, instancing the many ways in which the nonlover is more worthy of gratification than the lover.[22] Socrates, having first of all applauded the piece on technical grounds, criticizes it as an argument. He gives a speech of his own in the same vein as Lysias and on the same side. At its conclusion he is about to part from Phaedrus when he is prevented by his daemon, who warns him that both Lysias' speech and his own have been blasphemies. As expiation he delivers the famous speech in praise of love involving the picture of the soul as a charioteer and two horses.[23] When he has finished, he and Phaedrus spend the rest of the dialogue arguing about the criteria of good and bad in speech-making and writing and the relation of rhetoric to knowledge.

At first sight the dialogue seems simply concerned with two themes—love and rhetoric—and the bridge is the superficial fact that the criticism of rhetoric is based on examples taken from the three speeches on love in the first part of the dialogue.[24] It is my belief that further reflection shows the very close integration of the subjects.[25]

To understand Plato's treatment of love, we must turn from the dialogue of which we have been speaking to the *Symposium*.[26] Love is not simply an instrument for the attainment of higher ends, and it is not simply the satisfaction of lust. While it can be both of them, it is most importantly man's intermediary between his imperfect and mortal condition and the immortal and changeless existence which he constantly recollects or is made aware of as the completion or transfiguration of his human mold. Love, we hear from Diotima, is not a God or a mortal either but a daemon or spirit "through whose agency occurs all association and discourse between God and man."[27] The union of the physical and other-than-physical aspects of love is indicated in the parable of Love's birth from Poverty and Resource on the name day of Aphrodite as well as in the preoccupation with the physical aspects of love in the imagery of the horses and charioteer in the *Phaedrus*.[28] The sense of physical beauty, the magnetic quality of beauty, is for man the sign of an understanding which he partially lost at birth. The true course of love according to Plato—that is, the course which will lead to man's greater understanding of what he has lost and to his more effective efforts to regain it—is the merging of this physical attraction with a vision of a beauty not restricted to one body and then not restricted to body but finally discarding the beauty of body for the beauty of soul.

In this, the so-called "ladder of love," love is, as Diotima says, the daemon which effects communication between gods and men. The love of men for one another is more valuable than the love of man for boy, and the latter is better than the love of man for woman, according to Plato, simply because of the reciprocity of the intellectual relation which declines from man through boy to woman. It is not quite clear in the ladder of love whether in the first stages the physical satisfaction of passion is the necessary completion of a phase and whether the later ascent is helped or hindered by it. The impression left by the half-jesting foiling of Alcibiades' lust by Socrates is that Socrates has grown older and wiser than the young Alcibiades—that he knows that physical love is a slight and trivial matter in comparison with the inner power of beauty. The simile of the bad horse in the *Phaedrus* myth again suggests the transcendence of passion in the pursuit of the abstract. In all this there is plainly no reference at all to what is commonly called "natural" in sexual passion. The love of man for man is in every respect the same—except that it is better and higher than the love of man for woman as an inner monitor warning of a true communication between his imperfect self and what lies beyond it and behind his physical existence in this world. The emphasis lies, not on the difference between "natural" and "unnatural" love or really on the difference between the physical and psychological sides of passion, but on the transcendence and supersession of the physical by the other-than-physical.

Love, then, is the mark of divinity in man, or rather the sign which if truly followed will lead him to an understanding of beauty. But the power of beauty in one human being exercised over another calls for some sort of surrender or subjection of the one self to the other and a future union of the two. Whether that surrender must be of a physical character or whether, in some way, the physical consummation once accomplished, it did or did not significantly affect what followed can be momentarily disregarded. The tremendous emphasis on the distinction between loved one and lover built up in the *Symposium* and marked at the outset by the intentionally pedantic commentary on Aeschylus' use of the roles in the case of Achilles and Patroclus[29] shows the importance of the notion of surrender or submission on the part of the one to the other. It is as the instrument for this change that persuasion functions. And rhetoric is only the semitechnical—and for Plato falsely technical—name for Peitho: persuasion. That the surrender of the loved one should be brought about by violence or cupidity[30] or solely by bodily lust[31] is a bad thing. In persuasion there is an instrument which betrays the mark of divine origin as certainly as love which prompts its use. The two belong naturally together for Plato, and he has said so in the dramatic break in the *Phaedrus*. What is wrong about Lysias' oration is his assumption that persuasion is a tool neutral in character by which the inherently good or bad points of a case may be elucidated. An excellent argument can be made rationally for the position that it is to the advantage of the beloved to yield not to the lover but to the nonlover. But such rationality is in Plato's view a shameful and dead use of something which is only natural and vital when prompted by the passion of love, which is the guide given us to show us the image of our proper divinity in the loved one.

Since the physical beauty which inspired love is only the image capable of recalling the greater and more perfect beauty lost by man in his mortality, it is by convincing the loved one of the true kinship of the more and less perfect beauty that the lover succeeds in his ends. Thus, in the *Symposium*, both lover and loved, reverencing the feeling in both of them which is the sign of the God, attain an ever closer vision of true beauty. It is in this sense that rhetoric, which becomes the name for the discourse of the lover and the beloved, cannot be separated from philosophy.

7

Persuasion and surrender are, for Plato, the expression of something basic in human relationship and therefore peculiarly involve political life. This is a sexual relationship, and in its broadest aspect—that of political life—in which its expression is, of course, utterly different from that of the lover and the beloved in the *Phaedrus*, it is not merely analogically conceived.[32] It is the same driving force from within which makes use of persuasion, a human thing, as opposed to the violence of the animals. And in each case the love of the lover directed to the beloved is not for the sake of the beloved but for the image of beauty reflected in the beloved. The beauty which love teaches the lover to see in his beloved has a meaning which in turn he conveys to its possessor, the beloved. The fundamentally sexual nature of the relationship is indicated in the surrender: the persuasive force of the lover is aimed at inducing the beloved to yield, for without this there can be no learning on the part of the beloved and no achievement on the part of the lover and beloved together. This yielding cannot be an acquiescence in better reasoning power or a delicate balance of one choice over another. It must have the final decisive character which in its simplest form for human beings is involved in physical surrender.

Now the image of beauty which troubles the statesman with desire of creation is not localized in one other body. It is the image of a city which in its very meaning contains both governors and governed. But there can be no creation until there is a natural acquiescence by the governed in the designs of the governors. And herein lies the impossible obstacle in the way of the Platonic statesman, for he has no means of persuasion which would induce this voluntary natural acquiescence. In the world of human sexual relationship the strength of physical attraction visually experienced is a powerful reinforcement of the rhetoric of the lover. It is the living proof of the guidance of the God for both. The Platonic statesman has almost no means to show the other half of himself, namely, the people (since only he and they both can make up a city), the living proof of the love that guides him. He scorns the procedures of Themistocles and Pericles, who bribe the people into acquiescence by "ships and walls and dockyards."[33] And he is resolutely set against "murders and banishments."[34] Yet the actual instruction of large numbers of people in the inner mysteries of philosophy, which would alone permit a true understanding of the image of beauty in a city, is impossible. The best Socrates can suggest, when the model state is being constructed in the *Republic*, is rhetoric in the form of a "noble lie":

"I will try to convince first our rulers themselves and the soldiers and then the rest of the city that, for all the rearing and training they had at our hands, it was a kind of dream of what happened to them and what they experienced. That, in reality, they were in that time underneath the earth being formed and reared up, themselves and their arms and all their gear, in the process of artefaction and that in the moment they were completely wrought their mother the earth sent them up; and so now they must think of that earth as of a mother and nurse, for her counsel and defense against aggression, and of the rest of the citizens as brothers born likewise out of the earth. And we should tell them a tale to this effect: You are all brothers in this city, but the God in the case of those of you capable of rule mingled gold in their generation inasmuch as they are of the greatest worth. And in the helpers, silver, and in the farmers and other craftsmen, iron and bronze."[35]

We should notice that in the model state, which has been artificially constructed by the participants in the dialogue, those puppets who are rulers *might* also be convinced of the true-false myth, for then their task of convincing others would be easier. This is indirectly a commentary on the reality that confronted Plato in his lifetime. There was no noble lie which in easy physical and historical terms would lead people to true belief; still less was there any such image of value to himself. There is only the inexpressible vision of the completed city, given some perfunctory literary shape in the *Republic*, on the one hand, and the rejection of demagoguery, bribery, and violence, on the other. He is trying to find a road from his thought to its issuance in action, for love, which is his insight, without surrender, love without the other half of one's self, is empty and frustrated:

" 'The philosopher keeps quiet and minds his own business . . . content . . . if he himself shall live his life here in purity and free of injustice and deeds of impiety and take his departure finally with fair hope and in a spirit of graciousness and kindness.' 'In that case,' said he, 'he will have performed not the least of achievements before he departs.' 'But he will not have performed the greatest either,' said I, 'if he does not find a state that fits him: for in the state that fits him he himself will attain greater proportions and along with his private salvation will save the community as well.' "[36]

Since love and surrender and the life of the lover and beloved were for Plato the visible signs of the true road to the understanding of perfection, the picture of the ideal state (which is only the understanding of perfection written larger than in a single man) and the means toward approaching it in this world become sharply divided. Paradoxically, rhetoric belongs to the ideal state and cannot be used to bring it into being, for rhetoric postulates already a natural and good relation between the one who knows and the one who does not. Thus we have the seemingly absurd position that Plato emphasizes in the *Republic*, though he has often been misunderstood. The first part of the book contains the model state, including rhetoric in the form of the noble lie. But Books v and vi, which are concerned with the possibility of bringing the state to pass, declare that only by making a philosopher a king or an existing king a philosopher can the desired change take place. In fact, Plato is forced deliberately to ignore the comparatively easy inculcation of true opinion to bring his state into existence and throw himself on what he knew to be a near impossibility: that of finding a private person who by virtue of natural gifts and training can become a philosopher and simultaneously command the disposition and opportunities of a practicing politician, or a monarch who has talent and character such that he will abandon all the attributes of power in order that he may, almost scientifically, understand the abstract nature of his position.

True rhetoric, then, is the instrument of persuasion for inducing true belief. And true belief, politically, is what the community as a whole must possess. The prefaces to the *Laws*,[37] which he wrote later, are examples of what Plato meant by the true rhetoric. They do not, cannot, in fact, in the form of general preludes to particular ordinances, instruct in the philosophical grounds for belief. They can only assert that certain things are true and certain practices pious and link the specific law to these principles. True rhetoric in our world (though not necessarily in the puppet state of the first books of the *Republic*) demands that the governors should *know*. The truth of the true beliefs they convey must have an absolute command of their minds, and in this world Plato saw this command as largely dependent on rational understanding. Thus for political reconstructions there are two elements to reckon with—those few or even the single individual who can make the change and the people as a partner in the new partnership. Between the two newly created partners rhetoric is the instrument for creation. Philosophy, or dialectic, is, however, the only means for producing the man or men who will make the change. This is why in the early and middle dialogues, when Plato still sought a practical solution to his desire for bringing his state into existence, the stress falls on the criticism of false rhetoric (which the men of the fifth century knew as the only rhetoric) and on the difference between it and dialectic or philosophy; it is also why the Academy faced in the direction it did. When in Plato's old age, after the Sicilian experiment, he abandoned his practical ventures altogether, the *Laws*, with their prefaces, are born. They belong only to the new world, when the difficulties of the old shall have been solved.

CHAPTER XI

Constructions

1

THE *Republic* stands by itself among Plato's works in that it is the dramatic presentation of his own dilemma. That is, in the combination and composition of the parts he is laying bare the dilemma itself.[1]

An old man at the extreme limit of life speculates on what it is that makes men happy at the last. In the ensuing discussion it appears that happiness depends more on the character of the particular man than on various general conditions of life. Justice seems the most complete statement of the requisite human virtue which makes the soul of the possessor happier both in this world and in the next.

It is suggested that one will see more clearly the dimensions and outline of justice in a state than in an individual man.[2] And the model of justice in the state, and consequently the just state, is outlined. The interlocutors ask the essential question: *Can* it come into being in this world?[3] The answer is that it can— if a philosopher can become a king or a king a philosopher.[4] There follows a discussion of the progress toward knowledge which it takes to make the philosopher who will be king.[5] Lastly, Plato demonstrates that even the just state, if it should come to pass, will in course of time and at the juncture of the fulfilment of a certain number and a certain kind of man in the state decline.[6] An imaginary and highly schematic process is then described in which the original just state is transformed into the four variations of state Plato's world knew—timocracy, oligarchy, democracy, and tyranny—as the personal character of the inhabitants and the constitutional construction of the state interact. Here the identity of the big and the little, the state and the individual, in virtue and vice are very painstakingly articulated. The book ends with an epilogue amplifying the earlier treatment of the subject of art and government in the ideal state and with the myth which is the likeness of the journey of man's soul after death.[7]

Anyone who reads the *Republic* intelligently will see how clearly its outline reveals Plato's predicament in politics. The book has three phases, in its strictly political parts. In the first the model state is described with the clarity and certainty that belongs to Plato's vision of what should be. The second is separated from the first by the decisive question: Can it be made to work?[8] And Plato's answer is: It can. He vehemently asserts the truth and significance of the model even if it should never be born among men, but that there must be a *possibility* of such realization is essential to *him* if not to the truth of what he asserts.[9] Because if there is no possibility of it, his one function, that of an artist in the lives of men and women, is negatived. As to how the change can come to pass he has no detailed answer. That is, he is certain that the philosopher-king is to be the agent of change, and he shows how the philosopher-king can be trained, but he does not know (and later in Sicily did not know) how the conjunction of the trained philosopher-king and his future people can be accomplished. This, the moment when the dreams become actual life, he cannot see.[10] The third movement is the recognition that even the model state, brought as near realization among men as it can be, making allowance for the difference between word and act, will perish, like all things man-made, and enter into the cycle of imperfection inherent in its humanity. The whole political story of Plato is here: the picture of the model state, of the trained ruler, the faltering hesitation as to how to bring not one but two dreams together, the desperation at the thought that failure can be construed as precluding the possibility of success, the certainty increasing all the time as he grows older that there is an element in all man-made things that makes for death and change and that the dreams of static perfection are only dreams.

2

If we were to ask Plato, "What is the state?" in a certain sense the answer would not differ widely from that of Aristotle. The formulation of the latter, that the state is a combination of men that come together for the sake of living and continue for living well, is very nearly the best statement we could make in summing up the *Republic* to answer this question.[11] But a closer examination of the *Republic* will also show the important respects in which the expansion of the common statement would alter its meaning for Plato. It cannot be too much emphasized that in this dialogue the state is discussed only because it is felt that being larger than the individual, while still exhibiting precisely the same proportional dimensions, it may be easier to see justice in operation in the state than in the individual soul. Therefore, we are asked to join a kind of mechanical game in which the interlocutors create in the imagination a state, first in bare essentials and then with greater complexities, and set it to working. When it works and we set aside the virtues which can be most simply and unequivocally determined and named, the residual virtue, it is assumed, will be justice. It is very important to notice that this toy model created by the investigators of justice has in a sense a dual personality, for it is at once *a* state and the just state. These two aspects are combined in the dialogue, for good reasons as we shall see. But analytically we need to see them distinct to be clear as to what Plato is doing. When first Socrates and his friends set about "creating" the state, it would seem to have no "model" character. It appears to be only a question of how people come to live in communities and how the rules of the community increase in complexity as the community itself grows. But this is precisely the community in which we are going to find justice—as it is *not* possible to find it in the current Greek states. Therefore, when completed, the state created by Socrates will be the just state and as such will represent the theoretical projection, politically, toward which the philosopher-king, in the second half of the dialogue, will look when he tries to realize the true state in this world.

Of course, the assumptions here are so large that it is quite absurd to treat the argument of the *Republic* in logical terms. For instance, we must assume, to start with, that there is a limited number of virtues, four in this case, both in the organization of man's soul and in that of the state. When we have separated out three, the fourth is justice.[12] Moreover, in order to discover the nature of this fourth virtue, we are asked to agree, on the basis of of a rather unsubstantial argument, to the definition of three parts of the soul (and the state), the rational, the passionate, and the appetitive.[13] But all this is exactly as it should be. It must be said again: The dialogues are not treatises designed to teach the reader by the rigor of logic; they are not exhaustive as Aristotle tried to make his treatments of particular subject matters. They are rather designed to make the reader understand imaginatively one point of view and neglect others. He cannot learn Plato's doctrine from pieces of the dialogue; he cannot learn the methods of Plato's philosophic pedagogy. But he may be persuaded that one way of seeing politics is truer than another.[14]

Here, then, we see our mechanical model of a state being put together and into action. There is the hypothetical gathering of farmer, artisans, etc., and the formation of a community. In other words, economic needs dictate the formation of the state. Several men will survive, in unison, where one man will starve. So far we can call the origin of the state, according to Plato, and the thing created "natural."

There has been some discussion of whether one has any right to say of Plato that this is his theory of the "historical" origin of states. Some have thought that we must not assume this, that it is only a theoretical sketch, a working model designed to introduce to us the political elements which the argument requires.[15]

This is largely true, and yet we would do well not to forget Plato's description of historical cycles at a primitive level in the *Statesman*.[16] There we are told that as a result of flood and various forms of natural destruction the beginnings of civilization have been made many times over. The particular details of the initial organization in the *Republic* are admittedly chosen to illustrate the later argument. Plato certainly did not conceive of a civilization starting up with a full complement of necessary artisans. In fact, his discussion of the process in the *Statesman*, tracing the series of steps through the nomadic way of life to agriculture and beyond that, is a much more sophisticated analysis than this. But the notion of a state beginning with bare economic needs and out of them generating a social and moral order is, I believe, not purely a device of philosophic exposition but roughly approximates what he conceives of as a historical process.

When the organization of human beings in the community agrees to the principle of specialization and the peaceful combination of specialists, the seeds of justice are planted. Justice is, for Plato, the combinative virtue which exists not simply in the possession of one class in the community but in the union of all. It is, as he says, a kind of harmony; and the essential life of the state is in justice—is, in other words, in the need to be a harmony.[17] And since this, the higher organization of the state, is by agreement of men in accordance with certain principles to live peacefully with an end in view, we can also call the state "artificial." Yet neither "natural" nor "artificial" is a term which is useful applied to the Platonic scheme of the state. It is exactly Plato's purpose to convey in this dialogue that there is no true break between the first stage of man's economic association and his later more developed community. The need for the simplest economic co-operation already suggests the image of the harmony. All that is done later is to label the elements in the harmony, describe their most effective combination, and, of course, by the complication of the structure, render the whole working model more significant in ordinary human terms.[18]

This interpretation is further justified, perhaps, by observing the pains to which Plato goes to insist that the primitive city, that is, the city of simple economic needs and simple economic co-operation, is the healthy city—in spite of the title "city of pigs" which the interlocutor gives it.[19] The more developed, luxurious, "fevered" city is that in which our discovery of justice will have more importance for the discussion, for it will be more like an ordinary city, but the primitive city already exhibits the harmonic structure and as such is a *true* city and is "healthy." Thus we can see a considerable difference between the fashion in which Plato describes the state and Aristotle's statement. The latter conceived of a state bred of economic needs which in a second totally distinct stage of growth, a more "civilized" stage, discovers the principle of justice and "living well." For Plato the essential quality of the state is discovered when men combine in an economic unit, when a harmony, however crude, is born.

3

According to Plato, all objects in the world, and conceivably certain qualities or relationships between objects, are the image or reflection of ideas or perfect forms of the same objects, qualities, or relationships, eternally existent and immutable outside the world of sense.[20] There are various ambiguities in the scanty evidence of the theory that even the whole body of the dialogues affords us, such, for instance, as whether there are forms of both natural and artificial objects. In the *Parmenides* it looks as though only "natural" objects had correspondent forms; in the *Republic*, however, there is mentioned a form of such an artificial object as the bed made by a carpenter.[21] We will disregard these disputable matters and concentrate on the undoubted fact that Plato believed in the form of a state. Thus the true state in this world is that which would approximate most closely to the form of the state, eternal, immutable, and apprehensible by pure reason.

The great problem concerning the forms and the world of sense is, of course, and always has been to determine in what way the sensible objects "participate in" or "share in" or even "recall" their eternal and abstract forms.[22] This difficulty is peculiarly sharp in the world of politics, where the relation of the abstract harmony, governed by its principle of order, to the continuous confusion of the separate aims and separate interests of the aggregate of individuals in a political community is at its hardest to determine adequately.[23] Allowing for certain changes in emphasis, the pattern of Plato's political philosophy from the comparatively early days of the *Republic* to the period of the *Statesman* and *Sophist* and last of all the *Laws* is very consistent. The consistency is inherent in the belief that there is a true and vital relationship between the soul of the individual man, the state, and the perfect form, which is the pattern of both. In the *Republic* Plato conceives both of the individual soul and of the state as a combination of elements involving a natural hierarchy and a natural subordination and authority. This picture is exactly the same in the *Laws*. In both dialogues, just as the intellect exercises despotic authority over the passions and the appetites for the good of the unit, so in the state a class of guardians which represents the intellect controls the other classes of the community in the interests of the whole city.

The variable element in his political theory, as, for instance, determined by the *Republic*, is inherent in Plato's relation to its realization. For Plato the tantalizing and torturing thing is the gap between the inner stimulus and the creation to which it forces man. The prophet, the poet, and the lover are all men inspired; that is, the passion that possesses them makes them the vehicle of what in man is greater and more perfect than he. But these passions, like the capacity for recollection, are only the sign of what is hidden in the midst of human imperfection. When the poet would re-create in words or the statesman would try to transfigure in men and women and buildings and territory the image of beauty and human truth which has haunted him, he is moving from what is natural and independent of mortality to what is artificial, man-made, and doomed to imperfection and death.

It is for the moment of such creation that, in Plato's eyes, the rational understanding is all-important. That the poet or the statesman shall be able to give an account of himself is the only clear proof, in terms of his human fallibility, that he has not allowed his inspiration to exhaust itself and been self-impelled by vanity into the regions where he imitates "that which is not." So the statesman who would bring to life the model of the early books of the *Republic* must be a philosopher, one who by dint of training in abstract disciplines had acquired a critical, rational self-control. When, at the time that he wrote the *Republic*, Plato was still earnestly bent on trying, at least, to bring his state into existence, the training of the philosopher-king is all-important. The preliminary sketch of the model state in the *Republic* *can* be a mere sketch—for it is of the nature of the philosophic wisdom of the philosopher-ruler that he should be able to meet particular contingencies in the light of general principles. His will be the task of bringing the state into being and of formulating the manner in which it should conduct its affairs.

But there is another political domain in which Plato is interested—that which lies beyond the formation of the true state by the philosopher. Plato does not believe in the continuous emergence of rulers with the kind of original and creative gift which the first philosopher, who founds the state, possesses. There must then be provision for the future, with two political elements involved—laws which embody permanently whatever can be laid down as principles in the political wisdom of the philosophic founder, and one or more governors who continue to administer these laws in a spirit of devotion and constancy. Thus there is an inevitable coincidence between the model state of the early books of the *Republic* and the so-called "practical" state of the *Laws*. They are together, in theory, and only separated by the political tragedy of Plato's life—his total inability to bring his state into being. The "practical" treatise of the *Laws* can be deeply concerned about all the minutiae of administration—because it belonged to the never-never land that lay the other side of the failure in Sicily. It is more "practical" than the model state of the *Republic* only in that the early essay is really subordinate, in Plato's interests at the time, to the hope of realization which depends on the philosophic ruler and his education. When the drive to realization is spent, he can give thought and care to the details of what will never come to pass.

But from beginning to end the important thing in the earthly imitation of the perfect form is the harmony which is the objective if mechanical image of the true harmony of the perfect form. This harmony is very largely independent of the actual understanding of the truth by the lower members of the political unit and, strange as it may seem, partly independent of such understanding even by the rulers themselves. In the *Republic*, when discussing the mechanical toy model which develops from the city of pigs, Socrates urges the famous "noble lie" as the foundation of the community. This is the legend which we have already quoted which asserts that men are born gold, silver, or bronze and that their worth to the community and place in it must be determined in accordance with these "natural" characteristics.[24] Now it must be clearly understood that Socrates and his friends are acting like engineers with their model. They are pulling the strings, seeing the puppets work, and, on the basis of this, discovering what are their true and natural movements, always construing "true" and "natural" as pertaining to the interests of the community as a whole and viewing this whole as a kind of biological entity the destruction or survival of which constitutes the difference between good and bad, true and false, natural and unnatural. As an engineer of this kind Socrates says: Let us convince of the truth of this (noble lie) first and best the rulers if possible, but if not the rulers at least the rest of the people.[25] What matters apparently to the puppet reproduction of the "true" state is that certain motions should be gone through, almost ritualistically, and it is at least not of supreme importance that the people executing the motions do so out of an understanding belief in the truth of their doctrine. In other words, the harmony, in the mechanical toy, is the all-important element of resemblance between it and the eternal form, not the subjective understanding of the participants in the political unit. Socrates is at this point able to say "convince of the false-hood" first and best the rulers, because it is only the model that is being considered. When later the philosopher-king enters as the instrument of realization, the nature of the latter, we are told, will admit of no falsehood in any form. But the belief in falsehood on the part of the rulers does not interfere, from Plato's point of view, with the validity of the toy model as a suggestive representation of the eternal form of the state.

There are further hints in the *Republic* and elsewhere which reinforce this impression. For instance, in excising certain passages in the poets from the scheme of education in the toy model, Socrates says: We will not have the poets say such things, first, because they are not true, and, *even if they were*, it would not suit the interests of our state to have our young men taught them.[26] It is possible, of course, to explain this conditional statement by claiming that Plato cannot anticipate the question, "What is truth?" until he has written the parts of the dialogue on the knowledge line, but he is not writing a treatise in the fashion of Aristotle in which the steps follow one another logically. What is brought out by this passage is Plato's conviction of the value of certain beliefs and certain actions and ways of life resulting from them irrespective of whether the individual believers really understand what they believe or even of whether the things they believe are objectively so or not. The harmony and the ritual are the important elements in the earthly approximation of the eternal form.

The discussion of the philosopher-king, occupying the later

parts of the *Republic,* is introduced as the final wave of paradox.[27] After the sketch of the mechanical-toy state, his interlocutors ask Socrates for an expansion of certain details of that state and finally: Is the whole state possible? The answer to this is to investigate the smallest possible change in existing states which will permit the model of the ideal state to come to life. This change is the introduction of the philosopher-king, and the statement that the true state will exist only when and where the ruler becomes a philosopher, or a philosopher becomes a ruler, is Socrates' third and great "wave of paradox." It is therefore essential to notice that the philosopher-king—and that means the ruler who can admit of no compromise with falsehood, at least in his own understanding—belongs to the part of the work which deals with the realization of the eternal form in this political world.

Weak spots in the theory of the autocratic philosopher-ruler are already clearly apparent in the *Republic.* One is the difficulty of getting him into the position of supreme authority, and the other is keeping him there. The first is shown by the brilliant study of how easily a man of philosophic gifts can be corrupted in seeking power, the historical example in Plato's mind being, probably, Alcibiades.[28] The second appears in an appeal of Socrates to his auditors where one can hear the almost desperate anxiety of Plato himself: Do you not think, he says, that the many, when they understand that the philosopher-ruler wants nothing for himself and is not bent on robbing or plundering them but rules only for their good, will submit and gladly accept his leadership?[29]

These weaknesses in his plans affecting the inception and continuity of the philosophic ruler are to be painfully demonstrated in his experiment in Sicily. It is in accordance with the general picture of Plato that, faced with the necessity of using violence to impose something approximating his pattern, he is quite incapable of doing so. "No authority achieved with even the smallest number of deaths and banishments is any good,"[30] he says at the very end of his life; but in the *Laws*, in the projected state, once it is established, the heretic or rebel is to be cut off like a diseased limb.[31] The failure of his efforts to make of Dionysius the example of the existent ruler turned philosopher, and the failure of the government of Dion, Plato's friend and student, as the philosopher turned ruler, also left a very deep mark on Plato. What is powerfully suggested by the *Laws* is that, as Plato abandoned the possibility of realization for his state by the philosopher-king, the "first and best way,"[32] as he says himself, he turned back to the mechanical-toy state of the *Republic* and with minor modifications tried to convert this into another and more "lifelike" model (though one still belonging strictly to the unrealized), by a system of unchangeable laws freezing the life of the state into immobility.

This impression is strengthened if we notice that in the *Laws* again, as in the *Republic*, the devisers of the political structure are outside the framework itself. In the *Republic* Socrates and his friends were the engineers of the toy model. They say, "Let *us* convince, first and best, the guardians," etc. In the *Laws* a Spartan, a Cretan, and an Athenian are confronted with the task of constructing a system of laws for a new state. Thus, in both cases, political questions are not being raised from the inside of the drama, as it were—as, for instance, is the case in the *Gorgias* or the *Protagoras*—but from the outside. The harmonic structure of the state, the rigidity of the class system, the immutability of the several parts, are essential, mechanically and otherwise, to the state which would bear resemblance to the eternal form. The infallibility of the builder of the state must be assumed, and this holds equally well for both the philosopher-king, who may bring the toy model to life, or Socrates and his friends who set up the model itself. When we come to the *Laws*, we find that here, too, the three interlocutors are themselves thought of as *knowing* the truth, and this is now being permanently legislated into existence in a code of laws with preambles explaining in each case the general principles involved.[33]

But in the imitation of the eternal model it is the structure of the state and its unchangeability which are essential; it is not essential that from moment to moment or generation to generation even the ruler, much less the bulk of the population, should understand the truth which underlies this organization. It will do very well if they follow a pattern which in the first place was well laid out. It is perhaps because of this that in the *Republic* the ultimate downfall even of the perfect state is envisaged. At the completion of the appropriate number a deterioration will take place in the governing class, and the progress downward to timocracy, oligarchy, democracy, and tyranny has begun. It is not necessary to take this part of the *Republic* as a completely worked-out cyclical theory of history. There is no reason to assume that Plato thought that it was certain that each change in the social organization inevitably followed. Obviously, in his own time, certain states like Sparta had partially accepted all the changes and remained with a mixed constitution. Others, such as Thessaly, had frozen in one of the earlier stages. But it is probably important to notice that the perfect state, or the state which approaches the greatest perfection on earth, will necessarily one day change and change as a result of the emergence of a different and hence wrong kind of man in the governing class. And this I suggest is because the crucial value of the state is not in the understanding of its governing class or of the rest of the population but in the virtually ritualistic organization and functioning of the state as a whole.[34]

4

There is no doubt that, if Plato means this—as I believe he does—in his treatment of the ideal state in the *Republic* and in the *Laws*, it is nakedly at variance with the emphasis on understanding in the sphere of ethics as it appears in such parts of his work as the *Protagoras* and *Gorgias*. Yet I think that there is no real contradiction. There is a continuous split in his beliefs between the course of action desirable in the existent social organization as he saw it and a different and reformed social organization which he would have dearly liked to bring about.

In the fifth- and fourth-century corrupt state, democratic, oligarchic, or monarchical—and in the *Seventh Letter* he goes on record as saying that they were all corrupt[35]—the essential thing for the individual man became the saving of his own soul, and this for Plato is pre-eminently a matter of understanding. Greatest among such men, "wisest, justest, and best,"[36] is Socrates, who endured social disapproval, persecution, and death to find out the truth of things and the validity of current knowledge. Seen against the background of Socrates, the citizen of Athens, who in an ordinary and conventional fashion lived his daily life "in accordance with what is popularly considered virtue," deserves a low place in the moral hierarchy and in his next transformation is fit for some "gentle and political society of animals such as the bees."[37] It is essential that the break with a corrupt present, in social and individual terms, be made by the understanding, by a vision of the eternal model either of man's soul or of the state's organization.

But once the new society has been formed—or, if it can be formed—the true pattern for the individual life or the life of the state has been made. Henceforth the repetition of actions, the acquisition of habit, and the inculcation of belief prove safeguards against the formlessness and chaos of the corrupt society. The ritual of a life properly organized becomes a thing as beautiful and true as anything in this world can be. A Socrates cannot come to pass in such a society as this, because the conditions which made Socrates what he was will not exist.

Thus there are for Plato always two standards of ethics and two theories of social justice, the one belonging to the life and the society of here and now, and the other to that reformed life and that reformed society which he strove to create. In the one the object of his love and admiration is Socrates, the rebel, the diffuser of paradox, the man whose beliefs followed only that "argument which on examination proved to him the best";[38] in the other it is the ruler who works wholeheartedly for the preservation of an existing good society, obedient to the laws which are his masters, accepting them as the vehicle of a wisdom which admits of neither refutation nor investigation, devoting all his life to the maintenance of what is by definition a "good" government.

It is quite true that Socrates, as a dramatic character in Plato's work, is made to champion both points of view: the one in the *Apology*, which is, at least highly probably, a fairly faithful account of the trial, and in dialogues such as the *Gorgias;* the other in the *Republic*. Whether the historical Socrates, as well as Plato, held the same difference of opinion as concerns the present and the future politically we cannot say. Nor is it, in a certain sense, very profitable to speculate about it, since all we really know about Socrates we know through Plato. It would be hardly convincing to seek a solution in chronology and to mark off stages in Plato's development. We would then ascribe the view of Socrates in the *Gorgias* that he would choose rather "to suffer than to do injustice"[39] and the various views therein expressed which can be described as individualistic and liberal to Plato in his early days when under the influence of Socrates. The statements of admiration for the rigid and stratified society, the coercion of the governed, the deceptive propaganda of the governors, and such like, would then belong to the later Plato, who has moved far from Socrates, as can be seen by the omission of the figure of Socrates from the dialogues.[40] But in the *Republic*, which is the greatest argument for the objectionable views which Plato later entertained, Socrates is still the central figure. And in the last years of his own life, when writing the *Seventh Letter*, Plato ascribes to himself, in the days of his early youth, exactly the enthusiasm for a root-and-branch reform of society and the establishment of a new "total" order which characterizes the sketches in the *Republic* and the *Laws*.[41] This latter point can, of course, be discounted by those who think that Plato is unconsciously attributing to himself a consistency which the facts will not bear out. But it is possible and preferable, I should say, to take Plato at his word and assume that in

his last years he retained at least enough sense of what his youth
was like to know that the same vision of perfection had haunted
him always.

5

To see in Plato this division of political opinions, between the
intense interest in and concern with the individual of the ordinary Socratic dialogues, and the admiration of the caste society
and the unchangeable laws which would reduce the individual,
as such, to nothing, is both to broaden our understanding of
Plato himself and perhaps to broaden also the significance of the
problem involved in a discussion of Plato's political theory. For
the political aspect is for Plato only one aspect of his philosophy,
and its importance is great mostly because it is the key to so
much else. He is not a state worshiper in the ordinary sense of
that word. His feeling that the state, when a true state, is a
greater and more beautiful thing than the individual man is due
to his passionate desire for the pattern imposed upon disorder;
and the imposition of that pattern, the "harmony" of which he
wrote so much, is clearer and more certain in a large social
organization than in the rule of the intellect over the passions in
the particular man. Furthermore, precisely because of his
knowledge of human nature, Plato had a true understanding of
the power of passion, the weakness of will, and the fallibility of
intellect of the individual. He wished not for the greatest possible exploitation of passion, will, or intellect in the individual
but the true harmony of all of them, and for this, he thought, the
pattern imposed from the outside was the necessary condition.
Since he believed that the individual who ultimately found his
proper place in the stratified society was fulfilling completely
the role for which the design of his body and mind fitted him,
there can be no question of "happiness" involved. Or rather
Plato was sure that, when the interlocutor in the *Republic* asks
Socrates "if the guardians will be happy,"[42] the word "happy"
was being invoked in the special meaning ascribed to it conven-
tionally, which implies the fallacy that happiness is absence of

restraint. This for Plato is the typical fallacy of those who consider human life in its individual or social aspects. For him happiness, if it means anything, is the awareness of being a part of an order, not an isolated fragment whirling aimlessly in a great sea: this, the true happiness, will be only half-consciously realized by most of the members of the population of the true Platonic state; by the rulers it will probably, though not necessarily, be realized at a deeper level of significance.[43]

Yet the complexity of the individual's life, when not part of any imposed symphonic order, is just what Plato understood as almost no political philosopher tortured by the yearning for order has ever done. He knew, as we have seen, how the uniqueness of a Socrates is built up of his physical appearance, his odd habits, his manner of talking, of his love for Athens and her freedom, of his love for his friends, of his peculiar inverted egotism. And every fiber of Plato responded to this uniqueness with the certainty that this, this uniquely existing historically occurring person, is what he wanted to describe and fuse by his creative gift with his own dreams. He knew, too, that this man who affected him as friend and artist so intensely is psychologically an impossibility in the state which the other half of him wished to create. In this dilemma the figure of Socrates plays an all-important part. It is not exactly a conflict of artist and philosopher with the first in love with life and the second with order. It is rather a conflict between two kinds of artistic pattern, the first of which is that which artists, particularly dramatists and painters, have always sought, the fusion of an individual and something more general than an individual, and the other a pattern, like an architect's, of design upon unordered matter. The second involves treating men and women as bricks and timber to build a structure which implicitly expresses their individual lives but which removes individuality from each one of them. When in his last years Plato had come to feel that only this last pattern suited him, the figure of Socrates was bound to disappear. For Socrates cannot become the bricks and timber of a house greater than himself.

CHAPTER XII

Experiment in Sicily

1

SICILY and the Greek cities of southern Italy have, politically and socially, a particular position in the minds of the mainland Greeks of the fifth and fourth centuries. This area is not like Macedonia, which was largely "barbarous" and governed by a hereditary monarchy—a stable, savage sort of country, unenlightened except when one of its kings brought writers like Euripides and Agathon from Greece in an effort to build a literary circle there. It is not like the cities of the Asia Minor seaboard, the populations of which migrated from Greece in the ninth century before the onset of the Dorians. These cities represent for the Greeks a sort of luxurious and slightly degenerate sophistication in things material and intellectual. And it is not like any of the main divisions of mainland states—not like Thessaly and Boeotia, with their feudal landowner rulers, or the cities of the Isthmus, with their merchant oligarchies, or like Sparta, with its unique archaic constitution, or like the more primitive agricultural states Arcadia, Elis, Achaea, and Aetolia.

Sicily was a rich country and together with the Greek cities in southern Italy was settled fairly late. From the beginning their political consciousness was mature. There were no feudal or patriarchal states there but a too rapid succession of oligarchies, democracies, and dictatorships. The latter was so common as to be the predominant political institution through the fifth and fourth centuries. It was under the tyrant Gelon that Sicily fought off the assault of the Carthaginians in the 480's, about the time of the Persian invasion of the Greek mainland, and it was the Sicilian tyrants and those of Magna Graecia who were

Pindar's patrons for poems in celebration of their racing teams which carried off prize after prize at Olympia. It is the land of wealth, restlessness, and opportunity. Perhaps we are not wrong in reading the popular fifth-century Greek opinion in the words of Herodotus about the musician Arion of Lesbos, who, sojourning and playing in Sicily and the parts of Magna Graecia, and "having accumulated a great store of money, decided to go back home."[1]

It was the country of political experiment. It is to Thurii in Magna Graecia that the Athenians proposed to send in 442 the first international Greek colony—that is, a colony founded not by one of the great Greek ethnic divisions—Ionic, Aeolic, or Dorian—but by volunteers from any of them, combining together. Moreover, the laying-out of the new colony was directed by Hippodamos, "the man who invented the systematic division of cities."[2] And it was in Sicily in the early fourth century that the greatest venture in synoecism or combination of populations was made. Dionysius I, father of the young prince whom Plato tried to educate, in order to create one large metropolis, emptied other cities and forced the inhabitants to move to the new center of his administration, Syracuse.[3]

Plato saw Sicily for the first time in 387 when he paid a short visit to the court of Dionysius I. What he saw on this occasion he describes as follows:

"On my coming, their so-called happy life there was not at all to my taste. It consisted of a vast amount of eating Italiote and Sicilian cooking, stuffing one's self twice a day and never sleeping a single night alone, together with all the usual practices which go with this sort of life. If one were bred from boyhood up in habits like these and so lived, no man under heaven could ever have any self-control, much less become an intelligent and reasonable (*phronimos*) being, for there could be no nature so marvelously compounded as that. It would be the same story, of course, in regard to other sorts of goodness, but it is especially clear that no city will live in a stable condition and according to any laws, no matter what they are, if its inhabitants think that they ought to spend everything on excesses and that they may be lazy in everything except for the diligence they show in eating and drinking and making love. Cities like these must incessantly keep changing dictatorships, oligarchies, and democracies, and the governments in them must necessarily refuse to hear even the name of a just constitution with equality before the law for all."[4]

What he goes on to say describes his personal relation to the set of circumstances which brought him to Sicily later: "This was in my mind when I came to Syracuse, brought there by chance perhaps, though it seemed then as if it were by the contrivance of some one mightier than ourselves, to lay the foundations of the troubles which have now befallen Dion and Syracuse. . . . What do I mean when I say that my coming to Sicily was the beginning of it all? I met Dion, who was a young man then, and it may have been true that, as I told him what I thought was best for mankind and urged him to practice it, I may unwittingly have been in a certain way contriving the downfall of the monarchy."[5]

We do not know precisely what happened during Plato's visit in 387, except that it was a short one. There is a report that he quarreled with Dionysius I and that the latter sold him as a slave and that eventually he escaped. This may be true, but, if so, it is curious that, in this extremely long and detailed account of all that concerned him and Sicily, Plato does not mention it. In any case, Plato is certainly right that the most important thing about his stay in Sicily was his meeting with Dion. Dion was, in Plato's own words, "the most receptive and enthusiastic pupil I have ever met,"[6] and he says in regard to Dion's later political venture to control Sicily on his own behalf that about him he was quite sure—as far as one can be sure of anything human—that, had he succeeded, he would have established the true rule of law instead of despotism in his native city Syracuse and then freed such of the Sicilians as lived under Carthaginian rule.

his hands full in dealing with it. Eventually—it is not clear in what length of time but apparently it involved some months—matters were patched up between himself and Plato, and he proved ready to send Plato home. Before he did so, he made some apologies and explanations and begged Plato to tell Dion that he should look upon his banishment not as a punishment but as a holiday abroad. He said that he would be glad to recall Dion within a very short time and asked Plato to promise that he and Dion both would resume their plans of training him and reforming Sicily when he sent for them both. After an interval of establishing his government following the war, Dionysius requested Plato to come back—but not Dion. In the bald narrative as Plato tells it in the *Seventh Letter* it seems fantastic that Plato should have been willing to try again.

What Plato has to say of his own attitude to this request is painful in its reflection of his indecision. "Dion urged me very instantly to go, and there were many reports out of Sicily that Dionysius had again fallen marvelously in love with philosophy. That was why Dion was so strong in begging me not to refuse his summons. I know that in the pursuit of philosophy such things *do* happen to young men, but on the whole it seemed to me safer to have done with both Dionysius and Dion. They were both aggrieved when I said that, after all, I was an old man and that nothing that I had been promised by them had as yet happened. It seems that at this time Archytas came to Dionysius—before I left I had made Dionysius friends with Archytas and some associates of his in Tarentum—and there were some other people in Syracuse who had listened to Dion and some others to them and so were crammed full of lectures about philosophy. I think these people tried to talk to Dionysius about such matters assuming that Dionysius had heard all I had to say on the subject. He was, in a general way, not ungifted in his capacity to learn and was exceedingly ambitious. So probably he rather liked what they told him and was ashamed that it should be discovered that he had never listened to a lecture from

me when I was at his court. . . . So when I had got home again
and Dionysius asked me to come back and I refused, as I have
said, I believe that Dionysius was very anxious that people
should not think that I, who had had experience of his natural
qualities, disposition, and daily life, held all these in contempt
and so refused to go again. You see it is only just that I should
tell the truth and put up with it if someone hears what happened and despises my philosophy and thinks the prince was
sensible. . . . Dionysius sent a warship for me, to make my journey easy . . . and a very long letter . . . saying 'If you come to
Sicily now at my request first of all this matter of Dion shall be
arranged however you please. . . . I know that you will be
reasonable on the subject and I shall be ready to oblige you; if
you do not, nothing that affects Dion's property or person will
come out as you wish it.' "[14]

There were letters from all his friends in Sicily and Italy
urging him to go and various people in Athens "almost forcing
him on board," and "always it was the same story: that I must
not prove false to Dion and my friends and associates in Tarentum. It came to me, too, personally, that it was not so surprising
that a young man who had heard some lectures on significant
subjects and who was gifted besides should come to desire the
best life. So I had to prove definitely which way this thing was
and so not be untrue to my profession and be the cause of such
justified reproach if any of these reports were true."[15]

Dionysius never became a student of philosophy in Plato's
sense of the word. He had only one conference with Plato on
the subject. After lingering in Syracuse nearly a year and incur-
ring great unpopularity at the court, Plato set out for home.
The feeling against him was so strong and those who would
have had Dionysius make away with him so influential that
Plato was always curiously grateful to Dionysius for letting
him go unharmed. Dion, of course, never received any of his
money, nor was he allowed to return from banishment.

After Plato's final return from Sicily he had a meeting with

Dion in which the latter declared that he now proposed to dis-
possess Dionysius by force of arms and bring the new state to
birth after the revolution. He urged Plato to assist him. But
Plato refused and refused decidedly. "I said to him that he
should call on other friends and see if they were willing. 'For
my part, you and others in effect against my will made me break
bread with Dionysius, sit at his hearth, and share his rites.
Perhaps he did believe the many who told him that you and I
had plotted the overthrow of himself and his monarchy. But he
did not kill me for his conscience's sake. I am no age to join in
wars against anyone at all. I am with all of you at such time as
you bind yourselves in friendship to do good. But when you are
bent on doing hurt you had better call on others than me.' This
I said out of my bitter loathing for all my travels in Sicily and
their ill success."[16]

2

This is the story of the events as Plato himself tells us them;
it is in fact the whole narrative of the failure humanly. As we
have seen, the ambiguity of the relation of Dion both to Dionysius and to Plato effectively insured that failure. But it is perhaps
permissible to speculate on the possibilities of success under
better conditions. Granted, in fact, the best that could have been
expected. Let us assume, for instance, that Dionysius had been
amenable to instruction instead of being, as he was, a clever, vain
young man who wanted a reputation as an intellectual. Let us
assume that there was no Dion calculated to rouse suspicion in
the prince's mind and to confuse Plato's plans. Let us look as objectively as we can at Plato's strongly expressed hope for the
realization of a good state and ask ourselves whether under any
circumstances it would be possible. This is more than an interesting hypothetical case, for it reveals something quite fundamental in Plato's capacity as a political thinker. Plato says in the
Republic and repeats in the *Laws* that the easiest change whereby an existing bad state can be transformed into the good one is

by the convincing of "one of those who are now called kings or dynasts" of the value of philosophy or by the elevation of a philosopher to supreme rule or kingship.[17] The reason for this choice, according to the *Laws*, is that thus one needs only to convince one man or at most a very few, and, since philosophy cannot ever be taught to many, the practical advantage is clearly on the side of beginning in a state where there is one ruler who is actually the single source of governing authority in his state.[18] And therein lies the difficulty which Plato never overcame.

What he wanted, as he himself says in the *Seventh Letter*, was a state free and living according to the laws, these laws being as binding on the sovereign himself as on the people whom he ruled. And he wanted this sovereign to be a philosopher so that sovereign, laws, and people would form a harmonic whole which in a larger magnitude would parallel his philosophically conceived image of the soul and body of man in harmony. But there is an inevitable antithesis between a sovereign who is really a king in the historical sense of that word and a philosopher as Plato knew him. For the one lives in the atmosphere where his position must of necessity be unquestioned, where there is no alternative to having a king, since the king's relation to his people and its traditions is as objectively so, as incapable of being otherwise, as the people's individual possession of arms and legs and need of food and drink. The other, Plato's philosopher, is a creature whose whole existence is bound up with the search for an unfound truth, the continuous realization of partial failure, and the magnetic fact of persuasion.

These two political figures belong in different areas of history, and Plato's effort to combine them does not conceal how much he is a child of an exceedingly mature democracy and how far removed from the other conception of sovereignty as we have seen it historically represented in Egypt earlier or in the Byzantine empire later and certain of the monarchies which grew from it. Plato is in politics a sophisticated rationalist earnestly looking for a nonrational symbol in government, round which the whole community can gather itself. And this is not nearly all. He wants the king, who is the nonrational symbol, to do the things kings do and be the person kings are, not out of an inner unquestioned certainty but out of the mature result of reasoned speculation and training.

In such a psychological combination Plato is entirely at a loss in the face of the question of power, which was for him, as for any Athenian of his day, basic, politically—as it never would be for the Egyptian or the citizen of Byzantium. How to make the people obey your monarch, philosophic or otherwise, how to get them to continue to obey him, and how to prevent the king from becoming a tyrant are the life-and-death questions of fifth- and fourth-century Greek politics. For years Plato decided to sidestep this issue; in the *Republic* he created an entire state the other side of the gulf which separated him from reality. But for Plato the region which could not come to political life was still-born and ultimately negligible, and no amount of later disclaimers on his part can conceal his sense of that. The impotence of the philosopher politically is for him a desperate calamity—so desperate that he will try almost any means to bring his political plans to consummation. And hence the Sicilian experiment.

The best that could have come of it would have been an enlightened despotism: that is, Dionysius, had he been a philosopher in Plato's sense, might have singly and for his lifetime made Sicily look more like the model state of the early books of the *Republic*. But it would not have been a Sicily living free and according to the laws,[19] for that would have meant a traditional acceptance of Dionysius by his people, a kind of unself-consciousness in the prince himself, and a code of laws enforced by age and reverence, all of which are totally wanting. Instead we have a young uneasy dictator inheriting the hatreds incurred by his father, who had built the dictatorship out of violence and blood; he had an interest in and craving for an intellectual framework for his life and his work but was ultimately engrossed in the most difficult of positions—keeping himself in power—and saw everyone and everything that concerned him from this point of view.

The way of philosophy was, for Plato, necessarily the way of persuasion, for it was founded on love. The touch of violence is a deadly infection, and Plato recognized it as such. Yet the political situation in which Plato wanted philosophy and the philosopher to function was one made by violence and continued by violence and fear. There could be no true meeting of these two. The other solution, the true kingship, in which there is no philosophy but no violence either, was all but outside Plato's grasp intellectually and was in Sicily outside the range of historical possibility. But very strikingly in his last work, the *Laws*, when all hope of realization for his state had vanished and consequently he was able more completely to sketch it for us, he outlines, as far as he can in intellectual terms, the kind of monarchy and the kind of monarch that have nothing to do with intellectual analysis.

CHAPTER XIII

The Road to Dicte

1

WE HAVE a large block of dialogues from the last fifteen years of Plato's life, from 362, when he returned from Sicily for the last time, until his death in 347. The list covers the *Theaetetus, Parmenides, Philebus;* the *Sophist* and *Politicus;* the *Timaeus, Critias* (fragmentary), and the *Laws.* Of these, if we restrict our interest to the development of Plato's views on politics, the *Theaetetus* and *Philebus* concern us little. Neither, strictly speaking, does the *Parmenides.* But at two points it must be reckoned with even within our restricted subject. It is important in its indication of how in his later years Plato was disposed to think about the forms, and it is important in its handling of Socrates. In the *Parmenides* he is uniquely presented, for here he is shown when quite young. The dialogue, a conversation between the young Socrates and the old Parmenides, is given over to a criticism of the forms, at least in the fashion in which they were explained by Plato (or Socrates) in the earlier and middle Socratic dialogues. The questions are very searching and destructive. Whereas in the earlier and middle dialogues it is Socrates as the proponent of the theory of forms who is the object of dramatic sympathy and the winner in the argument, here he comes very close to losing it.[1] The chief objection of the old Parmenides is that Socrates has really not grasped all the intricacies and difficulties of asserting that there are abstract forms, totally separate from the world of becoming, in which objects "participate."[2]

It has sometimes been maintained that this dialogue constitutes Plato's explicit renunciation of the forms.[3] This can hardly be substantiated from the argument. It is to ignore the dramatic importance of the earlier part and also of certain key remarks of Parmenides, both of which, taken together, indicate no renunciation but a new attitude toward the theory. What Parmenides says in the dialogues is plainly to be taken very seriously; Plato, in other parts of his later works where the dramatic coloring is too slight to cause any ambiguity of interpretation, shows his admiration of him.[4] And Parmenides here is very old, and it is noteworthy that in the last dialogues Plato continually is emphasizing the wisdom of the old. The source of Critias' story, told to Timaeus, is a series of old men going back to Solon.[5] And it is the age of the old men that are the commentators in the *Laws* which makes them peculiarly suitable to plan the state and its laws.[6] In the *Seventh Letter* it is the old men that the Syracusans are advised to invite to frame their constitution.[7] The reverence for age is not restricted to persons. In the age of a tradition, as it divorces itself from the original historical stimulus which created it, is its wisdom. The Greeks, says the Egyptian priest in the *Timaeus*, are mere children; they know nothing of antiquity and of the accumulated wisdom of the past.[8] In the face of all these small bits of evidence, it is reasonable to assume that Parmenides, who is old, is supposed to exceed the youthful Socrates in wisdom.

Now Parmenides does not refute the theory of forms. It is not necessary to go into the entire argument, itself difficult and perplexed, but the summary remarks made by Parmenides at the beginning are clear indications of his position. "These difficulties, Socrates," said Parmenides, "and many others besides them are connected with the forms if there actually are forms of things that exist and if each form is defined as something separate; so that anyone who hears you say so must needs be perplexed and inclined to maintain that the forms do not exist and, even if they do, that they must be entirely incomprehensible to man's capacity. One who argues thus *must* seem rather sensible and, as I said before, is very hard to convince. It needs *a man of great natural talent* to be able to understand that there is a class of each thing and an absolute essence, and it needs a still more extraordinary person to find these things out for himself and to be able to teach another who can analyze them properly."[9] This is certainly not a denial of the forms. It is the judgment of an old man who, to Plato's mind, had come to a place on the road where he had himself arrived and had seen the difficulties of which he had not been fully aware earlier. This is clearest a little earlier in the dialogue:

" 'How is it, Socrates,' said Parmenides, 'about things which it might seem rather absurd to discuss—hair and mud and dirt or any other insignificant and trivial thing? Are you at a loss here or are we to assert that there is a separate form of each of these, distinct and different from the things we handle?' 'No,' said Socrates, 'I think that in this case these things we see are all there are. It would be too absurd to imagine that there is a separate form of *them*. Yet sometimes I am troubled and think that perhaps it *is* the same in all these cases: and then when I reach this point I turn away in haste in fear that I have fallen into an abyss of nonsense and am perishing there. So when I come to those things which we just now agreed *actually have* forms I stay and busy myself with them.' 'Ah, yes,' said Parmenides, 'but then you are very young still, and philosophy has not taken hold of you as she will yet, in my opinion. When that day comes you will not despise these things. Now you are young and pay more attention to men's opinions.' "[10]

This last picture of Socrates that Plato has given us is not only different by reason of his youth and his secondary position to Parmenides in wisdom. Plato has here tried to emancipate himself from the spell of the unique Socrates, the Socrates who was a kind of portent. Instead, he, the archetype of philosophic inquiry, is thought of as going through a stage which Parmenides characterizes as the general way of youth, and which Plato looking back thinks of as his own way from youth to old age. Nowhere else in all the dialogues is there this hint of development in Socrates. Only here as Plato looks back in his own old age does he try to bring Socrates into the concept of life as it changes and develops. And he tries to think of him changing and developing as he, Plato, changed and developed. It is, for Plato, the ultimate sacrifice of the historical element in his artistic work. As late as the *Symposium*, which probably did not precede the *Parmenides* by many years, the mystery and uniqueness of Socrates is still so close to the central life of his written work that he could build a dialogue round it. In the *Theaetetus*, which is probably even closer in time to the *Parmenides*,[11] Socrates is still something of his historical self, the intellectual midwife, with no growth of knowledge in himself, but the cause of knowledge in other men. Only in the *Parmenides* has Socrates been surrendered to the full tide which is sweeping from Plato everything and everybody singular into the world of quality, not action; rhythm, not fact; unending pattern rather than single beauty.

Moreover, although it is only in the *Parmenides* that Socrates himself has been brought into the process of change, it does look as though Plato in certain of the other of these later dialogues was anxious to tamper with his own earlier conception of the immutability of the figure. There is an elaborate comparison between the young Theaetetus and Socrates in the *Theaetetus*,[12] and there is the introduction of the colorless character known as the Younger Socrates in the *Statesman*. Though at first sight it would seem dangerous to build anything on such slight inferences as these, the more one reflects on these two phenomena, the more odd they appear. There is no discernible reason in the *Theaetetus* why there should be this comparison between the two men with such emphasis on their similarity; nor why in the *Statesman* another figure bearing the name which had become almost synonymous with the dialogues themselves should be introduced, while we are coolly informed that it is not the original Socrates.[13] Both of these cases need some serious explanation. My own belief—and there is of course no way of substantiating it—is that Plato was almost perversely bent on disclaiming his own artistic past. That is to say, he wished to obliterate traces of his early work and, in a spirit almost of bravado, to make clear the break between that and these later dialogues. These are only straws in the wind. They do seem, however, to have some bearing on the philosophical positions of certain of the later dialogues, notably the *Sophist* and the *Politicus* and perhaps the *Philebus*.

For in these dialogues—I do not seek and am not qualified to make a true philosophic appraisal of them—there is no doubt that Plato with a kind of desperate courage is seeking to give expression to his belief about the forms in a new way which will be free of what he now felt to be the inadequacies of his earlier work. This movement begins with the *Parmenides* in the direction that I have indicated. In a sense, that dialogue is more successful than the *Sophist* and the *Statesman*. For he has there managed to convey a possible truth for the theory of forms backed by the approbation of Parmenides in spite of the latter's objections to much of the earlier Platonic statement, if it is a Platonic statement, in the Socratic dialogues. In the *Sophist* and the *Statesman* we have, I think, a last effort to express the forms in a manner which will satisfy Plato's passionate belief in reason and in logic. They are among Plato's work unique in that they are dull. They are also uneven in texture and style, which in the case of an artist of such very sure touch is a clear sign that something is wrong. In the *Statesman* he combines a vivid and beautiful myth with pages of pedantic hair-splitting. That Plato himself realizes what he is doing and its probable failure is perhaps shown by a chance remark in the *Philebus*. There, in dividing knowledge into kinds, he makes Socrates say that, if he does not make the classification fearlessly, "our argument will be gone from us and lost, like a tale that is told, and we ourselves be saved on the raft of some irrational notion."[14] The "irrational notion" was to take shape and form later in the *Timaeus*. What we are looking at in these dialogues of the middle 350's are the last attempts to save the theory of forms by logic.

Perhaps it is also not too extravagant to see the same kind of emphasis in Plato's predominant logical fancy of the last years—the process of division. In the *Statesman* and *Sophist*, two dialogues are given over to the discovery of the true nature of the subjects explored by a continuous separation off of what appears to be essential from inessential elements. Thus the king emerges as the shepherd of hornless bipeds which do not cross-breed.[15] This method looks to us ridiculous. It might be said that this is only so because it is hard for us to think ourselves back into the infancy of logical method, and there is something to the contention. It is admittedly an easy matter to be misled about the caliber of speculation divided from us by a whole world of scientific discovery and so-called "scientific method." But the balance is still very heavily in favor of our initial impression, that division, considered as a serious logical or scientific procedure in Plato and taken at its face value, is absurd. But in the *Timaeus* he tells us that the true processes of division, in virtue of sameness and difference, are in accord with the motions of the world soul, as the Maker has formed it.[16] And in the passage from the *Parmenides* quoted above, Parmenides says that it needs an especially gifted man to understand that there are different classes among the ideas and that there is a relation between them and the classes of objects we can visually and sensibly distinguish. The most probable inference would seem to be that Plato is trying to make of logic a suggestive ritual in which the *process* of division as applied to subject matter became an imitation which awakened the liveliness of understanding of those other divisions in the invisible world. It is probably not the actual divisions of subject matter themselves that are so important—for indeed the participants in these dialogues handle them rather lightly—but the process itself. It is the preoccupation with quality, not individuality, rhythm not fact, that is all-important.

2

Nowhere is the disregard of the singular, the emphasis on quality and rhythm, in the later dialogues as marked as in Plato's expressed views on man's past life in the world and his political community. It cannot be maintained, of course, that this is really something new in Plato. He had never in his written work shown many signs of an interest in the actual events of political history. But the early and middle dialogues are saturated with a color and life of a single period—the last quarter of the fifth century—and the personality of a single man—Socrates. This does, in fact, tie them down to the atmosphere and intellectual climate of one time. With the abandonment of Socrates and the Socratic circle as the unit of discussion, Plato moves into an area where it is much more apparent that his concern is solely with what might be called the rhythmic sweep of civilization rather than with history or political life as such. It is only with political life in its broadest possible sense that he now deals. Except for the *Laws,* and this in a curiously modified way, too, there are no more discussions of rhetoric as a political force, of power as the object of political ambition, or the meaning of justice in political terms. Instead there is an attempt to consider in cosmic terms the meaning of political community and to render an account, in a kind of philosophic fantasy, of what the "ideal" history of such a political community could have been. Three passages in the later dialogues illustrate this tendency.

a) The first is the myth of the *Statesman.* While the most of the dialogue is concerned with the exact definition of the king or statesman through the continual application of the principle of division—so that the king is marked off finally as the caretaker of the hornless biped and so is schematically distinguished from shepherds of other varieties of animal—there is an interlude in which Plato explains the grounds of an error in the argument. We have not adequately grasped the meaning of "king," he says, because we are unaware of the changes that have befallen mankind and the world.[17] And this is the story he tells. All the older tales of the earth-born men, of the peace and automatic fertility of the earth in the time of Cronos, of the path of the sun and stars turned back by the gods to favor Atreus, have their roots in a great and shattering physical phenomenon. The world is being continuously turned in one direction, and at first it was so turned by "the Greatest Spirit," who is also called Demiurge or Father (as he is later in the *Timaeus*) and who is to be sharply distinguished from the Olympian gods. During this time generation was from the earth, since under the guidance of the God himself, who acted as a Divine Shepherd, creatures could come into being from different elements than themselves. And according to the myth there were no states and no possession of women and children. The processes of generation were also the exact opposite of those of our time, since, as we shall see in a moment, the circular movement of the world was opposite to that which now possesses it. These people were born old and large and grew younger and smaller until at last they disappeared. When they were born again from the earth, they had no recollection of their former existence.

But when "in the fulness of time there must needs be a change as each soul had fulfilled all its generations as it had fallen into the earth as seed the prescribed number of times, then the Pilot of All, abandoning as it were the rudder, retired to his lookout post, and its destined and native desire turned the universe backward."[18] At the same time the other gods, who under direction of the Greatest Spirit shared in his rule, let go their parts of the world.[19]

The result of the reverse swing of the world is a vast destruction of men and all living things in the form of a kind of earthquake. When conditions permitting life again are revived, the world pursues its reverse course entirely under its own guidance. It has "power and care over all that is in it and of itself."[20] But the only momentum it possesses is that generated by the reversal of the circular motion originally initiated by the Greatest Spirit. It must therefore inevitably at last run down. At the first, when the Greatest Spirit created it, he did so out of great disorder, and this disorder is a permanent ingredient in its material composition. Therefore, when the reverse movement has lasted a long time, the order and rhythm of the original designer grow fainter and fainter, and the material element in the world, without control, becomes predominant. In the time of the reverse swing of the world, generation, as we know it, of human beings in their own kind and of other animals according to their kind originates. For "it was not possible any more for any living thing to be born in earth of the union of other elements; but as the universe was commanded to be master of its own course, so in the same way and according to the same principles the parts too were instructed, as far as they could, to grow and beget and nourish themselves under the same guidance."[21]

The myth goes on to say that, in the end of this stage, the Greatest Spirit, perceiving that the world was growing weaker and weaker and fearful lest it should entirely perish, once again took the tiller, and all became as it had been before.[22]

b) The second passage is the Preface to the *Timaeus*. The dialogue opens with a brief recapitulation of a few points in the early books of the *Republic*, notably those dealing with the separation of function in the inhabitants of the model state and the community of women and children.[23] These are only cited, apparently, to call before our minds briefly the outline of the model state. Socrates would now like to see his model state in action but professes himself unable, from inexperience, to imagine it in a supreme crisis of action—a war or something of this sort.[24]

Critias answers that history has actually provided an example that is particularly suitable. He had heard of this state, now long forgotten, from his grandfather, who as a boy had heard of it from Solon, who in turn had heard of it from an Egyptian priest. This state, which existed on the site of the fifth-century Athens, paralleled Socrates' sketch of the model state in all particulars, according to the Egyptian, and it saved the European continent from an invasion of the inhabitants of the island empire of Atlantis. The fuller account of this exploit is to be reserved for Critias' narration in the second dialogue of the projected trilogy (*Timaeus, Critias, Hermocrates*).[25] The *Critias* was only partly finished and the *Hermocrates* never undertaken.

But the most interesting thing is the renewal of the reference to the historical cycles separated by cataclysms, this time, however, without the metaphysical explanation of the change which is given in the *Statesman:*

" 'Solon,' said the Egyptian priest, 'you Greeks are all children and, as to an old Greek, there is no such man.' 'What do you mean?' said Solon. 'You are all young in soul,' said the priest, 'for you have in your souls no ancient opinion rooted there by old tradition or any learning gray with time. The reason is this. Many are the times of destruction that have befallen man and many the ways it has destroyed him and shall be so again. The greatest of them came with fire and water, but there are other lesser forms of devastation by thousands of other means. So the story that is told among you that Phaëthon was the child of the Sun and harnessed his father's team and, being unable to drive his father's road, crashed and was burned up himself and scorched a part of earth as well, this is said among you to have the appearance of a fable, but the truth is that it refers to the deviation of the bodies that revolve around the earth and the destruction wrought by the enormous fire which thus at long intervals overtakes all that is on earth. At this time those that dwell in the mountains and high places and deserts are more completely destroyed than those that are neighbors of rivers and sea; for us Egyptians the Nile in this as in all else proves our savior and delivers us from trouble. But when the gods purify the earth with water and flood it, it is those in the hills that are saved, the shepherds and tenders of cattle, and it is those of you who live in cities that are swept down to the sea by the rivers; but in our country neither at this nor any other time does the water fall from above on the fields: on the contrary it is its nature to rise always from below. That is the reason why what is preserved here is the oldest that is on record. The truth is that where inordinate heat or cold does not prevent it, the race of man always survives in more or less numbers. So anything that happened among you or here in Egypt or in any other place of which we have hearsay knowledge, any deed of greatness beauty or pre-eminence, are all written from of old time and preserved here in the temples. But among you and other people letters and all the other necessaries of civilized life are always just new, and again and again after the wonted cycle of years the stream from Heaven descends like a plague among you and carries you off leaving only the unlettered and uncultivated among you, so that again and again you become as it were children from the beginning, knowing nothing of what has happened in your own land or in ours in the old time. At least, Solon, the genealogies you Greeks have of what happened among you are little better than children's stories, seeing that first of all you tell of one flood upon the face of the earth, though there were many earlier, and secondly, the fairest and best race of men that were ever among you, you do not even know existed. . . .' "

This is followed by the account of the primitive Athenians' defeat of the invaders from Atlantis.[26]

c) The last passage, from the *Laws*, starts by referring again to the cycle of destruction and the kinds of remnants of civilization that survive there.

ATH.: Shall we then say that at the time when the destruction happened human affairs were something like this: there was a vast and fearful wilderness and a great mass of empty country and when the other animals had perished there were left only a few herds of cattle and some remnants of flocks of goats and these gave a scanty living to the herdsmen at the first.
CL.: Yes.
ATH.: And of cities, constitutions, and law enactment with which our discussion is now concerned are we to think that these people retained any knowledge of these things at all, so to speak?
CL.: No.

ATH.: And so from these men, in this position, have sprung all that we have now, cities and constitutions, and skills and laws, and a great deal of both vice and virtue?

CL.: What do you mean?

ATH.: Well, are we to think, my friend, that those who in those days knew nothing of the many fine things that go with cities—and of the many other than fine things—were perfect either in vice or virtue?

He then goes on to describe how among such men there was no strife, civil disputes or war, etc., and their want of economic distress. He concludes:

Now whatever community has neither wealth nor poverty it is in it that the noblest characters are apt to grow; for there is engendered no violence nor injustice nor envy and grudges. So these people were good for these reasons and because of what is called simplicity; that is, what they heard spoken of as fair and foul they believed most truly to be so and were convinced—because they were simple-minded. For no one had wisdom to make him suspect a lie as now, but believing the traditions about gods and men to be true they lived by them. And that is why they were entirely of the character we have described.[27]

It does not matter much whether we are to assume that Plato believed literally in the recurrence of natural catastrophes which destroyed some civilizations and set the stage for the birth of others. Indeed, the first passage in the *Statesman* and the second in the *Timaeus* are not easily harmonized in this respect, for the *Statesman* implies that the reverse swing of the world affects the entire world and so would involve catastrophes which would destroy virtually all parts of the world at once, while the *Timaeus* directly asserts that there are large areas, such as Egypt, which survive undamaged. The important aspect of both these passages is not their assurance that Plato believed in the occurrence of such destruction of man and civilization. He may have or he may not, in the literal sense of a historical phenomenon.

What is important is the manner in which in both the *Statesman* and the *Timaeus* and the *Laws*, too, he feels it necessary to tell the story. There was a world of order and design which, since it was a created thing and therefore not immortal, had an admixture of disorder in it. It was once as near perfection as its nature permitted when the design controlled its material composition. That stage, whether conceived of temporally or otherwise, is no more. It ceased to exist through a combination of inner necessity—the fulfilment of the allotted number of births—and outer mechanical violence—the destruction by natural forces which followed on the change in direction of motion. It is the fact of separateness, of the ultimate loss of design and order, which is of passionate significance for the later Plato. It does not matter whether he tells the story on the grandiose scale of ten, twenty, or thirty thousand years and involves all mankind, or dwarfs it relatively to the destruction of a great pre-Greek civilization. What is essential in both pictures is the loss of a former or other world of design and order. It is absolutely irretrievably lost. What remains of it are the echoes which haunt the minds of the men who came after the catastrophe, and the echoes are listened to in the half-obliterated evidence of design in the world of natural phenomena. Recurrence and uniformity become the simplest tokens of design, and in the singleness of man, animal, or event there is only negation until this microcosm can itself yield signs of the order that is inherent in the greater unit. Thus not only the individual but the span of human life, and perhaps one should add the significance of human life, became for Plato of less and less interest.

At the same time the physical world and the intellectual processes of man, interacting, are all he has to look at. Of that he is now quite certain. In the days of the *Republic* and the *Symposium* an ascent was possible; the process of dialectical thought, however necessarily crude, still, involving as it did a turning-away from the sensible to the intelligible, led to an understanding akin to the understanding which mathematics afforded at a lower level. Now, however, the material object must itself furnish all the evidence; the trace of design and the brute vitality must simultaneously be always remembered. And so there comes to be in Plato the frame of mind expressed in the words of the *Seventh Letter* in the very last years: "In one word, the student who is not akin to the subject cannot be made so by any readiness to learn nor yet by memory; for this kind of knowledge does not grow at all in tempers alien to it. . . ."[28] For it is not expressible as other kinds of knowledge are, but from constant association with the subject itself and living with it, suddenly like the light that is kindled like a leaping flame it is born in the soul and nourishes itself."[29] The true world of design is lost; the finding of it again, even fragmentarily, is the product of chance, or God's guidance, of anything except regularized instruction in the nature of reality.

Let us turn, for the time being, from the more general aspects of these passages to their particular meaning in Plato's political speculation. When these passages are put side by side with the *Laws* as a whole, it is clear that there is in all these later dialogues no longer the break that earlier existed between arguments and themes appropriate to the world of Greek political life and those belonging to the possible approximation, in action, of the ethical and political forms.[30] Instead there is a single kind of study of political life, and it runs all the way from the metaphysical explanation of the reverse swing of the world in the *Statesman* to the projected future state in the *Laws*. This is clearly marked in the plan for the uncompleted trilogy and the written introduction to the *Laws* itself. The project in the *Timaeus* is that Timaeus shall cover the origins of the world to the birth of man; Critias is then to tell the story, in detail, of the Athens of ten thousand years ago which is to represent Socrates' ideal state in action; Hermocrates probably was to cover the age of cataclysms and the ensuing slow development through nomadic peoples to the foundation of cities in approximately their fifth-century form. The *Hermocrates* was not written, but this is exactly what is done in the introduction to the *Laws*, that is, in Books ii and iii. The *Laws* is to go on from there, with the old men who participate in the argument setting up the best institutions for the future on the basis of the whole study of the past, as these three written dialogues have outlined it. There can be very little doubt indeed that we are correct in thus seeing the *Laws* as the completion of the scheme begun in the *Timaeus*.[31]

With this to guide us, let us look at the *Republic* beside the *Timaeus* and *Laws*, viewing the latter as the completion of the trilogy. The comparison reveals so much that is common that the difference in tone and emphasis stands out strongly. The "ideal" state of the first books of the *Republic*, which we have elsewhere called the model, has an "ideal" origin in the simple economic needs of man at the most primitive level. The interlocutor says that this is a "city of pigs,"[32] but Socrates insists that this is the sound and healthy city and that justice can as truly be found there as anywhere. He agrees to complicate the picture and take up the fevered state only because, as the political conditions described are closer to contemporary Greece, the discussion of justice becomes more valuable.[33] This is exactly what is said in the *Laws:* the simple nomads who survive the cataclysm have virtue in the highest degree. They achieve this largely because, since neither their training nor their environment make them suspect a lie, they entirely believe what is told them about gods and men and so live virtuous lives.[34] We are reminded of the "ideal" state in the *Republic* where we would convince first and best the rulers, but, failing that, the rest of the people, of a kind of noble falsehood which when accepted would maintain the pattern of society as a thing to be revered and lived by for every member of the society.

But in the *Republic* there is a cleavage in Book v.[35] In that book Socrates tries to answer his friend's question on the possibility of achievement for the ideal state. It is understood that the ideal state already sketched is an engineers' model; that the philosopher who becomes a ruler will adapt and adjust an existing state in the light of it; and that the model itself must, of course, be adjusted to meet the needs of an actual emergence into life. In the *Timaeus* and *Laws* trilogy the ideal state has become historical; somewhere in the past it can be thought of as having been, and its past actions can be imagined and fitted into a scheme which will lead all the way to the "best" state of the future. But for the earlier Plato, the Plato of the *Republic*, there could be no assertion, lightly made, that his model city had been achieved, or even that it would be, exactly as outlined, the "best" state for the future. The possibility of its actual existence meant far too much to him. He was at this time genuinely haunted by the impotence of the philosopher in action, "being ashamed lest I should seem always only a kind of argument, never venturing to put my hand to any action."[36] Once only in the *Republic* one can catch a hint of what is to come and see the shadow of the comfort he was building for himself against the assaults of reality: no one can say our state is an impossibility, he declares, "if in the infinite reaches of time past or today in some barbaric region beyond our knowledge" it has ever come to pass.[37] In the *Laws* the importance of the actual historical past is gone; history can become myth rich in meaning, and myth, history; and both can point to the future, which has no hopes of fulfilment and no agonies of frustration.

3

It is at the junction of the human and divine that Plato's genius expresses itself most clearly at this time, for it is on this level and this level only that he still contrived to maintain the balance between the unordered and the design. This is no subject on which even the greatest writer can be wholly intelligible, but here Plato at least conveys the old sense of profundity and his old power to render it in artistic form, parable, allegory, and naked fact combined. In speaking of the universe, he says:

"To turn itself forever is scarcely possible for anything except that which guides all moving things; and that the universe should move now in this way and now in that is impious to believe. So from all of this we must assert that the universe does not move itself nor yet that in its entirety it is being continuously turned by God in two opposite and contrary circular courses nor again that there are any two gods with opposite views one to another turning it. What is left as the only alternative is what I said just now: that there is a time when the universe is guided and accompanied by some Divine Cause which is not its own and that it thereby gains the power of living again and attains a recovered immortality from its Fashioner. But there is also a time when it is let go by him and proceeds on its own course, being released at such a moment that it travels backward many cycles of ten thousand years, because it is immensely large and most evenly balanced upon the smallest pivot."[38]

To deny the unity of design in the world was always, for Plato, impious. And so at this moment when he is speaking theologically, if this strange parable can be called theology, there may not be two different gods, and there may not be two different directions in the universe, to account for his undying sense of the difference between brute vitality and that which has form. The way he seeks is life which is in between the two —vitality with the echo of something other than itself which gives it precision, beauty, and meaning.

He had never written much in the dialogues which bore on the conventional religion of fifth- and fourth-century Greece, but in what we have there are hints of this, the explicit statement of the latest phase. It is the impression of discordance in divine government that he rejects as a feature of education in the *Republic*[39] when Socrates expresses himself in favor of censoring the myths, and it is the humanization, the excision of the other and incomprehensible cause, that Socrates dismisses in the passage in the *Phaedrus*[40] when he discusses the rape of Oreithyia.

In his last years the Olympian gods and the tales about them have receded from any share in his interest. Though the sacred stories have in them what he would probably regard as germs of truth, these are few and heavily overlaid with almost political colors, of factions and disputes, hates, friendships, and separations. Immortality and consistency sit strangely on the Olympian gods. We can never quite believe in the *Iliad* that Ares cannot ultimately be killed, and indeed the poet plainly wants to lead us as far in the other direction as possible with his story of the war-god's wounds. Consistency is not even to be thought of in this medley of dissonant personalities. In his last years Plato, perhaps, felt about the Homeric stories and the myths much as he did about current political life. There was a truth to be found there amid so much that was superficial, but it was exceedingly obscured and was no longer the kind of story or the kind of situation which stimulated the imaginative response by which he lived. In the *Timaeus* the Olympian gods are quite removed from the Demiurge;[41] in the *Statesman* the other gods, coregents with the Fashioner, who, under him, created various parts of the universe, are also probably not the Olympian gods.[42] The Olympian gods are thought of, I believe, as a markedly imperfect image formed by man of a God. They are more powerful than man but otherwise no different. Their immortality is no true immortality but an inability to succumb to death which defeats their pygmy brother, man. They are no wiser, no happier, and no more complete than those whose minds have contained their picture.

In the *Laws* Plato stresses repeatedly the significance for human worship of the heavenly stars in their courses.[43] Here he finds the symbol he wants: motion, consistent and changeless, and an object immortal with no human attributes to blur the sense of otherness. The stars themselves are, of course, only provocations of the religious imagination. They are not the inner mystery; they are not the true objects of reverence. But they recall him.

The *Timaeus* is often spoken of as a myth in Platonic terms, and this is to some extent justified by Plato's own words. The account of the universe, he tells us, can only be a likely story, a "mythos."[44] But that it is a myth different from the other myths is proved by the very next words after those just quoted.

Since the physical universe is of the nature of the perishable and changing, says Timaeus, no account of it can be more than a likely story. Professor Cornford in his famous edition of the *Timaeus* comments that this is, as far as we know, a purely Platonic notion. The Pythagoreans had no theory that it was impossible to describe the physical world exactly.[45] And it is plainly a misconstruction to imagine that what Plato is saying is that his is a provisional account of the universe, an account which will be made more exact and rigorous by later investigators.[46] At first sight there seem to be parallel disclaimers in certain of the earlier dialogues. In the *Phaedo* we are given some account of the afterworld, and Socrates says first that no man of sense would pretend to speak exactly on such a topic.[47] In the conclusion of the *Republic* the story of Er, which is concerned with the voyage of the soul in the afterlife, is told as the dream dreamed by this man as he lay on the funeral pyre.[48] In these two earlier examples, however, the apology for inexactitude is almost conventional. The subject is one where human reasoning and experience are completely at fault. But the Preface of the *Timaeus* describing his account of the universe as a likely story is of a more complicated significance. It is precisely the elements in the physical universe which make it physical, which for Plato means that the story must be only likely and necessarily inexact. We cannot overestimate the importance of this. It is the things we can touch and see, and the organs with which we apprehend them, which make for the confusion.

Yet the most startling feature of the likely story is the relative roles of reason and the instruments other than reason in the attainment of what man can call "truth." There is in the *Timaeus* a tremendous sense of the direct revelation to man from the outside; and in one of the most extraordinary parts of his extraordinary account of the human body he speaks of it like this:

"Now that part of the soul that has desire of food and drink and has need of it because of the nature of the body they [the gods] established within the boundaries of the midriff and the navel, contriving in all this region what we could call a manger for the nourishment of the body. And they tethered this there, like a wild beast, untamed but necessary to be maintained with the rest, if the race of man was to continue to exist. . . . They knew it, that it would not understand reasonable discourses and even if it should attain to some perception of such it would not be in its nature to take heed of them but that it would chiefly be under the spell of shapes and phantoms by day and night. And so the God taking thought against this very thing formed the shape of the liver and placed its dwelling there."[49]

Then follow some sentences the exact purport of which is difficult to determine. Apparently the liver receives impressions cast upon it by the mind, which it then gives back, like a mirror, as visible images. But the following passage leaves no doubt of the position of reason and inspiration:

"This is sufficient testimony that divination is a gift given by God to human witlessness; for no one in his senses lays hold of the true inspiration of divination save either when in sleep the potency of his intelligence has been fettered or he has been rendered distraught by sickness or by some immediate possession by God. It is for the man in his ordinary senses to reflect upon what he remembers to have been said by the inspired and divining nature, either in sleep or waking, and to resurvey with reason the phantoms he may have seen as to what they betoken and for whom, either of present, past, or future and for good or evil. When a man is still in frenzy there is no advantage in his judging what he has seen or spoken. There is a good old proverb to the effect that it is only the sane on whom it falls to attend to his own concerns and know himself."[50]

The reasonable inference from this passage seems to be something like this. At the time that he wrote the *Timaeus* Plato still retained his old conviction that man's reason was that which was closest to the divine—that is, it was closest to whatever in man was nonmaterial and consequently shows form and design clearly. On the other hand, the bodily functions of man furthest removed from reason are still subject to the influence of whatever is not material and consequently peculiarly form or design. This outside force Plato will call variously "the God" (who is not always the Demiurge) or "the Gods" or "They." A form of direct communication can and does exist through the least worthy of man's bodily instruments—for instance, the liver—and, under inspiration from without, truth is grasped as it never can be grasped by the intellect. The function of reason in such connections is to sift the communication received and discover its exact pertinence. This feeling just described is part of the general doubt of the clarity and certainty of anything human, even the human intellect, which is deep in the older Plato. In the *Timaeus* the universe is described as an *agalma* of the gods— a thing in which they find delight.[51] This is the favorable way to see it. The other side is shown by the passage in the *Laws* in which Plato says that the universe is a puppet show in which we, the puppets, are moved by strings held by the gods. We perform dances and acts of all kinds, each executing his appointed part, with none capable of understanding the meaning of what he does in the dimension outside it all.[52]

It is with this in mind that we must see this strange cosmic drama, the *Timaeus*—a creation which does not occur in time by a God incapable of our comprehension for a purpose unknown.[53] And as in the theater the actions and voices of the players establish the indispensable link between the artificiality of the dramatic design and the formless realism of life outside the theater, so in the *Timaeus* the analytical description of body, blood, brain, and other organs is the link between the precision of the unknowable cosmic design and the meaninglessness of the known physical world. This is the medium which holds our sense of reality; it is through the fantastic interpretation of this, the body, that our belief is induced in his cosmic design. It is in the nature of the subject, of course, that he must give the greater mystery first: that the Demiurge and the gods, the mixing bowl and the proportions of world soul and world body, the basic triangles and harmonic intervals should precede the charting of the human body and human soul as microcosms of the greater unit. But it is the latter which when grasped finally transport us, in a dramatist's sense, into complete understanding and momentary belief in the weird fancies of this sketch of the universe. Yet not the least frightening aspect of this dialogue is that Plato is clearly interested in the human body and the human soul only as they give evidence of the greater design. Take, for instance, his story of the differentiation of the sexes:

"And now it seems we have almost completed what we said at the beginning we would do, to tell the story of the universe until the generation of man. . . . And let this be the account of it. Of the men that are born, such as are cowards and have lived a life of injustice were, according to a probable account, transformed into women in the second generation. And at that time for this reason the gods devised the love of copulation, fashioning within us men one living creature and another instinct with life in women. From the channel of our drink when it receives liquid that has passed through the lungs by the kidneys into the bladder and ejects it with the air that presses upon it they pierced an opening communicating with the compact marrow which runs from the head down the neck and along the spine and has indeed in our earlier discussion been called seed. This marrow, being instinct with life and finding an outlet, implanted in the part where the outlet was a lively appetite for egress and so brought it to completion as an Eros of begetting. Wherefore it is that in men the sexual member is disobedient and stubborn like a creature that will not listen to reason and through its frenzied appetite would master everything. And in women the matrix or womb, for the same reason, a living creature within them with a desire for childbearing . . . until at last the desire of the one and the Eros of the other bringing them together pluck as it were the fruit from the tree and sow the field of the womb with creatures alive but invisible, by reason of smallness, and unformed, and again differentiating their parts nourish them till they grow large within and after that bring them forth to the light of day and so complete the generation of living things."[54]

There is here a preoccupation with physical images merely to heighten the reality of the systematic design. The marrow and the brain must be connected with sexual intercouse because man's physical immortality by reproduction must be linked with the immortal soul. And there is something horrible in the vividness with which he presents the sexual organs as somehow autonomous animals. In this picture as in much else that deals with man's body there is a dreadful combination of intimacy and an impersonal hatred for the body which can only be allevi- ated by the assurance of a design which overrules the material. This design in titanic proportions is the story of the creation and conservation of the universe. And if there is in us fear and uneasiness as we read Plato on the body, there is something great and entirely terrifying about his uncanny personalization of the universe. Through the account of the basic triangles, the har- monic intervals, and the blending of sameness and otherness one comes suddenly to the finality of his few great poetic sentences describing the world. If the mood is right, they somehow con- vey completely an image: it may be a madman's image—perhaps only a madman will try to sum up the qualities of the universe in an image—but it brings the reader to the very brink of the incomprehensible and lets him, momentarily, glance beyond. "The universe then is an ensouled animal. Because there is nothing outside it, it has no need of support and therefore neither hands nor feet, and, being alone and single, it needs neither neighbors nor acquaintances with which to converse."[55] On such a level of communication there is nothing further to be said about man as an individual or in a community. When Plato abandoned the *Timaeus* trilogy halfway in the middle of Critias' account of the "ideal" state which had been historically extant many thousands of years before, it is because the subject has lost interest for him. In the *Timaeus* he has succeeded for the last time in a total picture in which man, although a minor figure in the universe, still had a place.

4

"Now as we make our scrutiny and examination of this subject at the present, a kind of sober old man's game with laws, we should travel on our road painlessly, as we said when we started the journey."[56] The fictitious scene in the *Laws* is the road from Cnossus to Dicte, but the imagery is pointedly chosen. For Plato the road had been a long one and the traveler was tired. This, his last work, has hanging over it the sunlit haze of the end of a summer day. There is heat and light, but it is near the end, and the end is not coming violently. At the last he had his period of peace when the love of the colors and movement of life mercifully deserted him and left him to form serenely the death mask of his thought.

It is no accident that this, his last work, should be concerned with the laws and the political community. Of all that he now could touch, there was nothing that engaged him less in life; there was nothing that was more susceptible to his fashioning and molding. And it was full, too, of recollections and echoes of his past, so that the shapes were familiar and welcome. The failure in Sicily did not irk him any more: it was hundreds of years away; and the state described in his *Republic* is implicitly equated with the perfect state of the age of Cronos, which was ruled by daemons or demigods.[57] This his second-best community, as sketched in the *Laws*, is truly at the end of the road. He had represented the live reality for the last time in the *Timaeus* on a cosmic stage; when he turned to man in the *Laws*, he could not see him, politically, alive, as the world is alive in the *Timaeus*. The way was barred by the loss of all that he had surrendered to write the *Timaeus*. But he also could not see man in political community as he had been in the *Republic*, the phantom of his dreams just touching the edges of realization. Political man of the *Laws* must be the object of a sober old man's game, in which the stakes are nonexistent, for he cannot come to life, but with the outward appearance of the city-state, with his judges and soldiers and market wardens and priests, with all the appurtenances of living which the hope of realization in the *Republic* derided as useless and a waste of time.[58] And the focus must be on the laws, for here is where his workman's fading interest still is strongest—in the form of persuasion, of embodied reason, to create a form and pattern in human life.

"Let us think of each of us living creatures," says the Athenian, "as a puppet of the gods, whether contrived to be a plaything of theirs or for some serious purpose. For this we do not know. But we do know that the emotions that are with us are like sinews and strings that draw us along and pull against one another toward different actions and therein lies the difference of vice and virtue. For, as our argument declares, there is one of these strings which each of us should always follow and never let go, resisting the pull of the other sinews. This is the holy golden leading string of reason which is called the public law of the state."[59]

It is indeed this public law of the state which is the center of the dialogue and rightly gives it its name, for the laws have taken over the function both of the philosopher-king and, in a sense, of philosophy itself. In the *Republic* the model state had been projected in the first books as a crude image of political community in which justice would be found. Its foundations, however, are in philosophy, in the divided line and the nature of the soul as they are expressed later. The philosopher-king is the connecting link, for he is the one hope of realizing the approximation of the true state, and so the nature and training of the philosopher himself absolutely condition the state. If he shall be, and if he shall find the opportunity, the true state shall be and not otherwise. And that he shall be and shall be the man required is dependent on the concept of philosophic wisdom and training in it which Socrates describes.

In the *Laws* the image has become autonomous. The laws are, it is true, written by one man, the lawgiver, but he is divorced from the exercise of the ruling function. What has led him to the truths which are expressed in written, unalterable form is wisdom acquired in a way Plato would now not have cared to describe. It was wisdom, that is all; and its principles and applications can be combined together in all manner of particular ordinances affecting every moment of people's lives. The wisdom involved in ordering a political community and being part of it is indeed a divine thing. "We ought then by all means to imitate life in the age of Cronos and, obeying the immortal element in us, contrive both public and private government, both of our households and our cities, giving to the ordinance of reason the name of law."[60] Yet it is only the motions of the puppets, the actual imitative acts which embody the application of the laws, that interest Plato any more. And consequently we are always being reminded of the early books of the *Republic*, never the later. The persuasion which was the golden key of the earlier dialogues has been transformed, too. It is no longer the product of passionate understanding; it is now the gentle voice of reason speaking across the years which have taken from it self-interest or human limitation, one with the past only in its opposition to force and violence: "What we seek is the rule of law over willing subjects, according to nature: there must be no violence therein."[61]

In the brief sentences in which he tells of the possibilities of the good state the relation to the earlier political dialogues is at its most striking. For what is needed is a prince who will invite the lawgiver, obey him, and then obey his creation, the laws,[62] and leave them after him for his successors likewise to love and obey. Gone is the Plato who disbelieved in written words, "for if you ask them . . . they just say the same thing and the same thing always."[63] And gone is the Plato who refused, in the *Republic*, to sketch the laws which the philosopher-king would draw up, since such would be dead and lifeless before the living knowledge of the ruler.[64] If Plato's image in the *Laws* were to come true, it would be like the other kind of monarchy he had never known. There would be a king who was half-magical, for to his subjects he was in the place of the gods who once ruled them; yet in his own eyes humble before the sanctity of the laws. There would be the laws which were unalterable and also unquestioned, for they would be a creation so old that no one could say that they were not the laws of nature herself; and there would be subjects who could not divorce their human personality from the attribute of being subjects. But though Plato's state in the *Laws* recalls such a monarchy, it no more than recalls it. For the structure is intellectual and belongs in the world of intellectual dissection and creation where the other monarchy cannot live. It is indeed an old man's "dream in the daylight."

In this work of fading strength—for the style and the color and the glory of the words are all going or gone—there is only one stabbing gleam of light—of a Plato different from any we have known. I think that, as the human world with all its ambiguities melted away from him, there was a moment when the unity of the direction of the world lost its value; when the blending of the good and the bad, always subordinate to another description which in our crude human way we could call good, ceased to be that which gave him peace. The sentences are short, obscure, and utterly unexpected.

"It is Soul then that we must say dwells in all things that are moved and controls them and since this is so must we not also say that it controls Heaven? Yes. And is there one soul or several? *Let me answer for you too:* there are more than one. Anyway let us assume that there are no less than two, one the Beneficent Soul and the other that can effect results that are just the opposite. . . . Soul drives all things in heaven and earth and the sea with its own motions and the names of the motions are will, reflection, forethought, counsel, true judgment, false judgment, joy, sorrow, confidence, fear, hate, and love . . . all these qualities Soul employs when it governs all things happily like a true God with reason to aid her, but when she dwells with unreason she does the opposite of all of them."[65]

But this is but a moment. The mood of the whole dialogue

is otherwise and is somehow summed up in one of the conversations between the old men:

. . . Men shall then live according to the fashion of their nature like puppets, for the most part, yet with some occasional share in truth.

MEG.: You have surely a very poor opinion of humanity!

ATH.: Do not wonder, my friend, but pardon me. For my thoughts and my feelings were set on God when I said what I did. Let out kind of creature be no mean thing, if you please, but even worth some serious attention.[66]

5

In the later dialogues the hunger for the perfection of form and design, the desire to force the naturally unco-ordinated in the direction of design and pattern, is blunted by the sense that pure form is beyond the reach of life, is beyond even what life should seek. The mass permeated by fragments of design is all that Plato cares to consider any more—for here is all that there is of reality. Yet it is the hints of design that drew him on. It is the brute vitality which at last disgusts him. Though the love of pure abstraction is gone, all that in the end has meaning for him is the evidence of design, so much more subtly, so much more doubtfully accepted than in his early days. There is a direction in his last works from the *Parmenides* to the *Laws*, and it is always moving one way to the half-lit world where eyes grown used to the light can see the regularity of the shadowy figures, blurred and unsubstantial though they are. In this last movement the *Timaeus* and the *Laws* stand on opposite peaks. In the *Timaeus*, for a brief moment, perhaps his greatest, in a cosmological setting the two forces of life and design can really be fused, and the strange dream of their combination has force, beauty, and eloquence. In the *Laws* life has at last been superseded: this old man had at last exhausted the tension of his creativity. He can find his design at last and be passive and unafraid. For there is nothing any more to hold him in life.

Notes

CHAPTER I

THE WORLD OF THUCYDIDES

1. Cf. Herodotus vi. 9–10, 48–52, 102–4; viii. 140–44.
2. Cf. *ibid.* viii. 142–43; ix. 45.
3. Thucydides ii. 41. 1.
4. Cf. H. Frankfort, *Ancient Egyptian Religion* (New York: Columbia University Press, 1948), pp. 30–58.
5. Cf. C. N. Cochrane, *Christianity and Classical Culture* (London, New York, and Toronto: Oxford University Press, 1944), pp. 27–73.
6. See p. 22.
7. It must be remembered that this is a statement of the Athenians. However, on the whole there seems to be no reason to question its accuracy (cf. Herodotus v. 92A; Thucydides i. 18. 1, 19; Isocrates iv. 125; Aristotle *Politics* v. 1312 b 7). Some scholars have nevertheless tried to modify the Athenian statement, e.g., G. Busolt, *Die Lakedämonier und ihre Bundesgenossen*, I (Leipzig: Teubner, 1878), 212–15, 304 ff.
8. Thucydides i. 75–76.
9. *Ibid.* iii. 82–83.
10. *Ibid.* v. 89–105.

CHAPTER II

OUR KNOWLEDGE OF THUCYDIDES

1. In addition to this, we get some very scanty information from Suidas, from a short *Life*, and from a biography by Marcellinus, the reliability of which is marred by the fact that the historian is often confused with the politician, Thucydides son of Melesias. Furthermore, we get information on certain specific points from Plutarch's *Life of Cimon* and from Pausanias.
2. Thucydides i. 1.
3. *Ibid.* iv. 104. 4.
4. *Ibid.* v. 26. 1. The facts of Thucydides' death are most uncertain and obscured by legend. The most probable version is perhaps that which Marcellinus (*Life of Thucydides* 33) credits to Cratippus, according to which the historian died in Thrace and was buried in Athens (cf. also Plutarch *Life of Cimon* iv) shortly after the Peloponnesian War. The statement by Marcellinus (*op. cit.* 34) that Thucydides was over fifty years old when he died fits in well with the other data we have and places the date of his death at about 400 B.C. According to a tradition preserved in Pausanias i. 23. 11

and by Didymus (Marcellinus *op. cit.* 32), he met a violent end. For a thorough analysis of the sources on the life of Thucydides and what we can extract from them see John H. Finley, Jr., *Thucydides* (Cambridge, Mass.: Harvard University Press, 1942), pp. 5-17.

5. Thucydides v. 26. For an authoritative treatment of the problems of the composition and revision of the *History* see Wolfgang Schadewaldt, *Die Geschichtschreibung des Thukydides* (Weidmann, 1929).

6. Thucydides viii. 97.

7. *Ibid.* iii. 82-83 *passim.* No one single English word quite covers the meaning of the Greek *stasis*, for, in addition to a number of non-political connotations, it designates in its technical meaning in Thucydides a party organized for seditious purposes as well as the violent discord of party warfare.

8. *Ibid.* i. 138. 3-6 (Themistocles); ii. 65. 5-13 (Pericles); iv. 21. 3 (Cleon); viii. 73. 3 (Hyperbolus); viii. 68. 1 (Antiphon); vii. 86. 5 (Nicias).

9. E.g., ii. 65. 4; iv. 28. 5; vi. 24. 3-4, 60; viii. 1. 4, 47. 2, 48. 3, 89. 3. Cf. also on democracy, p. 41.

10. Thucydides i. 22. 1, 2.

11. It is hard to imagine that such a speech as the Corinthian analysis of the Athenian character (i. 68-71) was delivered at Sparta in exactly the form in which Thucydides reports it. Nor could one think of the Melian Dialogue (v. 85-111) as embodying the minutes of the actual meeting.

12. E.g., iii. 37-48, speeches of Cleon and Diodotus about Mitylene; vi. 9-23, speeches of Nicias, Alcibiades, and again Nicias about the expedition to Sicily.

13. See p. 12.

14. Cf. F. M. Cornford, *Thucydides Mythistoricus* (London: E. Arnold, 1907), pp. 174-87.

15. A good example of what confusion may be caused by too carelessa differentiation can be found in Charles N. Cochrane, *Thucydides and the Science of History* (London: Oxford University Press, 1929), p. 103: "Thucydides is fully aware that, for democracy, expediency is the rule of state, and there are many passages which could be cited to illustrate this fact. Of these, one, in particular, may be noticed: the passage in which *he* analyzes the problem of crime and punishment (iii, 37, 40)." (Italics mine.) This statement is the more remarkable because in an earlier part of the same book Cochrane, in what I admittedly found a very ambiguous passage, says: "In another sense they [the speeches] are genuinely objective in so far as each of them constitutes an analysis conveying to the reader the attitude of representative individuals or groups in relation to the facts which came up for discussion" (p. 26). Earlier Cochrane said

that the speeches represent Thucydides' thought as well as style. Now, can these statements really be reconciled? If what we have is Thucydides' thought and if we can speak of the speech of Diodotus as revealing Thucydides' analysis of the problem of crime and punishment, in what sense does the reporting of such a speech constitute "objective" reality? Surely the latter phrase would only be correct if there actually was a speech delivered by Diodotus substantially on the lines indicated by Thucydides, and in that case we have no grounds for assuming that what is said, taken in itself, constitutes Thucydides' point of view. Paul Shorey, too, in his essay "On the Implicit Ethics and Psychology of Thucydides," in the *Transactions of the American Philological Association*, XXIV (1893), 66–88, exhibits similar instances of ambiguity in his treatment of the speeches. For instance, though in this case, as in the Cochrane passages, the meaning is not entirely clear, the series of statements beginning "the Athenians, so their envoys at Sparta declare . . ." (Shorey, *op. cit.*, p. 67), almost all taken from speeches, are apparently being treated as evidence of Thucydides' own philosophy.

16. Thucydides i. 72. 1.

17. *Ibid.* vii. 10.

18. *Ibid.* iii. 36. 6 and 41.

19. *Ibid.* i. 22. 1.

20. The evidence is chiefly contained in the crucial i. 22 already discussed and in such subsidiary arguments as are used by A. W. Gomme in his essay on "The Speeches in Thucydides," in *Essays in Greek History and Literature* (Oxford: B. Blackwell, 1937), pp. 156–89, a definitive treatment of this whole subject on which the preceding pages have drawn heavily. Cf. Gomme's discussion in his *Commentary on Thucydides*, I (Oxford: Clarendon Press, 1945), 139 ff., in which he also adequately deals with the position of August Grosskinsky in "Das Programm des Thukydides," *Neue deutsche Forschungen, Abteilung klassische Philologie*, III (1936), 24–43. Grosskinsky differs from Gomme on some points; I agree with them both, however, in rejecting as untenable the interpretation of i. 22 given by Eduard Schwartz in *Gnomon*, II (1926), 65 ff., and in his *Das Geschichtswerk des Thukydides* (Bonn: F. Cohen, 1919), p. 25.

CHAPTER III

The Problem of Thucydidean Politics

1. R. C. Jebb, "The Speeches of Thucydides," in *Essays and Addresses* (Cambridge: Cambridge University Press, 1907), pp. 359–445.

2. *Ibid.*, p. 409.

3. Paul Shorey, "On the Implicit Ethics and Psychology of Thucydides," *Transactions of the American Philological Association,* XXIV (1893), 66–88.

4. *Ibid.,* p. 66.

5. *Ibid.,* p. 75.

6. Thucydides ii. 53. 4: "Neither fear of god nor law of man restrained them. For the former, they judged that piety or its opposite had much the same consequences when they saw all equally meeting their doom; and for the latter, no one expected to live until the day of judgment when he would pay the penalty for his misdeeds: rather they assumed that a far greater penalty had already been assessed against them and even now impended, which to forestall and gain some enjoyment from their life became their natural object."

7. *Ibid.* iii. 37–40.

8. *Ibid.* v. 85–111.

9. Shorey, *op. cit.,* p. 66.

10. *Ibid.* (The italics are mine.)

11. See chap. vi.

12. Thucydides viii. 68. 1 (see chap. vii).

13. The Greek word used here is *epitechnesis.*

14. Thucydides i. 71. 2–3.

15. *Ibid.* iii. 82.

16. *Ibid.* iii. 42–43.

17. *Ibid.* 44.

18. *Ibid.* 45–48. Cf. C. N. Cochrane, *Thucydides and the Science of History* (Oxford: Oxford University Press, 1929), pp. 115, 124.

19. The transfer of the treasury from Delos to Athens in 454 B.C. is not recorded by Thucydides. The evidence is found in Plutarch's *Life of Pericles* xii. 1 and in his *Life of Aristeides* xxv. 3, in Aristodemus Frag. 7 (Jacoby), and in several passages in Diodorus: xii. 40. 1, 54. 3, and xiii. 21. 3.

20. In addition to the statement of the Athenians in Thucydides i. 77. 1, there is some inscriptional and very scattered literary evidence, with which A. W. Gomme deals most satisfactorily in his *Commentary on Thucydides* (Oxford: Clarendon Press, 1945), I, 239–43.

21. Only such settlements as happened during the war are mentioned by Thucydides, e.g., in Aegina (ii. 27. 1), in Potidaea (ii. 70. 4), in Mitylene (iii. 50. 2), etc. For earlier settlements of Athenian citizens in allied territory see Plutarch *Pericles* xi. 5; Diodorus xi. 88. 3; Pausanias i. 27. 5; Andocides iii. 9; and a number of inscriptions. Cf. Gomme, *op. cit.,* pp. 373 ff.

22. Plato *Gorgias* 490A.

23. Cicero *De senectute* xvi. 55 ff. Cf. Léon Homo, *Roman Polit-*

ical Institutions (London: Kegan Paul, Trench, Trubner & Co.; New York: Alfred A. Knopf, 1929), pp. 123 ff.

24. See Sallust's account in his *Jugurthine War* 63–65, 73, 84, and especially the speech of Marius in chap. 85.

25. See chap. i, p. 11.

26. Thucydides vi. 92. 4.

27. *Ibid.* 85. 1.

28. *Ibid.* ii. 63. 2; iii. 37. 2.

29. Plato *Republic* viii. 562A ff.; 564A; 569C.

30. Cf. K. J. Hermann and H. Swoboda, *Lehrbuch der griechischen Staatsaltertümer*, Part III (6th ed.; Tübingen: J. C. B. Mohr, 1913), pp. 92 ff.; see also T. Lenschau's article on "Tyrannis" in *R.-E.*, Zweite Reihe, 14. Halbband (1943), pp. 1821 ff.

31. Aristotle *Constitution of Athens* xix. 6.

CHAPTER IV

THUCYDIDES AND THE ATHENIAN DEMOCRACY

1. Thucydides viii. 68. 4.

2. There is, of course, a good deal of evidence also in such works as the pseudo-Xenophontic *Constitution of Athens*, a political pamphlet of the fifth century, which is also quoted under the name of the *Old Oligarch* in many of Aristophanes' comedies and in inscriptions. Yet we find there only elucidation on certain points without comments on the larger political development which Aristotle's *Constitution of Athens* and the relevant *Lives* of Plutarch give us.

3. The clans and brotherhoods were, of course, not dissolved as such and continued to exist as religious units (cf. Aristotle *Constitution of Athens* xxi. 6).

4. Cf. H. T. Wade-Gery's account of the Dorian tyrannies in the *Cambridge Ancient History*, III (Cambridge: University Press, 1925), 548–69.

5. See also A. W. Gomme, *Commentary on Thucydides* (Oxford: Clarendon Press, 1945), I, 380 ff., as cited below, n. 11.

6. Thucydides ii. 37. 1.

7. *Ibid.* vi. 89. 6.

8. *Ibid.* iii. 47. On the reliance of the Athenians on the democratic elements in the subject states of the empire see also Plato *Letter VII* 332B, C.

9. Thucydides iii. 37.

10. *Ibid.* 37. 2. Compare with this the argument of the Athenian envoys at Sparta in i. 77.

11. There is no conclusive evidence to prove the establishment of

permanent Athenian garrisons in allied territory during the fifty years between the end of the Persian Wars and the beginning of the Peloponnesian War. Such garrisons as were established in Erythrae (M. N. Tod, *Greek Historical Inscriptions* [2d ed.; Oxford: Clarendon Press, 1946], No. 29), Miletus (Oliver in *Transactions of the American Philological Association*, LXVI [1935], 177-98), the Thracian Chersonese (Plutarch *Life of Cimon* xiv. 1), Chalcis (Tod, *op. cit.*, No. 42), and Samos (Thucydides i. 115. 3) seem to have been of a temporary nature only. For a full treatment see Gomme, *op. cit.*, I, 380-84.

12. Aristophanes *Acharnians* 17-26; Aristotle *Constitution of Athens* xli. 3.

13. The character of Cleon is admirably parodied in the *Knights* of Aristophanes, and allusions to him are frequent in the *Wasps* and the *Peace*. For a description of his character see also Plutarch *Life of Nicias* iii-ix *passim*.

14. Actually, the lot was drawn from a list of candidates previously chosen by the various tribes. This process, called *Klerosis ek prokriton*, was instituted by Solon (Aristotle *Constitution of Athens* viii. 1). It fell into disuse during the tyranny and was reintroduced with slight modifications in 487 B.C. (*ibid.* xxii. 5); eligibility for the office was extended to the Teamster class in 457 B.C. (*ibid.* xxvi. 2); and it remained in this form until the revolution of the Four Hundred (*ibid.* xxx. 5).

15. Aristotle *Constitution of Athens* xliii. 3-4.

16. Whether this was done regularly is most uncertain. We do not know either how frequently appointments of these so-called "strategoi autokratores" were made. The way in which Plutarch describes the office of Aristeides (*Life of Aristeides* viii) and of Themistocles (*Life of Themistocles* xii) makes us believe that they did not hold a special title. There is no doubt, however, that occasionally one general was appointed as commander-in-chief over his colleagues. Even if Herodotus is unreliable in reporting certain details about the office, we may infer from a number of passages (Herodotus vii. 173; viii. 4, 61, 131; ix. 28, 46, 117) that something like that was the practice during the Persian Wars. We know that Pericles held a similar position in the war against Samos (Thucydides i. 116. 1) and in the first year of the Peloponnesian War (*ibid.* ii. 13. 1), but we have no conclusive evidence that such an appointment was ever made in times of peace; we only possess Plutarch's testimony (*Life of Pericles* xvi. 3) that during the period of his pre-eminence the official position of Pericles was that of a *strategos*.

17. To what degree separate functions were allocated to the various generals is not known. For detailed information about their duties in the fifth century see Walther Schwahn in *R.-E.*, Supple-

mentband VI (1935), pp. 1076 ff. The statement of Aristotle, *Constitution of Athens* lxi, seems to apply only to the fourth century.

18. Plutarch *Life of Pericles* xi; xvi. 3; *Life of Nicias* ii. 2. Cf. also Wade-Gery's excellent article on "Thucydides, the Son of Melesias," *Journal of Hellenic Studies*, LII (1932), 205–27.

19. Aristotle *Constitution of Athens* xxviii. 1.

20. Thucydides viii. 97. 2.

21. *Ibid.* ii. 65. 4.

22. *Ibid.* viii. 1 and ii. 65. 11.

23. *Ibid.* vii. 14. 2.

24. *Ibid.* 14. 4.

25. *Ibid.* 15. 2.

26. *Ibid.* ii. 65. 8.

27. *Ibid.* viii. 86. 5.

28. *Ibid.* ii. 65. 9.

29. C. N. Cochrane, *Thucydides and the Science of History* (London: Oxford University Press, 1929), pp. 94–97; cf. John H. Finley, Jr., *Thucydides* (Cambridge, Mass.: Harvard University Press, 1942), pp. 33–35.

CHAPTER V

THUCYDIDES AND THE ATHENIAN EMPIRE

1. Thucydides i. 69, 1 ff.; iii. 62–64.

2. *Ibid.* i. 68–71.

3. *Ibid.* iv. 61. 5–7.

4. E.g., Archidamos in Thucydides i. 82. 1; Sthenelaidas in i. 86. 2, etc.

5. *Ibid.* iv. 85. 1, 5; 86. 1, 4; 87. 4–5.

6. Aristotle *Constitution of Athens* xxiii. 4–5; xxviii. 2.

7. *Ibid.* xxvi. 1 and xxviii. 2.

8. Cf. especially such a work as the pseudo-Xenophontic *Constitution of Athens*.

9. Plutarch *Life of Pericles* xi. 1–2; xii. 1–2.

10. *Ibid.* xii. 2.

11. Thucydides v. 14–15.

12. *Ibid.* vi. 9–14.

13. *Ibid.* i. 144. 1.

14. *Ibid.* ii. 65. 11.

15. *Ibid.* vii. 85. 1; cf. 86. 3.

16. *Ibid.* vii. 86. 1–2.

17. *Ibid.* viii. 47. 2–48. 3.

18. *Ibid.* 70. 2–71.

19. *Ibid.* 91. 3.

20. Pseudo-Xenophon *Constitution of Athens* i. 1–12.

21. Plato *Laws* iv. 705A.

22. Aristophanes *Knights* 214–19; Aristotle *Constitution of Athens* xxviii. 3.

23. We do not know to what degree landed estates were held inside or outside Attica. For landed estates in Attica see B. Büchsenschütz, *Besitz und Erwerb in Alterthume* (Halle: Buchhandlung des Waisenhauses, 1869), pp. 57 ff.

24. Investment in the mines of Laurion was the source of Nicias' wealth, for example, according to Plutarch *Life of Nicias* iv. On private interests in the mines see also Xenophon *Poroi* iv. 14–17.

25. Cf. Thucydides vii. 19. 1–2, 27. 3, 28. 4.

26. As, e.g., in the case of Antiphon (cf. Thucydides viii. 68. 1–2).

27. This is the name given to the first twenty-two chapters of the first book of Thucydides. Similarly, the account of the events between the end of the Persian Wars and the beginning of the Peloponnesian War (i. 89–118) is usually referred to as the "Pentekontaëtia" or *Fifty Years*.

28. Thucydides i. 8. 3.

29. *Ibid.* 23. 6.

30. It is not necessary here to go into the question of whether *prophasis* or *aitia* are being cited here as "primary" and "secondary" causes or "real" as opposed to "assumed" causes. The important thing is that there *is* a contrast between what Thucydides thinks is the important underlying cause, not much brought into the open, and one that was extensively publicized.

31. E.g., causes for Agamemnon's power over the suitors: Thucydides i. 9–10; causes of the length of the siege of Troy: i. 11; and the general statement on method: i. 21.

32. Thucydides iii. 10. 3, people of Mitylene; iii. 63. 3, Thebans against people of Plataea; iv. 85. 5, Brasidas before the Acanthians.

33. Herodotus viii. 140A.

34. *Ibid.* 141–42.

35. *Ibid.* 143–44.

36. Thucydides iii. 62. 1–2.

37. *Ibid.* iv. 59–64.

38. *Ibid.* i. 19, 76. 1.

39. *Ibid.* 23. 1–2.

40. *Ibid.* 82. 1.

41. *Ibid.* viii. 47.

42. *Ibid.* ii. 65. 12.

43. Aristophanes *Acharnians* 180–81; *Clouds* 985–86.

44. Thucydides iii. 67. 2.

45. Cf. above, chap. i, n. 9.

46. Thucydides viii. 97. 2.

47. *Ibid.* 73. 3.

48. *Ibid.* iv. 28. 5.
49. *Ibid.* vii. 30. 3.
50. *Ibid.* 86. 5.
51. *Ibid.* iii. 82-83.

CHAPTER VI

HISTORICAL NECESSITY

1. Thucydides i. 11.
2. *Ibid.* 21.
3. *Ibid.* 9. 1.
4. *Ibid.* 9. 4, 10. 3.
5. *Ibid.* 8. 2-3; 11. 1; 13. 1, 5-6
6. *Ibid.* 75. 3. There is a striking parallel between these three motive forces and the three passions listed by Hobbes (*Leviathan*, Part I, chap. xiii) as causes of the war of all against all; i.e., competition, diffidence, and glory: "The first maketh men invade for gain; the second, for safety; and the third, for reputation." The fact that Hobbes himself translated Thucydides makes it reasonable to see a direct influence here—as well as a basic similarity in the two men's views of human nature, especially with reference to the nature and sources of political power.
7. Thucydides i. 8. 3.
8. *Ibid.* v. 26. 5.
9. *Ibid.* iii. 42-48.
10. *Ibid.* 45. 4-7.
11. *Ibid.* i. 22. 4.
12. *Ibid.* iii. 82. 2.
13. *Ibid.* i. 77. 6.
14. *Ibid.* v. 25, 27 ff.
15. Plato *Republic* i. 338C-339A; 343B-344C; *Gorgias* 481D-484C.
16. Thucydides i. 76. 3.
17. *Ibid.* v. 85; Plato *Republic* i. 349A-B.
18. Thucydides i. 22. 4, the war; ii. 48. 3, the plague; iii. 82. 2, *stasis*.
19. *Ibid.* iii. 82. 2.
20. *Ibid.* ii. 54. 4.
21. *Ibid.* 52.
22. *Ibid.* i. 22. 4.
23. Cf. *ibid.* iii. 82. 2.
24. *Ibid.* ii. 48. 3.
25. *Ibid.* i. 138. 3.
26. *Ibid.* ii. 65. 5-13.
27. *Ibid.* v. 45. 3; vi. 17. 2-6; vi. 91. 4-5, 6-7.
28. *Ibid.* i. 14. 3, 93. 3.
29. *Ibid.* 90. 3—92.
30. *Ibid.* ii. 65. 8.
31. *Ibid.* i. 140-44.

32. *Ibid.* ii. 60–64.
33. *Ibid.* vi. 48; 91. 6–7.
34. *Ibid.* v. 45, 3–4; vi. 16–19. 1, 89–93. 2.
35. *Ibid.* vi. 15. 4.
36. *Ibid.* ii. 60. 6.
37. *Ibid.* vi. 53. 3—60. 2.

CHAPTER VII

Chance and Pity

1. A fourth passage, the assessment of Antiphon, will receive a separate treatment in chap. vii.
2. Thucydides vii. 29.
3. *Ibid.* 27. 2.
4. *Ibid.* 29. 4–5.
5. *Ibid.* 30. 3.
6. *Ibid.* 85–86.
7. *Ibid.* 75. 5.
8. *Ibid.* 86. 5.
9. *Ibid.* viii. 66. 2.
10. *Ibid.* 97. 2.
11. *Ibid.* 68. 1.
12. *Ibid.* vii. 29. 1–2.
13. *Ibid.* vi. 8. 4.
14. *Ibid.* 61. 6–7, 103. 3.
15. *Ibid.* vii. 15.
16. *Ibid.* 16–17.
17. *Ibid.* 50. 3–4.
18. *Ibid.* v. 16. 1.
19. *Ibid.* vii. 86. 5.
20. *Ibid.* iii. 82. 2.
21. *Ibid.* viii. 97.

CHAPTER VIII

Beyond Necessity

1. E.g., J. B. Bury, *The Ancient Greek Historians* (New York: Macmillan Co., 1909), p. 119.
2. See p. 72 above.
3. Thucydides viii. 68. 1.
4. See p. 71 above.
5. Thucydides viii. 70. 2.
6. *Ibid.* vii. 77. 2.
7. *Ibid.* ii. 60. 6–7.
8. *Ibid.* i. 138. 3.
9. *Ibid.* ii. 63. 2.

10. *Ibid.* i. 138. 1-2, 4.
11. *Ibid.* ii. 65. 3-4.
12. *Ibid.* viii. 68. 2.
13. *Ibid.* i. 138. 3.
14. *Ibid.* ii. 65. 8-10.
15. *Ibid.* viii. 68. 1.
16. *Ibid.* i. 140-44.
17. *Ibid.* ii. 35-46.
18. *Ibid.* 60-64.
19. *Ibid.* 65. 8.
20. *Ibid.* i. 140. 1.
21. *Ibid.* ii. 62. 1, 2.
22. *Ibid.* 64. 2.
23. *Ibid.* vii. 69. 2.
24. *Ibid.* ii. 38. 2.
25. *Ibid.* 37. 2-3.
26. *Ibid.* 139.
27. *Ibid.* 44. 3.
28. *Ibid.* 42. 2.
29. *Ibid.* 64. 3.
30. *Ibid.* 64. 5.
31. Herodotus i. 1.
32. Thucydides ii. 65. 10.

CHAPTER IX

The Word and the Deed

1. There is not much more known of Plato's life than he himself tells us in the *Seventh Letter* (see n. 14 below). For our other sources see A. E. Taylor, *Plato, the Man and His Work* (New York: Dial Press, 1936), pp. 1-9.

2. For an attempt—unconvincing to the present writer—to turn the dialogues into commentaries on fourth-century affairs see G. C. Field, *Plato and His Contemporaries* (London: Methuen & Co., 1930), chap. ix, pp. 122-31.

3. Concerning the authenticity of the dialogues, as distinct from their dating, there are no longer any serious problems. It was fashionable among German scholars in the nineteenth century to doubt not only obviously spurious dialogues like the *Theages* or the *Alcibiades I* and *II* but such indubitably authentic ones as the *Parmenides* (see F. Ueberweg, "Der Dialog Parmenides," in *Jahrb. f. klass. Phil.*, 1863, pp. 97-126) or the *Laws* (see Eduard Zeller, *Platonische Studien* [Tübingen: C. F. Osiander, 1839], pp. 112 ff.). Such pseudoproblems can be taken as settled, as least in general, by Grote (G.

Grote, *Plato and the Other Companions of Socrates* [London: John Murray, 1888], Vol. I, chaps. vi and vii, pp. 264-341). See also Taylor, *op. cit.*, pp. 10-15.

4. The "stylometric" method of dating the dialogues was initiated by Lewis Campbell in his edition of *The Sophistes and Politicus of Plato* (Oxford: Clarendon Press, 1867). His work was not much noticed until it was expanded and elaborated by W. Lutoslawski in his *Origin and Growth of Plato's Logic* (London: Longmans, Green & Co., 1897). Parallel research by Ritter and others served to confirm the conclusions of Campbell (see C. Ritter, *Untersuchungen über Platon* [Stuttgart: W. Kohlhammer, 1888] and *Neue Untersuchungen über Platon* [München: Oskar Beck, 1910], pp. 183-227). For a summary of the results now generally accepted see Taylor, *op. cit.*, pp. 16-22.

5. It should be mentioned, however, that the great majority of German scholars put the *Protagoras* extremely early, sometimes even before the *Apology*, not in the great group of middle dialogues, as I have done here. This seems to me, in view of the extraordinary dramatic skill and subtlety of the dialogue, quite fantastic (see Taylor, *op. cit.*, pp. 20 and 235, with whose view on this point I should entirely agree).

6. Among the foremost modern commentators perhaps the only one who appears to date the dialogues *exclusively* on the basis of doctrine is Natorp (see Paul Natorp, *Platons Ideenlehre* [2e Auflage; Leipzig: Felix Meiner, 1921]). In his case it is not, as is more frequent, a question of Plato's dropping the ideas in his later dialogues but of the continuous elaboration and development of the "Ideenlehre." Some odd datings result; in particular, the *Theaetetus* (p. 90) is placed after the *Gorgias* and *Phaedrus* but before the *Phaedo*, *Symposium*, and *Republic*: "Die drei Schriften *Gorgias, Phaedrus, Theaetet*, können nicht anders als in dieser Folge, und sie können sehr gut in unmittelbarer Folge entstanden sein" (p. 96); and "... dass die Prämissen, die der *Phaedo* vom ersten Anfang an also schon festgestellt annimmt, nirgendwo anders festgestellt sind als im *Theaetet;* dass die beiden Dialoge *Theaetet* und *Phaedo* sich genau zusammenschliessen zu dem radikalsten und vollständingsten Beweise der Ideenlehre, den wir von Plato besitzen; einem Beweise, auf dem dagegen das *Gastmahl* und der *Staat* . . . bereits fussen und weiterbauen" (p. 132). Cf. pp. 164-67. Now, while the *Theaetetus* is not a dialogue which in itself can be placed "stylometrically," there are numerous other bits of evidence to tie it to the *Sophist* and *Parmenides*, which doubtless *are* later. So, for example, Natorp has to associate the reference to a possible critique of Parmenides at *Theaet.* 183C, not with the *Parmenides*, but with a projected work that was never written. Moreover, even though the evidence with regard

to the battle in which Theaetetus was wounded is inconclusive (see *Theaetetus*, ed. H. N. Fowler [Cambridge: Harvard University Press, 1942], Introduction, p. 5), still the explicit linking of the *Theaetetus* with the *Sophist* (*Soph.* 216A), which is undoubtedly late (see Campbell, *op. cit.*), the likeness between the *Theaetetus* and the *Parmenides* as critical dialogues—the one approaching the forms from the side of the advocates of motion or change, the other from the side of the believers in permanence or being—the strange pre-occupation of Plato in the *Theaetetus*, the *Parmenides*, and the *Statesman* with a younger Socrates or copy or even namesake of Socrates (see chap. xiii below)—all these matters must be ignored or twisted to support Natorp's dating. Such violence must result from the attempt to trace a univocal line of doctrinal development in the dialogues.

7. *Seventh Letter* 341C. For the general question of the authenticity of the *Letters* see n. 14 below.

8. Among English scholars the best-known exponent of this kind of view was John Burnet (see his *Greek Philosophy*, Part I: *From Thales to Plato* [London: Macmillan & Co., 1914], pp. 154-55, 247-48, and *Platonism* [Berkeley: University of California Press, 1928], pp. 35-47). Burnet goes so far as to consider the theory of ideas entirely Socratic, and the later doctrines, which substitute "categories" for "ideas," Platonic. Lutoslawski (*op. cit.*) had applied his "stylometry" to the development of a not dissimilar theory, though attributing both the earlier and the later doctrines equally to Plato.

9. *Timaeus* 51C. Burnet (*Greek Philosophy*, Part I, p. 155, and *Platonism*, p. 34) dismisses this statement because it is brief and made by a Pythagorean! It has, however, too important a place in the articulation of the dialogue to be so lightly dismissed. Besides, the later dialogues generally seem to involve rather a restatement than a dismissal of the forms; see, e.g., the One and the Many and the Four Classes of the *Philebus* 15A–E, 16D; or *Sophist* 253D. See chap. xiii, esp. Section 1.

10. Lutoslawski's attempt to date each dialogue exactly is a *reductio ad absurdum* of Campbell's method (cf. Burnet, *Platonism*, p. 11).

11. Cf. Burnet, *Greek Philosophy*, Part I, p. 303, n. 1. The ancient sources for this tradition are Plutarch *Adv. Col.* 1126C and Book iii of Diogenes Laertius.

12. See chap. xii.

13. *Seventh Letter* 328E.

14. The *Seventh Letter* seems to me undoubtedly genuine. It is accepted, e.g., by Burnet (*Greek Philosophy*, Part I, pp. 206-7), by Wilamowitz-Moellendorf (*Platon* [2e Auflage; Berlin: Weidmannsche Buchhandlung, 1920], II, 281-82), and by Robin (Léon

Robin, *Platon* [Paris: F. Alcan, 1935], p. 31), and even, in principle, by Ritter (*Neue Untersuchungen*, p. 404). To save his extremely systematic interpretation of the Platonic philosophy, Ritter *must* reject the "philosophical digression," though he admits that it entirely matches the rest of the letter in style and fits coherently into its context, and though he admits the genuineness of the rest of the letter. For a thorough treatment of the whole problem of the authenticity of the Platonic *Letters* see R. Hackforth, *The Authorship of the Platonic Epistles* (Manchester: University Press, 1913).

15. Not much can be made, I think, of the attempt to fix the relative dates of the *Theaetetus* and *Parmenides;* see, e.g., Burnet's discussion in *Platonism*, pp. 50–54.

16. Cf. Taylor, *op. cit.*, pp. 371 ff. Cf. also the analysis of the later Plato which has been given wide currency by the work of Stenzel (Julius Stenzel, *Plato's Method of Dialectic*, trans. D. Allan [Oxford: Clarendon Press, 1940]). This is a variant of the conventional view, in which the moral interest of the younger is contrasted with the scientific interest of the older Plato.

17. Cf. A. E. Taylor, *A Commentary on Plato's Timaeus* (Oxford: Clarendon Press, 1928), pp. 18–19 *et passim*.

18. Cf. Wilamowitz-Moellendorf, *op. cit.*, I, 630.

19. *Ibid.*, p. 658: "dass er sich auf den Boden des Realisierbaren stellen will"; Taylor, *Plato*, p. 463: "The purpose of the whole is severely practical"; Burnet, *Greek Philosophy*, Part I, p. 303: "The purpose of the *Laws* is an eminently practical one."

20. The only actual "evidence" here is the famous reference by Aristoxenus (*Harmonics* 30–31) to Aristotle's comment on Plato's "lecture on the Good." As Professor Cherniss has amply shown in the work cited below (nn. 24 ff.), the fact of this single public lecture offers no proof that Plato was in the habit of delivering regular lectures in the Academy.

21. On the interpretation of the *Timaeus* as Pythagorean, and therefore not Platonic, cf. the theory of Taylor, *A Commentary on Plato's Timaeus*, p. 11.

22. E.g., in Natorp, *op. cit.*, pp. 4 ff.

23. *Seventh Letter* 341C.

24. Harold Cherniss, *The Riddle of the Early Academy* (Berkeley and Los Angeles: University of California Press, 1945). Professor Cherniss concludes a long and careful argument analyzing the "evidence" for Plato's "unwritten doctrines": "If your opponent asserts a thesis which you undertake to refute, you do not begin by *proving* that he asserts it. That you do only when you wish to refute him by refuting the inferences which he does not himself draw. Such is the practice of Aristotle here, a method which he habitually em-

ploys. In this particular case, as in a good many others, the inference which he draws depends upon misinterpretation; but—and for our problem this is still more important—it is misinterpretation of the doctrine in the Platonic dialogues. So the Plato reflected with different distortions in the criticism of Aristotle and the heterodox systems of Speusippus and Xenocrates is not a hypothetical Plato of lecture platform or seminar, but the Plato of the dialogues still extant in their entirety" (p. 54).

25. *Ibid.*, p. 70.

26. *Ibid.*, p. 81.

27. *Ibid.*, pp. 32 ff.

28. Although I accept Professor Cherniss' conclusions as part of the historical basis for my own interpretation of Plato's development, I am by no means suggesting that he would necessarily—or even probably—agree with that interpretation itself. For one thing, he does not accept the *Seventh Letter* (*ibid.*, p. 13) and can therefore, if he likes and the *Phaedrus* permits him, take the dialogues as presenting Platonic doctrine in a sense in which I cannot. He should be absolved, therefore, from any responsibility for such superstructures as I have erected on the foundation of his theory.

29. Cherniss, *op. cit.*, Lecture II (pp. 31–59).

30. This is the position, essentially, of systematic commentators like Robin (*op. cit.*), Ritter (*Die Kerngedanken der Platonischen Philosophie* [München: Ernst Reinhardt, 1931]), and R. Demos (*Philosophy of Plato* [New York: Charles Scribner's Sons, 1939]).

31. Cf. Burnet, *Greek Philosophy*, Part I, p. 179: "If Plato's Sokrates is not meant for the real Sokrates, I find it very hard to imagine what he can be meant for."

32. Cf. n. 7 above.

33. *Meno* 80A. It is unnecessary for my present purpose to examine the much-discussed question of the "Platonic" as against the Aristophanic or the Xenophontic Socrates (see, e.g., Burnet, *Greek Philosophy*, Part I, pp. 126–50).

34. *Symposium* 215E–216C.

35. Cf. *Theaetetus* 144A; *Symposium* 220A–221C.

36. *Apology* 21A.

37. *Symposium* 216E–217A.

38. Cf. Karl Reinhardt, *Platons Mythen* (Bonn: Friedrich Cohen, 1927), p. 27.

39. *Apology* 24C.

40. *Seventh Letter* 326A–B.

41. *Ibid.* 314C. On the inauthenticity of this letter see Hackforth, *op. cit.*, "General Introduction," pp. 1–35, and "Epistle II," pp. 40–51.

42. Cf., e.g., *Symposium* 174A, 215E ff., 221E; *Gorgias* 490D.

43. *Symposium* 217A.

44. *Ibid.* 209E–212A.

45. *Theaetetus* 149A–151D. This supports the usual view of the *Theaetetus* as a transitional dialogue; see n. 6 above and chap. xiii, pp. 177 ff.

46. *Seventh Letter* 341B–E.

47. *Ibid.* 342A–343A.

48. *Phaedrus* 275C ff.

49. Cf. Romano Guardini, *The Death of Socrates* (New York: Sheed & Ward, 1948).

50. *Republic* 472D. This passage marks the articulation between the first and second major divisions of the dialogue (see chap. xi, pp. 147 ff.).

51. Cf. *Phaedrus* 250B and D–E, where beauty is singled out as the one of the forms most immediately recalled, through vision, by the human soul, in contrast to justice, temperance, etc.

52. F. C. S. Northrop in his essay, "The Mathematical Background and Content of Greek Philosophy" (*Philosophical Essays for Alfred North Whitehead* [London, New York, and Toronto: Longmans, Green & Co., 1936], pp. 1–40), goes so far as to identify the ideas with mathematical concepts or ratios: "The idea of the Good, the idea of God, and the idea of the soul, can be expressed; ... being constituted of the elementary ideas or ratios, they can be expressed in terms of them. Since there is no ineffable contribution of the 'Boundless' in them, they can be expressed in terms of the elements of all form which mathematics reveals" (p. 30). This, of course, contradicts Plato's own description of his method in the *Seventh Letter* (see p. 111 above); yet Professor Northrop's argument is provocative and illuminating in stressing the importance of "ratio" and proportion for Plato and in taking seriously the place of mathematics as propaedeutic to dialectic. On the other hand, to say that "the key to the epistemological, as well as the ethical and political, problem is to be found 'only' in the natural sciences" (p. 21) is to view Plato as a systematic and scientific philosopher in a manner which this whole essay is in a sense intended to refute.

53. This is clear from the statements of the *Seventh Letter* (342–43) and the *Phaedrus* quoted above (pp. 111–13), understood in relation to the dialogues themselves. See also *Cratylus* 349A–B, *Laws* 895D.

54. *Republic* 473A.

55. There are numerous "scientific" interpretations of the forms, which stress only this "epistemological" aspect of their nature. Cf., e.g., Ritter (*Kerngedanken*, p. 77): "Ich fasse die platonische Idee als Ausdruck des einfachen Gedankens, dass jede richtig gebildete Vorstellung an der objektiven Wirklichkeit ihren festen Halt habe." In the light of this interpretation Ritter considers phenomenology a modern rebirth of true Platonism (*ibid.*, pp. 185–90). Cf. also Natorp's conception of the ideas as "reine Denkbestimmungen"

(*op. cit.*, p. 133): "Als Reinergebnis der bis hierher geführten Untersuchungen lässt sich aussprechen: Ideen bedeuten nicht Dinge, sondern Methoden" (*ibid.*, p. 221). On the idea of the good as "das Gesetz des Gesetzes" (p. 194), cf. pp. 188-201. That this is a mere attempt to show that Plato anticipates Kant or the Neo-Kantians, Natorp indignantly denies in the *Anhang* to the second edition (*ibid.*, pp. 462-63). There is, as a matter of fact, in both these views an important core of truth; they are, in a sense, minimal interpretations of the forms—though Ritter's, despite his avowals to the contrary (cf., e.g., *Kerngedanken*, p. 84 n.), is narrower and less illuminating than that of Natorp. But for a definitive argument on the ultimate inadequacy of all "scientific" interpretations see F. M. Cornford, *Plato's Theory of Knowledge* (London: Routledge & Kegan Paul, 1935), Introduction, pp. 1-13.

56. *Republic* 592A-B.

57. *Ibid.* 499C.

58. The intimate union of the drive to thought and action in Plato is not often taken sufficiently serious account of; it is in a sense the theme of a study by Kurt Hildebrandt, *Platon: Der Kampf des Geistes um die Macht* (Berlin: Georg Bondi, 1933). Cf. p. 311: "Platons Geheimnis und Zauber ruht in der ursprünglichen Einheit seines Willens zur Tat und zum Denken." The "practical" interpretation of the dialogues is here, however, much *too* literally applied. Cf., e.g., Hildebrandt's interpretation of the *Phaedrus* (*ibid.*, pp. 274 ff.) or, even more extreme, of the *Republic* (*ibid.*, pp. 225 ff.). Cf. chap. xi below, n. 10.

59. *Philebus* 15A-18D; cf. *Republic* 509D ff.

60. Cf., e.g., *Republic* 392C-398B.

61. Although the treatment of art as imitation is given at length in Book x of the *Republic* (595A-608B), it is implicit also in the discussion of poetry in education in Books ii and iii, and is stated there explicitly, e.g., at 402 B-C. The metaphysical basis for it, however, can be discussed only in the later exposition, coming after the "knowledge line" of Book vi. For discussions of Plato's view of art which do not make imitation central in this fashion cf., e.g., R. G. Collingwood, *The Principles of Art* (Oxford: Clarendon Press, 1938), pp. 46 ff., and Edgar Wind, "Theios Phobos, Untersuchungen über die platonische Kunstphilosophie," *Zeitschr. für Aesth. und allgem. Kunstwissenschaft*, XXVI (1932), 349-73. Collingwood holds that Plato considered only some art to be representational, while Wind divorces the Platonic theory of art entirely from the concept of imitation—accepting the common view of the later Plato as dropping the theory of ideas, and then showing that the whole Platonic theory can be found in the *Laws*, and therefore independently of "ideas" and the "imitation" of ideas.

62. Cf. Hermann Reich, *Der Mimus* (Berlin: Weidmannsche Buchhandlung, 1903——).

CHAPTER X

The Teamster and the Team

1. *Republic* 328E ff.

2. F. M. Cornford, *Plato's Theory of Knowledge* (London: Routledge & Kegan Paul, 1935), p. 2.

3. Cf., e.g., R. H. S. Crossman, *Plato Today* (London: G. Allen & Unwin, 1937), or in part even the much more illuminating book of Karl Popper, *The Open Society and Its Enemies*, Vol. I: *The Spell of Plato* (London: G. Routledge & Sons, Ltd., 1945). Popper, as a matter of fact, considers that he is chiefly carrying further the work begun by Crossman (*ibid.*, p. 28).

4. Aristotle *Politics* 1260 b 30.

5. Cf. the reference to the origin of the Cretan and Spartan legal systems in the opening of the *Laws* 624A ff.; also Book iii. 682E ff.

6. Cf. chap. xii.

7. Cf. chap. ix, n. 11 above. On this characteristic of Plato's political views cf. also Wilamowitz-Moellendorf, *Platon* (2e Auflage; Berlin, 1920), I, 394: "Es ist keine Reform des Bestehenden, sondern ein Neubau, der kein anderes Fundament haben soll als die Natur des Menschen."

8. *Republic* 421D–423B.

9. *Ibid.* 368D–369B.

10. *Seventh Letter* 324B–326B.

11. *Apology* 32C–E.

12. *Crito* 50B–53A.

13. *Gorgias* 503C, 515E ff.

14. *Republic* 420B–C.

15. Cf. Otto Apelt, *Platonische Aufsätze* (Leipzig and Berlin: Teubner, 1912), pp. 185–86. Apelt comments on the passage in the *Gorgias:* "Er stellt an die Staatsmänner höchst sonderbare Forderungen. Sie sollen selbst Muster der Tugend sein und sollen ihre Mitbürger zu tugendhaften Männern machen. Nun weiss jeder, dass es beim *sittlichen* Handeln anderen gegenüber nicht auf den Erfolg ankommt, sondern auf die Gesinnung, aus der die Handlung entspringt und in der sie wurzelt. Anderseits beurteilt den Staatsmann allerdings jeder nach dem Erfolg, und Platon macht es eben nicht anders. . . . Politik und Sittlichkeit fallen ihm in Eins zusammen." But Apelt is here separating "Politik" and "Sittlichkeit" in a modern Christian fashion in order to observe the oddity of Plato's putting them back together; what is unique, among his contemporaries, is not the identification or unification of "politics" and "morality" but the direction and emphasis given the identity.

16. *Gorgias* 516B.

17. *Laws* 709E ff.

18. *Gorgias* 479A–E; *Republic* 566D ff., 579D, 587E.

19. *Gorgias* 519A.

20. Cf., e.g., Thucydides iii. 38.

21. *Republic* 493A–B.

22. *Phaedrus* 230E–234C. It is quite immaterial, for the interpretation of the dialogue, whether, as some scholars have supposed, this is really a speech by Lysias rather than an imitation by Plato (cf. A. E. Taylor, *Plato, the Man and His Work* [New York: Dial Press, 1936], p. 302). That Plato *could* have written it we know, e.g., from the superb stylistic imitations of the *Symposium*.

23. *Phaedrus* 246A ff.

24. Cf. Taylor, *op. cit.*, p. 300; Léon Robin, *La Théorie platonicienne de l'amour* (Paris: Félix Alcan, 1908), p. 45.

25. When a closer connection of the two parts is suggested, it is usually something to the effect that the dialectic of the Academy involved an erotic relation between teacher and pupil (cf., e.g., Wilamowitz-Moellendorf, *op. cit.*, I, 487). Wilamowitz also suggests that the first part is necessary to the second, since "Psychology belongs with Psychagogy"—a rather far-fetched and external link. What seems to me most important, however, is not so much the sense in which, for Plato, the true rhetoric, or dialectic, demands love, as the sense in which love itself is, or has, a kind of rhetoric.

26. For a detailed analysis of the *Symposium*, with special reference to the relation of *eros* to philosophy, see Gerhard Krueger, *Einsicht und Leidenschaft* (Frankfurt: V. Klostermann, 1948), pp. 77 ff.

27. *Symposium* 202E.

28. *Ibid.* 203B ff.; *Phaedrus* 251A–E.

29. *Symposium* 180A.

30. *Ibid.* 184B–C.

31. *Phaedrus* 251A.

32. For some brief suggestions of other sorts of connection between *eros* and political life see, e.g., C. Ritter, *Die Kerngedanken, der Platonischen Philosophie* (München, 1931), p. 55 n., on love among citizens as a possible political bond between them, or Robin, *Platon* (Paris: F. Alcan, 1935), pp. 79 and 262–63, on the role of love in training the philosopher.

33. *Gorgias* 517C.

34. *Seventh Letter* 351C.

35. *Republic* 414D–415A.

36. *Ibid.* 497A.

37. *Laws* 719E ff., esp. 722B–E.

CHAPTER XI
Constructions

1. The *Republic* can be dated only very roughly. John Burnet, for example, puts it "either before the foundation of the Academy or very shortly after" (*Greek Philosophy*, Part I: *From Thales to Plato* [London, 1914], pp. 223–24)–i.e., in the 380's. Wilamowitz-Moellendorf (*Platon* [Berlin, 1920], I, 393) places it "about 374." For the popular German hypothesis that the first book formed an earlier, unpublished dialogue, the *Thrasymachus* (cf. Ritter, *Untersuchungen über Platon* [Stuttgart, 1888], pp. 34–47; Wilamowitz-Moellendorf, *op. cit.*, II, 81–85), there is not sufficient stylistic evidence, and there is every philosophic and artistic evidence against it.

2. *Republic* 368D ff.

3. *Ibid.* 471C ff.

4. *Ibid.* 473D.

5. *Ibid.* 474C–483E, 504A–511E.

6. *Ibid.* Books viii and ix (543A–588A).

7. *Ibid.* 614B ff.

8. The sharp break in the dialogue marked by the "three waves of paradox" is seldom given sufficient attention; apparently the third wave is thought simply, as Wilamowitz explains (*op. cit.*, I, 446–47), "to set metaphysics at the center of the dialogue" (cf. also Ritter, *Die Kerngedanken der Platonischen Philosophie* [München, 1931], pp. 48 ff.). The introduction of "metaphysics," however, does not serve so much to complete a dialectical structure of being or reality as to turn our attention from the formal articulation of the model state to the need for its realization (cf., e.g., 502C, 540D); it is for the purpose of realizing the model that the philosopher-king, with his knowledge of the really real, is necessary.

9. *Republic* 499C.

10. It is precisely the desperate concern with the problem of realization, without the sure means of accomplishing it, that characterizes Plato's argument. Hildebrandt's analysis of the *Republic*, as the last appeal to his city by a Plato quite seriously wanting and even half-expecting to be made philosopher-king of Athens, involves an amazing misunderstanding both of the spirit of the *Republic* and of the possibilities of Athenian politics (cf. Kurt Hildebrandt, *Platon: Der Kampf des Geistes um die Macht* [Berlin, 1933], p. 271). It was one thing to try to turn a Sicilian tyrant into a philosopher-king—though that was itself a sufficiently dubious undertaking—but it was inconceivable (as Plato himself has said: *Republic* 407A–B) that the philosopher-king should be superimposed on any of the totally antimonarchical (as well as antiphilosophical) constitutions of Greece proper.

11. *Politics* 1252 b 5, 1252 a 25. Cf. 1279 a 30.

12. *Republic* 432B.

13. Even if, because of the resemblance to the *Phaedrus* myth, the tripartite division of the soul is generally taken as a constant of Platonic "psychology" (cf., e.g., Burnet, *op. cit.*, Part I, p. 177, where it appears as Socratic; or Wilamowitz-Moellendorf, *op. cit.*, I, 396), the whole apparatus here (four virtues and three parts of the soul) is introduced much too arbitrarily to be taken as "proved." It is rather, as most Platonic arguments are, intended to turn the interlocutors' attention in the proper direction; in this case, to the nature of justice as a harmony.

14. Cf. Leo Strauss, "On a New Interpretation of Plato's Political Philosophy," *Social Research*, XIII (1946), 326–47: "Plato composed his writings in such a way as to prevent for all time their use as authoritative texts. His dialogues supply us not so much with an answer to the riddle of being as with a most articulate imitation of that riddle" (p. 351).

15. This view is implicit, e.g., in the discussion of Paul Shorey, "Introduction" to *Republic* (Loeb ed.; Cambridge: Harvard University Press, 1937), pp. xiv and xv.

16. *Statesman* 269C–274E.

17. It is hardly necessary to point out the importance of the conceptions of order and harmony for Plato. This has been done and overdone in the discussions of the connections of Plato and Pythagoreanism from Aristotle and the Neo-Platonists on (cf., e.g., Burnet, *op. cit.*, Part I, p. 91, and F. M. Cornford, *Plato's Theory of Knowledge* [London, 1935], pp. 9–10). All that is needed is to point, for example, to the tenor of the argument against Callicles in the *Gorgias* (cf. 506D) or the whole treatment of the well-ordered soul in the *Republic* itself: 399E–401A, the effect of rhythms on the soul; 430E, the definition of temperance; 443C–444E, the definition of justice—to mention only a few of the many relevant texts.

18. It is the conception of the state as existing in and through a harmony that accounts for Plato's emphasis on the rigid division of labor, for in a harmony the component parts must be pure and distinct. Cf. *Republic* 433A–434C, also 414B ff. (the "noble lie") and 421A.

19. *Republic* 372D.

20. See chap. ix, n. 55, and the analysis by Cornford cited there.

21. *Parmenides* 128E–F; *Republic* 597A; cf. *Seventh Letter* 342D.

22. The best text for this problem is Plato's own: *Parmenides* 130E ff.

23. *Phaedrus* 250B (cf. chap. ix, n. 51 above).

24. *Republic* 414B ff.

25. *Ibid.* 414C.

26. *Ibid.* 378A.

27. *Ibid.* 472A.
28. *Ibid.* 490E–495B.
29. *Ibid.* 499E; 500C.
30. *Seventh Letter* 351C.
31. *Laws* 907D–909D.
32. Cf. *ibid.* 710A–B; *Statesman* 297E.
33. *Ibid.* 719E ff.

34. On the other side, in contrast to this highly formalized conception of the best state and the philosophic necessity for its decay even were it once realized, it is interesting to notice the very particular and Athenian character of Plato's account of the shifts from one form of degenerate state to the next. The change in the constitution is brought about by the change in psychological conditioning in the individual, and that, in turn, is brought about by the continuous sense of other people living around him in a fashion different from his own: that is just the mark of a democracy, which, as Socrates says, exhibits within herself a pattern of every sort of state—and he is certainly thinking of Athens as the supreme example of a democracy. As Pericles said in the Funeral Speech: "We bear our neighbor no grudge for going his own way even if it is not ours, and we refrain from inflicting on him not only legal penalties but private animosity which may or may not be painful but is always vexatious." The oligarch who perceives the power of money to be more powerful than the old value of honor is not a figure taken from Thessaly or Corinth; instead he is a certain kind of young Athenian, a son of the older order. He is tempted, obviously, by seeing all around him young men and older men who have more influence than his own father, in virtue of the money they possess. The democratic son of this oligarch emerges amid the general atmosphere of license within his society and the sense of the cramping restrictions of his money-hungry father. Lastly, the tyrant son of the democratic father appears as the *reductio ad absurdum* of the liberty and want of discipline of his democratic father.

35. *Seventh Letter* 326A; cf. *Republic* 496C and 497A–B.
36. *Phaedo* 118A.
37. *Ibid.* 82B.
38. *Crito* 46C.
39. *Gorgias* 469C.

40. On the more "humanitarian" Socratic Plato of the *Gorgias* as against the "totalitarian" Plato of the *Republic*, cf. Karl Popper, *The Open Society and Its Enemies*, Vol. I: *The Spell of Plato* (London: G. Routledge & Sons, Ltd., 1945), pp. 91–92 and 171 ff. Professor Popper, taking account of the importance of Socrates in the very dialogue which sets forth such "unscientific," totalitarian ideas, believes that Plato was trying to solve his own conflict by "implicating" Socrates in his (Plato's) new reactionary position. This is clear-

ly an attempt by Professor Popper—the plausibility of which the reader can judge for himself—to extricate himself from the kind of difficulty I have described.

41. *Seventh Letter* 326A.

42. *Republic* 419A.

43. The interpretation of Plato's "ethics" in the *Republic* as "eudaimonism" (Ritter, *Kerngedanken*, pp. 54-55) is based on the acceptance as Plato's literal and conclusive "doctrine" of the purely conventional level of discussion at which his arguments frequently start, or rest at stopping points in the dialogues. It is a traditional misinterpretation as old as the *Nicomachean Ethics* of Aristotle.

CHAPTER XII

EXPERIMENT IN SICILY

1. Herodotus i. 24.

2. Aristotle *Politics* 1267 b 22; cf. Diodorus xii. 10. 7.

3. Cf. *Seventh Letter* 332C.

4. *Ibid.* 326B-C.

5. *Ibid.* 326D-327A.

6. *Ibid.* 327A.

7. *Ibid.* 327C-328C.

8. Cf. chap. ix, n. 1, on the sources of our knowledge of Plato's life. Plutarch's *Dion* itself is principally based on this letter.

9. *Laws* 709E.

10. *Republic* 473D.

11. *Seventh Letter* 336A.

12. *Ibid.* 330A-B.

13. *Republic* 473A.

14. *Seventh Letter* 338B-339B.

15. *Ibid.* 339D-340A.

16. *Ibid.* 350C-D.

17. *Republic* 473D; cf. *Laws* 709E ff.

18. *Laws* 711C.

19. Cf. *Seventh Letter* 324B and 336A.

CHAPTER XIII

THE ROAD TO DICTE

1. Cf. *Parmenides* 135C.

2. *Ibid.* 133B ff.

3. John Burnet, *Platonism* (Berkeley, 1928), pp. 44-45; cf. also Harold Cherniss, *The Riddle of the Early Academy* (Berkeley and Los Angeles, 1945), p. 5.

4. *Theaetetus* 152E.

5. *Timaeus* 20D–21E.

6. *Laws* 625B.

7. *Seventh Letter* 337B.

8. *Timaeus* 22B.

9. *Parmenides* 135A.

10. *Ibid.* 130C.

11. Cf. chap. xi, nn. 6 and 15.

12. *Theaetetus* 143E–144B; cf. *Statesman* 257D.

13. *Statesman* 257D.

14. *Philebus* 14A. This is not, strictly, a division by dichotomy like those of the *Sophist* and *Statesman*, but it is a division in the broader sense and typical of the arguments in the later dialogues.

15. *Statesman* 267A–C.

16. *Timaeus* 37B. Cf. also discussion in F. M. Cornford, *Plato's Theory of Knowledge* (London, 1935), pp. 170 ff. and 184 ff.

17. *Statesman* 269D.

18. *Ibid.* 272E.

19. These powers were also probably not the Olympian gods.

20. *Statesman* 273B.

21. *Ibid.* 274A.

22. *Ibid.* 273E.

23. *Timaeus* 17C–19B.

24. *Ibid.* 19C.

25. *Ibid.* 27A–B.

26. *Ibid.* 24E–25D.

27. *Laws* 679B.

28. *Seventh Letter* 341D.

29. *Ibid.* 344A. The description of Plato's method here may, as I have said earlier, be held to apply to the whole body of the earlier dramatic dialogues as well; but the emphasis in this passage is undeniably that of the older Plato.

30. Cf. chap. xi, Sections 1 and 2, above.

31. Cf. F. M. Cornford, *Plato's Cosmology* (London: Routledge & Kegan Paul, 1937), pp. 7–8.

32. *Republic* 372D–E.

33. *Ibid.* 373A.

34. *Laws* 679B–C.

35. Cf. chap. xi, n. 8, above.

36. *Seventh Letter* 328C.

37. *Republic* 499C.

38. *Statesman* 270A.

39. *Republic* 377C ff.

40. *Phaedrus* 229D ff.

41. *Timaeus* 40D–E. Cf. Cornford, *Plato's Cosmology*, pp. 138–39.

42. The evidence seems to point this way. In the myth we are told of certain gods who are coregents with him and are intrusted with

certain spheres of authority by him. When the Supreme Spirit let go control of the world, these likewise let go (*Statesman* 272E). In the reverse swing of the world, we learn of the activities of Prometheus (*ibid*. 274D–E). It is a mistake to take this as dogmatic theology, yet what I think is being suggested is that the Olympian gods belong in the reverse swing of the world, i.e., that they have the same relation to the divine helmsman and his assistants of the previous era that the politicians and statesmen of the period of the reverse movement have to the original political authority.

43. *Laws* 899B ff.
44. *Timaeus* 29C–D.
45. Cf. Cornford, *Plato's Cosmology*, p. 28.
46. Cf. A. E. Taylor, *A Commentary on Plato's Timaeus* (Oxford, 1928), p. 19.
47. *Phaedo* 114D.
48. *Republic* 614B ff.
49. *Timaeus* 70D.
50. *Ibid*. 71E–72A.
51. *Ibid*. 37C.
52. *Laws*, 644D–E.
53. Cf. Cornford's discussion of the Demiurge (*Plato's Cosmology*, pp. 34–39).
54. *Timaeus* 90E–91D.
55. *Ibid*. 30D–34A.
56. *Laws* 685A–B.
57. *Ibid*. 713C–714A.
58. *Republic* 425C–E; cf. *Statesman* 294B.
59. *Laws* 644B–E.
60. *Ibid*. 713E.
61. *Ibid*. 690C. We must remember, however, the ruthless cutting-off of the heretic, should persuasion fail (*ibid*. 907D ff.).
62. *Ibid*. 710A–B.
63. *Phaedrus* 275D.
64. Cf. n. 58 above.
65. *Laws* 896D–897B.
66. *Ibid*. 804B.

PHOENIX BOOKS
in Philosophy